WE CALLED IT
MACARONI

WE CALLED IT MACARONI

An American Heritage

of Southern Italian Cooking

by Nancy Verde Barr

Illustrations by Kathe Helander

 ALFRED A. KNOPF NEW YORK 1996

THIS IS A BORZOI BOOK
PUBLISHED BY ALFRED A. KNOPF, INC.

Copyright © 1990 by Nancy Verde Barr
Illustrations copyright © 1990 by Kathe Helander
All rights reserved under International and Pan-American Copyright Conventions.
Published in the United States by Alfred A. Knopf, Inc., New York,
and simultaneously in Canada by Random House of Canada Limited, Toronto.
Distributed by Random House, Inc., New York.

Library of Congress Cataloging-in-Publication Data
Barr, Nancy Verde.
We called it macaroni : an American heritage of southern Italian cooking /
Nancy Verde Barr. — 1st ed.
p. cm. —[The Knopf cooks American series; 4]
ISBN 0-394-55798-0
ISBN 0-679-76577-8 (pbk.)
1. Cookery, Italian—Southern style. I. Title. II. Series.
TX723.2.S65B37   1990
641.59457—dc20   90-53114   CIP

Manufactured in the United States of America
Published November 15, 1990

First Paperback Edition, February 1996

For all those first Italian-Americans
who knew that food meant so
much more than eating.

If children wish to see the future more clearly,
they should stand on their parents' shoulders.

ANONYMOUS

Se i figli volessero vedere il futuro più chiaramente,
dovrebbero mettersi sulle spalle dei genitori.

ANONIMO

CONTENTS

ACKNOWLEDGMENTS

Many people made this book possible. Unmeasurable thanks for their caring and support belong to my family—to Philip, the wind beneath my wings, who enthusiastically accepted the care and nurturing of the boys while I traveled; to Brad and Andrew, who always let me know that everything I did was "awesome"; to my mother, Billie Higgins Verde, who enrolled herself and all her friends in my very first cooking class; and to my brother, Tom Verde, who contributed generously from his expertise in journalism and hand-holding. I owe my awakening to the richness of my culinary heritage to Italo Scanga and Dale Chihuly and the many happy, colorful times we spent cooking and eating "alla italiana." The fact that I ever began to put pen to paper I credit to Julia Child, whose friendship allowed me to see the most gracious form of professionalism. In her ever practical and endearing way she simply assumed that I would do this —and do it well. Still, this book might have been forever unseen had it not been for the generosity of Jean Anderson, who shared so much with me including her agent, Julie Fallowfield, whose help was so valuable. "Bravissime" to Jody Adams and Marlene Diamond, who tested and retested recipes with expertise and ever-pleasant demeanors. I am grateful to my dear friend, Mary Higgins, who tasted and retasted and advised and whose opinion I always value. Kathy Zuckerman, editorial assistant at Knopf, should know how much I appreciate her enthusiastic assistance. Gratitude and fond memories belong to my favorite traveling companion, Dagmar Sullivan, whose passion for Italy matches my own and whose copious notes on every meal are legend. And, "mille, mille grazie" to my editor, Judith Jones, whose judgment, encouragement, and feeling for this project made me happy that it was mine.

INTRODUCTION

Something happened to Italian food on its way to American citizenship. It adapted and adjusted, recipes changed their names, some foods were added and some discarded—but good Italian cooking never completely disappeared. Although what we call pasta today was called macaroni by the old-timers, it is still the same, basic comforting food. A contemporary restaurant may serve us a "designer pizza," but fundamentally it's the same flat circle of dough that Neapolitans have been baking for generations.

We called it macaroni when I was growing up because that was the generic word that my grandparents used for pasta. They came from Ischia, off the coast of Naples, in the late 1800s and settled with fellow Ischiani in the Little Italy of Providence. Like most of their countrymen, they were eager to adapt to the new land, its people, its culture, its opportunities—but not its food. They clung tenaciously to their own ways of cooking. So when my mother, who is Irish, married my father, it was natural that she learn from his mother and his sisters how to prepare the foods that he had grown up with. Consequently, my brothers and sister and I grew up surrounded by the wonderful smells, sights, and tastes that were part of the legacy of southern Italian cooking. Nevertheless, I tended to take that food for granted. It wasn't until I left home and studied classic French cooking, and then started to teach cooking, that I realized how rich my own culinary heritage was. It made me determined to learn more about the origins and evolution of the southern Italian cooking style, one which has often been denigrated in America.

Surely if I had known that one day I would write this book I couldn't have asked for a more perfect place to grow up in than Rhode Island. The largest ethnic population in the state is made up of people of Italian descent. Almost twenty percent of the population of Providence is Italian and we have towns with Italian-American populations as high as forty-four percent. The Italian influence is so strong that last St. Joseph's Day, one bakery alone sold fifteen thousand "zeppole" (deep-fried cream puffs), the traditional sweet that Neapolitans have always made to celebrate that saint's day. The same sweet is made on the same day in neighborhoods settled by Sicilians who called the cream puffs "sfinge." And there are hundreds of bakeries and food shops in towns and cities along the East coast that continue to turn out specialties that have long been associated with feast days. So I grew up with an understanding of how Italians feel about their food and the important role it plays in their lives, not just here in the Northeast but wherever groups of Italians have settled in America.

The majority of immigrants came during the late 1800s and early 1900s and mostly from the areas south of Rome. They emigrated with fellow villagers ("paesani") and settled together in the new country. Almost immediately, the immigrants formed mutual aid societies to meet the needs of "paesani" who found themselves bewildered in a strange land. The original purpose of the societies was to provide financial assistance for their own people when unemployment, death, or temporary setbacks made it impossible for them to provide for their families and to offer the comradeship of others from their particular corner of the world. Often the societies were named after the village the immigrants came from, or its church or patron saint, and the social activities kept alive the customs and culture of the old country village. Membership was stringently restricted to fellow "paesani," which is not surprising considering that in southern Italy during the time of the heaviest emigration, there was a tremendous mistrust of outsiders, usually defined as anyone who did not live within hearing of the local church bell. "Campanile" is the Italian word for bell tower and "campanillismo" translates as "localism." This sense of localism followed the Italians to America.

The Italians did their best to reproduce the food of their homeland. Those who remember the early times speak of family members and fellow countrymen who would return periodically to the old country and bring back prosciutto and salami and cases of macaroni from their villages. Here in America they would manage to raise their own animals or purchase them live to be killed and dressed under their supervision so they would have fresh pork fat or the necessary ingredients for "soffritto" (southern Italian stew of pork or chicken heart, liver, and innards). They would purchase eels from the fish cart, "capretto" (baby goats) sometimes live from farmers or the market, hazelnuts on ropes. Everyone had a dirt cellar or a cool entryway and used it to store foods of their own making—wine, sausages, salume.

The early Italian-Americans had a passion for gardening; no matter whether it was backyard, front yard, windowsill, or rooftop, a garden was a necessity. They grew and preserved whatever they could coax from the soil. Most of the early southern immigrants had been gardeners in Italy, so they were extremely resourceful in learning to cultivate a strange soil. I know an elderly man, from the Naples area, who lives in Providence with a very tiny garden. He has

a fruit-bearing fig tree that he buries every winter to protect it from the frost, and resurrects it each spring. I was amazed at his expertise and one time told him that he had certainly learned to garden well in Italy. "Oh no," he said. "I learned to do this from the early Italians here. *They* had to learn to do these things, not those in Italy." Because of the time and care given to raising produce and seeking resources as close to the original as possible, the original dishes had all taken on a decidedly regional flavor in America.

As long as the first generation of immigrants dominated the Italian communities numerically, the village-oriented social life and food preferences prevailed, in spite of the United States government's rather aggressive attempts to alter the Italians' eating habits. Social workers were sent to Italian-American homes to convince the immigrants, according to the prevailing nutritional opinion, that too many vegetables in the diet were not good for a person and that meat should accompany starch at every meal. Their efforts were gradually rewarded as the second generation of Italians grew in numbers and reached maturity. These Italian-Americans knew little or nothing of life in "the old country" and felt comfortable relinquishing the old village bonds to form a society that reflected a national Italian, or Italian-American, sentiment rather than a village consciousness. Whereas my grandparents only referred to a fellow villager as "paesan," my father referred to many friends from all parts of Italy as "paesani." Writer Tom Maresca uses the term "double melting pot" to describe the fact that these early Italians had first to melt with one another and then melt into American society. As the groups began to intermarry and merge, many of the regional food differences began to fade. Calabrian wives might well add their own touches to their Sicilian husbands' family recipes. Holiday meals were always traditional but they gradually included traditional foods of more than one region of Italy. Once the groups melted together, they were ready to melt into American society and a new Italian-American cooking emerged.

Italian-American cooking found a welcome home in the numerous restaurants that opened to serve cheap Italian food in a homey setting. The Momma and Papa proprietors were eager to please their public and did as the Americans did. They served meat and starch together so that entrees came with a side of spaghetti, or spaghetti and meatballs arrived in the same dish—practices unheard of in Italy. They also substituted meat in traditional vegetable dishes. Veal

Parmesan did not arrive with the Italians; they brought eggplant or zucchini Parmesan and later created veal or chicken Parmesan to satisfy a meat-eating nation. Salads began to be served before the meal, an American custom, rather than in the Italian fashion of after or with the entree. For most of the year in sunny Italy the Italians were able to make quick tomato sauces with ripe garden tomatoes, but in America, with its shorter growing season, restaurants began to rely more on long-simmered tomato sauces that could be made with canned tomatoes or tomato paste. Americans began to associate these heavier tomato sauces with all of southern Italian cooking. And, since abundance was the American way, restaurants made sure that their clientele could count on being well fed. In Italy these Italians had never known such large portions and certainly the early immigrants had never experienced such ample servings. Few of these restaurants offered any true regional specialties.

It was the search for these original dishes that sent me on several trips to Italy. I wanted to discover, or rediscover, the foods that had been part of our culinary heritage. It was then that I became aware of the richness and variety of the cooking of southern Italy. Fortunately, contrary to those misguided social workers, it is a cuisine that is also healthy.

Today, I am tremendously optimistic about this "rebirth" of authentic Italian food. If you visit Providence's Federal Hill, or Boston's North End, or New York's Little Italy, you will certainly be met with an Italian feeling. We can still buy live chickens, baby goats at holiday times, a huge variety of imported olive oils, fresh Italian cheeses, fish from a pushcart, a variety of homemade sausages, "zeppole," "sfogliatelle." The merchants that I deal with tell me that they are selling more and more Italian products every year and people are demanding better quality. Many new restaurants identify themselves as serving food from a particular region—even when that region is a southern Italian one. I see the overwhelming interest in the original foods of our ancestors in the changing attitudes of my students. At one time they wanted only classes in "Northern Italian" food. Now they are delighted to learn about *all* the regional dishes and want to learn to recreate some family specialties that had become merely taste memories. Because of our strong beginnings, our Italian roots are deep and our food connections strong. This book looks at those beginnings and at the changes and offers a modern restoration of what might otherwise have been lost.

WE CALLED IT
MACARONI

Chapter One

APPETIZERS

.

It is a curious thing that for years antipasto in Italian-American restaurants was synonymous with a plate of cold cuts, stalks of celery, a mound of tuna fish, anchovies, and a few olives. Although this is indeed an antipasto, it is merely one choice of a selection that could fill a few cookbooks. Many of those early restaurants were little more than spaghetti houses and they offered only a few simple dishes. Fortunately, good Italian restaurants today offer a variety of starters. At home, antipasti were never a part of the daily meal, but were reserved for holidays and celebrations. I have found that most Italian-American families relied on a few family favorites that appeared at every holiday meal. Snail salad, stuffed mushrooms, and preserved vegetables are among the most popular ones I encountered in old Providence, Rhode Island, Italian families.

Traditionally an antipasto is served on a plate, at the table before the first course. Pasto means "meal" and antipasto means "before the meal," not "before the pasta" as many people think. Restaurants often serve a small selection of antipasti on the same plate but this is seldom done at home. I have altered some of the traditional recipes so that the antipasti may be passed as finger foods. This is in keeping with the way I entertain today and certainly not part of the culture of the early Italian-Americans who ate their antipasti only at the table. I like to pass two to three different antipasti when I have prepared a simple meal, perhaps a one-dish pasta or soup dinner. When I serve a more elaborate meal, I do not offer anything more filling than some olives or nuts beforehand and serve the antipasto at the table.

Actually, there is a southern Italian tradition, especially in Naples, of eating food outdoors on one's feet. Along the streets that wrap around the Bay of Naples are numerous stands that offer miniature pizzas, seafood salads, fried vegetables—all meant to be eaten standing up. Neapolitans call these snacks "passatempi" (pastimes). The Italians in America continue this tradition of street food at their numerous outdoor festivals.

Italians have always loved to feed people. Social workers who visited the early immigrants were amazed that no matter how little a family might have, they would always offer a visitor something to eat. If you enjoy feeding large groups of people, consider serving a buffet with a selection of antipasto foods along with recipes from the vegetable and salad chapters. So many of these foods are meant to be served at room temperature that you are relieved of the hassle of trying to keep food hot for a crowd. Best of all, your table will be alive with bright, vibrant colors and flavors.

Crostini with Sun-Dried Tomato Sauce

CROSTINI CON SALSINA DI POMODORI SECCHI

I have taken a bit of "cucina" license with this antipasto recipe. Traditionally the tomato mixture would be served on an individual plate with a small scoop of fresh cheese, some black olives, and the crostini. I created the following presentation because I am always in need of terrific recipes for casual entertaining or cocktail parties. This is one of my most requested recipes and a personal favorite. The tomato mixture may be made and the cheeses blended together three days ahead.

1¼ pounds salad tomatoes (about 2 large), halved, seeded, and juiced
3 medium garlic cloves, chopped
½ cup sun-dried tomatoes, drain and reserve oil (see note)

¼ cup fresh basil leaves
Salt
1½ pounds fresh ricotta cheese
6 ounces mascarpone cheese
36 garlic crostini (page 7)

1. In a food processor, combine the fresh tomatoes, garlic, sun-dried tomatoes, and basil. Process, turning the machine quickly on and off and scraping down the bowl as necessary until everything is minced. Add enough of the reserved oil (or fresh olive oil) to make the mixture spreadable. Taste for salt.

2. In a clean processor bowl, combine the ricotta and mascarpone cheeses and process until blended and smooth.

3. To serve, place the cheese mixture in the center of a serving dish. Drain any liquid from tomato mixture and spoon around cheese. Garnish with fresh basil leaves and serve with garlic crostini. *Makes 36.*

· · ·

Note: Most sun-dried tomatoes are sold in jars covered with olive oil. If you buy them loose, you will have to reconstitute them in boiling water for one minute and use fresh olive oil in place of oil reserved from jar.

Appetizer Toasts Neapolitan Style

CROSTINI NAPOLETANI

For a more defined anchovy taste, for the real anchovy lover, leave the anchovies whole and put two fillets on each toast. If you don't like anchovies at all, try the roasted pepper variation, and don't hesitate to create your own toppings. Proportions are not critical as long as the flavors are good. A variety of small crostini are wonderful for cocktail parties.

About ½ cup extra-virgin olive oil

16 slices Italian bread, ½ inch thick

16 slices mozzarella cheese, ¼ inch thick

32 anchovy fillets, rinsed and patted dry, chopped

1 pound fresh plum tomatoes, cut into 16 thin slices

Salt and pepper

1. Preheat the oven to 400°F.

2. Brush oil on one side of bread slices and place oiled side up on flat baking sheet. Cover each piece of bread with a slice of mozzarella, sprinkle with chopped anchovy and top with a slice of tomato. Brush with oil and sprinkle with salt and pepper. Bake 10 minutes. *Serves 8.*

• • •

Variation: In place of anchovies and plum tomatoes, use ¼ cup black or green olivada (olive puree) and 2 large roasted red peppers cut in ¼-inch strips. Spread bread with olivada, lay on mozzarella cheese, and cover with 2 crossed strips of pepper. Bake as above.

CROSTINI

Crostini are pieces of bread that are toasted or fried. They are used in soups or for an antipasto topped with something delicious. For the southern Italian, antipasto crostini were a rare treat, but crostini in soup was a mainstay of the diet—the frugal use of stale bread providing substance to a soup that might be the only dish of the meal. The bread replaced macaroni that the cook could not afford, and the soup was called a "zuppa." Once this extreme poverty disappeared in the United States, soups thickened with bread began to fade from the immigrants' diet. It is a shame because they are among the most delicious (see recipes called "Zuppa"). Rejecting them was a way the immigrants had of showing how removed they were from "la misuria" (the impoverished condition) of the "old country."

Bread for crostini may be cut into any size or shape. I like to cut Italian bread into ½-inch-thick slices about 2 inches in diameter. If the round slices are larger than that, I simply cut them in half, making half circles. Put the slices directly on the rack of a preheated 400°F oven and toast, turning once, until browned on each side (total cooking time about 4 to 5 minutes). Immediately brush one side with olive oil. If you want a garlic flavor, before brushing with the oil, rub the same side with the cut side of a clove of garlic. The toasts should be made the same day they are to be used or they will develop an "off" taste.

Some antipasto crostini do not require that you pretoast the bread (see Appetizer Toasts Neapolitan Style, opposite page), but you can do so if you wish.

Fried Cheese-Filled Antipasti

PANZAROTTI (PANZEROTTI) DI FORMAGGI

Panzarotti are filled pieces of dough that, when fried, swell up so they resemble a small "pancia" (belly)—hence the name. They may be square raviolis as below or fluted half moons as in Panzarotti di Funghi. In the olden days, panzarotti were almost always made with a simple bread dough and fried in lard because that was the most affordable way to make them. Pasta dough produces a more delicate result and any pieces that are not fried may be stored and then boiled like any filled pasta.

FILLING

1 egg
1 egg white
½ pound mozzarella cheese, grated
2 ounces mild provolone or pecorino cheese, grated

¼ pound boiled ham, minced
Salt and pepper

———

Pasta dough made with ½ cup flour and 2 large eggs (page 122)

Vegetable oil or lard for frying

1. For the filling, beat the egg and egg white together just until blended. Mix in cheeses and ham and season with salt and pepper.

2. Roll and fill the pasta dough according to the directions for ravioli on page 130–31.

3. In a deep, heavy frying pan, heat 1 inch of oil to 360°F–375°F, or hot enough to brown a bread cube. Add panzarotti a few at a time, being careful not to crowd the pan. Fry until golden, turning once (about 1 minute per side). Drain on paper towels and sprinkle with salt before serving. *Makes 60 panzarotti.*

• • •

Note: Panzarotti should be served hot. If necessary, they may be reheated in a 400°F oven for 3 minutes, or until hot. Do not salt until ready to serve.

Fried Mushroom Pasta

PANZAROTTI (PANZEROTTI) DI FUNGHI

I like to pass panzarotti as hors d'oeuvres and have given a recipe here that will make enough of these half moon–shaped panzarotti for a large party. The recipe may be cut in half, or any unfried panzarotti may be frozen to be fried at a later time or to be boiled and served with a simple butter and cheese sauce. If you fall in love with panzarotti, as I have, try a variety of fillings. Pieces of chopped, marinated artichoke hearts for hors d'oeuvres are particularly good.

FILLING

1 pound mushrooms, cleaned, trimmed, and minced
½ small onion (about 2 tablespoons), minced
Salt and freshly ground pepper
2 tablespoons extra-virgin olive oil

½ cup ricotta cheese, drained in a sieve ½ hour
1½ ounces prosciutto (about ¼ cup), minced
1 ounce mozzarella cheese (about ½ cup), finely shredded
1 large egg, lightly beaten

Pasta dough made with 3 cups flour (page 122)

Vegetable oil or lard for frying

1. In a sauté pan over medium-high heat, sauté the mushrooms, onions, salt, and pepper in the olive oil until mushrooms are brown and juices evaporate, 5 to 10 minutes. Mushrooms should be as dry as possible. Cool slightly and combine with the cheeses, prosciutto, and beaten egg. Adjust seasonings.

2. Divide the dough into 10 pieces and roll each piece out in a pasta machine to the thinnest setting according to directions on page 123. Cut fluted circles approximately 2½ inches in diameter from the dough. Place a generous teaspoon of filling in the center of each circle. Fold in half and press edges together using a bit of cold water to help seal the dough. Lay the pieces on a lightly floured towel in one layer, pieces not touching, to dry. Turn to dry the second side. Repeat with the remaining dough and filling.

Fried Mushroom Pasta (continued)

3. In a deep, heavy frying pan, heat 1 inch of lard or oil to 360°F–375°F, or hot enough to brown a bread cube. Add panzarotti a few at a time, being careful not to crowd the pan. Fry until golden, turning once (about 1 minute per side). Drain on paper towels and sprinkle with salt before serving. To reheat, place the pieces before salting them in a 400°F oven for 3 minutes, or until hot and crisped. *Makes 140 panzarotti.*

Collars

COLLARI

In southern Italy deep-frying dough was part of the traditional winter pig killing. As the lard was being rendered, mothers would break off pieces of bread dough, fill them with a snack, and deep-fry them in the hot lard for the children. Sometimes they would fry pieces of dough without any filling and then brush them with honey or sprinkle them with sugar while still hot. This tradition survives in "dough boys," the deep-fried, sugared pieces of dough seen at Italian-American street fairs. The fillings for the Calabrian version of these treats are merely suggestions—you can use what appeals to you.

BREAD DOUGH	FILLINGS
1 package dry yeast	Anchovies or
1 cup warm water (110°F)	Prosciutto in thin strips or
3 cups all-purpose flour	Thin slices provolone or
1 teaspoon salt	cacciocavalo cheese or
½ cup lard, at room	Pitted black olives, coarsely
temperature, diced	chopped

Lard or vegetable oil
    for frying

1. Dissolve the yeast in ¼ cup of the warm water. Put the flour on work surface and toss in salt. Scatter the lard over the flour and

work it in with your fingertips. When all the fat is incorporated, make a well in the center and add the dissolved yeast and the remaining water. Gradually incorporate the flour into the liquids and knead well for 8 to 10 minutes, or until a firm, smooth dough is formed. The dough may also be made by food processor or electric mixer with dough hook. Put the finished dough into an oiled or floured bowl, turn to coat, cover with towel, and let rise until doubled in bulk (about 2 hours).

2. Pinch off walnut-size pieces of dough. Either with a rolling pin on a floured surface or in a pasta machine, roll each piece into a 5 x 3-inch rectangle no thicker than ¹⁄₁₆ inch. Put one of the selected fillings, or a combination such as ham and cheese, on a rectangle of dough, leaving a ½-inch border, and roll up loosely, jelly-roll fashion. Form a ring (a collar) by pinching the ends together. Use a little water if necessary to make the dough stick. Shape and fill the remaining dough.

3. Heat lard or oil in a deep skillet to 1 inch depth and heat to 370°F. Cook the collari a few at a time so as not to crowd the pan. Cook until light brown, about 45 seconds per side. Drain on paper towels. Sprinkle with coarse salt if desired and if filling is not already salty. Serve hot. May be reheated in 400°F oven 2 to 3 minutes. *Makes about 40.*

• • •

Note: Lard is the traditional fat used for collari. When I want to make the collari in a hurry I often buy ready-made dough from the Italian baker. That dough is made without lard and the results are different but equally delicious.

Rice Croquettes

ARANCINI

"Arancini" translates to little oranges and that is what the Sicilians think these appetizer croquettes resemble. I don't remember these from my own childhood since we didn't know too many Sicilians, but if I had I might have named them "little delights"! I discovered them in Italy but many American-Sicilians remember eating larger versions of these as a main course. Arancini may have a number of different fillings—tomato sauce and a bit of meatball, ham and tiny peas, chicken livers and tomatoes. Saffron is often added to the rice mixture to increase their golden color, but I prefer them without.

1½ cups Arborio rice
5 tablespoons unsalted
    butter
1⅓ cups freshly grated
    Parmesan cheese
    (about 4½ ounces)
5 eggs
½ carrot (about ¼ cup
    minced)
¼ small onion (about 1½
    tablespoons minced)
1 cup plus 2 tablespoons
    all-purpose flour

1 cup warm milk
1 bay leaf
¼ teaspoon freshly grated
    nutmeg
Salt and freshly ground
    black pepper
¼ cup finely diced Italian
    Fontina cheese
¼ cup finely diced prosciutto
2 cups dry breadcrumbs
Olive oil or vegetable oil
    for frying

1. Stir the rice into 3½ cups of boiling salted water. Cover and let simmer until rice is tender but still "al dente" and water is absorbed, 18 to 20 minutes. Remove from heat and immediately stir in 2 tablespoons butter and 1 cup Parmesan cheese. Let cool slightly, then lightly beat 3 eggs and stir them in.

2. Meanwhile, in a heavy medium saucepan, melt the remaining 3 tablespoons butter. Add the carrot and the onion and cook over moderately low heat until softened but not browned, about 8 minutes. Off the heat, blend in the flour and return to heat for 2 to 3 minutes, stirring so flour cooks but does not brown. Off the heat, whisk in the warm milk, return to heat, and bring to a boil, stirring until thick and smooth. Reduce heat to low, add bay leaf, nutmeg,

salt, and pepper and simmer for at least 10 minutes. Remove from heat, discard bay leaf, and stir in remaining ⅓ cup Parmesan cheese, and let sauce cool. Mix in diced Fontina and prosciutto.

3. To form the rice balls, wet hands and place about ½ tablespoon of cooled rice in the palm of one hand. Press with a finger to form an indentation. Place 1 teaspoon of the cheese and prosciutto filling in the center of the rice. Cover with another ½ tablespoon of the rice and form a ball completely encasing the filling.

4. Roll the rice balls in flour. Lightly beat the remaining eggs. Dip the rice balls in the eggs, and roll them in the breadcrumbs to coat. Set them on a tray. For best results in deep frying, cover and refrigerate 2 hours or overnight.

5. Heat 1 inch of oil in a deep pan to 375°F. Fry the arancini in the hot oil a few at a time without crowding the pan, turning, until golden brown (about 1½ minutes). Drain on paper towels and serve immediately. *Makes 4 dozen.*

• • •

Note: Arancini should be served hot. If necessary, they may be reheated in a 400°F oven for 3 to 5 minutes, or until crisped and hot. I have refrigerated leftover arancini and reheated them the same way a few days later and found them quite good. They can also be formed up to 3 days ahead, refrigerated on a tray, and deep-fried at the last minute. They may be frozen, unfried, for 3 months.

Festival of the Madonna della Civita, Knightsville, 1921.

OLIVE OIL

The flavor of olive oil is so important to southern Italian cooking that the character of the food would be completely altered without it. It is a natural complement to such southern staples as garlic, eggplant, peppers, tomatoes, anchovies, and the like. In the past, olive oil was not restricted to culinary uses. It was used in oil lamps for light and was a medicine with almost magical qualities. Everyone's Italian grandmother rubbed olive oil on burns and rashes and dribbled a few warm drops into an aching ear.

At the time of the greatest emigration, olive oil was available in southern Italy but it was costly for poor families. Many people reserved it for salads or cooked vegetables and used pork fat for cooking. Some fortunate families had olive trees on their property and picked their own olives and either pressed them themselves or brought them to a common olive press. They were fortunate because, if they kept the first cold-pressed oil (extra-virgin), they had the best possible flavor. The commercial olive oils that were sold in shops were of a lesser quality and lacked the full flavor of the more carefully produced product. These commercial oils (known as "pure olive oil") were from the second or third pressing of the olives and were chemically treated to reduce what would be high acidic levels. Some first pressing oil was added to pure olive oil to boost its flavor.

It was this commercial pure olive oil that the southern Italian immigrant brought to the United States. Unfortunately, this practically tasteless oil became the basis of Italian-American cooking and the all-important olive flavor disappeared from the food of almost everyone except those Italians who continued to bring back their own olive oil from family farms in Italy.

Fortunately, today many extra-virgin olive oils are

available on the market. The salumeria where I shop has served the southern Italian community for years. After decades of selling one common brand of pure olive oil, the owner finds that now Italian-Americans are sampling his large variety of full-flavored extra-virgin olive oils.

Not all extra-virgin olive oils are equal. The quality depends on the quality of the olives and on whether they were picked from the tree or allowed to fall to the ground where they were bruised. "Extra-virgin" on the label will assure the buyer that the oil has no more than 1 percent oleic acid, but the buyer must judge the taste.

I choose different oils for different reasons. I select southern Italian oils, such as Colavita and Sclafani, for most cooking and frying. The flavor is full and it is economical enough to use daily. I use a top-quality olive oil, such as the Tuscan Badia a Coltibuono or the Umbrian Mancianti, for salads and dressing cooked foods. The simpler the dish, the greater need for a better oil. Some southern Italian oil producers are beginning to use the same careful techniques as the Tuscans and I think we will soon see some extraordinary southern extra-virgin olive oils on the market.

Handle all olive oil with care. Keep it away from heat and light. I buy large cans of my "everyday" olive oil and transfer smaller amounts to a small stainless oil can for easier use.

Fried Breaded Mozzarella

MOZZARELLA IMPANATA

Fried breaded mozzarella shows up on such eclectic menus that it is hard to remember that it is a traditional southern Italian antipasto. If you cannot get freshly made mozzarella, do as the immigrants did and substitute scamorza or mild provolone. Serve on a plate with fresh basil leaves and chopped fresh tomatoes seasoned with oil and basil, or with a spoonful of either fresh tomato sauce or anchovy sauce (pages 82 and 108).

1¼ pounds fresh mozzarella
   cheese
¼ cup flour
2 eggs, beaten with
   ½ teaspoon salt

1 cup dry breadcrumbs
Olive oil for frying
Salt

1. Cut the mozzarella into ½-inch-thick rounds. There should be about 18 pieces. Coat the pieces well, including sides, with flour. Pat off excess and dip into the eggs. Drop into breadcrumbs and coat completely, pressing bread to be sure it adheres all over cheese. It is absolutely necessary that the cheese be completely coated or it will seep out during cooking. Pieces may be refrigerated if desired for later cooking.

2. Put the olive oil into a deep frying pan to ½-inch depth and bring to 375°F. Using a slotted spoon, carefully place the mozzarella pieces in the hot oil, a few at a time so as not to crowd the pan. Cook, turning once, until golden on both sides (about 1 minute). Remove to paper towels to drain. Salt and serve while still hot.
Serves 6.

MEMORIES

*"Your nose has to feel all the different
perfumes and fragrances from the food."*

The basic Italian ingredients are easy to find here because of the large Italian population. The problem with getting foods here like you could back in Italy is with the vegetables because they have a different taste. For example, I used to cook a lot of eggplant when I was in Sicily because they are different there—they are sweet and white and here they are very bitter. Tomatoes are not as tasty here either.

Regarding the herbs, I import them from my house. My grandmother prepares all the herbs every summer. She dries them and it is a very easy process. She dries oregano and sage, mint and basil and rosemary. She does this in a very dry and dark place, not in the sun because the sun burns them and makes them yellow. She dries them in the attic because there is ventilation there.

Herbs are important because in Sicily you cook a lot with the fragrances, with the herbs, so your nose has to feel all the different perfumes and fragrances from the food. Actually sometimes we use flowers such as jasmine because our cooking has been influenced by the Arabic domination [of Sicily] so we use a lot of sweet and sour, a lot of sugar and vinegar, lemon. The Arabic domination is why the Sicilian people are very famous for their sweets as well.

We would start always with a first dish, which was pasta, or a soup, a minestrone, and then you would have maybe a kind of sandwich steak or veal or pork cutlet maybe alla griglia, grilled, with a salad or vegetables as a side dish. Then just fruit at the end, or cakes on occasions such as parties.

My mother would do the fresh tomato sauce during the summer to use for the winter and also the kind of dried sauce. You would strain your tomatoes and put it under the sun. You turn it so the sun would dry it and it becomes like a tomato paste. You did this in big dishes which are called congotti. These are typical Sicilian dishes which are very large. In the old ages, they used to have one dish for the family and they would eat all from this dish. When I was young I would take turns with my sister turning the tomatoes in the sun while we were sunbathing. We would use it to season minestrone in the winter, or even to make the tomato sauce stronger because it has a nice flavor. We call it sugo.

My father loved to cook as well and he would do the shopping, as a lot of men in Sicily did. He would do the vegetable shopping every day. He would go to the market and buy everything. He would teach us a lot of northern Italian recipes as well because he was a partisan during World War II. He fought and he was a prisoner. He lived in Veneto for many, many years during the war, with a family there, and so he learned how to cook according to that region— risotti and polenta. So we were the only Sicilian family in Caltagirone to eat polenta in winter because of my father.

When my mother or my father would show me how to cook, they never made me try, they always let me see or watch what they did.

Italian men often did the shopping.

It is a kind of ritual—on Sunday, for example, everybody pre-pares this important lunch. A ragu sauce, or a roast pork or a roast veal with rosemary, basil, polenta, roasted potatoes on the side or onions. And everybody knows that Sunday at one o'clock is the most important appointment for the family because everybody is reunited. The grandparents come, or the uncles and whatever. And after you drink your coffee, you talk about the main events of the week, and then you go out for a walk.

My grandparents had a big farm. I loved their house. During the harvest they would put all the wheat in the house and we would play on the grano, on the wheat. Then they would bring that to the mill and make flour out of it, but it was kind of a game for us. And they would also make a sweet for us out of cotonia, which was a sweet apple, and out of them they would make a dry mustard, mela co-tonia. These were our big treats—no toys, no presents.

My father would grow tomatoes, eggplants; we had a small vine-yard and olive trees. He also grew a kind of zucchini which you cannot find here, which is very exquisite. One summer he came here and he grew it here in Rhode Island.

When my mother would teach us how to cook, she would always tell us the ingredients first. For a soup, for example, we had to cut all the onions and potatoes and tomatoes, or whatever, and wash them. Then we would watch her putting these things together and we would be in charge of stirring it or being sure that it had enough salt. She would always ask first how it tasted, then we would tell her, and then she would correct our taste. It was always by word, never with recipes.

My grandmother had a wood oven and she would make all the bread. She would make it once a week and keep it for the whole week. Then, on Sunday again, she would make more bread and pizza. She would also make calzone with spinach or broccoli and olives. We would always help her kneading the dough and make it rise. She would teach us that food is precious, you do not waste it. She would take the fresh baked bread, a round loaf, and cut it in half. In it she would put some pecorino cheese, black olives, olive oil, a little bit of salt, some rosemary, herbs, or oregano, and you would eat it right away and it would be fantastic. It is called pane consato.

In Sicily, the Christmas season coincides with the oranges and tangerines, so you have the house full of them and it would have a beautiful fragrance. You always decorated the nativity scene with oranges or tangerines. We also made these cookies which were very exquisite. It was a type of rolled dough, very, very fine and thin, filled with honey and nuts, pinoli. And you would roll it and make nice shapes and these are called colorelle. Each family exchanged the colorelle, each one had a different flavor. You can also make it with wine. It is called mosto. You boil it and it has a heavier flavor, but it is still good.

A Sicilian tradition it is a shame to lose here is the breakfast. In the summer, because it is so hot, instead of having a hot breakfast you would go to a bar, which is like a cafe here in America, and you would have la granita, which is a kind of slush but it is very different. You would have different flavors, like almond, lemon, or mulberry. Then you would have coffee with heavy cream on top with a brioche or a croissant. This is the Sicilian breakfast, and it is so good and refreshing.

SANTINA FORTUNATO
(from Caltagirone in Catania)

ASK FOR THURBERS' S.I. (SPECIALLY IMPORTED.) SPICES.

Eggplant in the Style of Modugno

MELANZANE ALLA MODUGNO

These Apulian eggplant rolls are more or less a variation of eggplant Parmigiana. They make a wonderful antipasto as well as a delicious luncheon dish. Serve them at room temperature in order to enjoy their flavor to the fullest.

1 large eggplant, about
  1½ pounds
Salt
Olive oil for frying
¼ cup dry breadcrumbs
3 garlic cloves, minced
½ cup parsley, chopped
8 ounces grated mozzarella
  cheese

2 ounces grated Parmesan
  cheese
1 egg, beaten
Freshly ground black pepper
1 cup marinara sauce
  (page 82)

1. Cut the eggplant in half and then slice lengthwise into ¼-inch-thick slices. (There should be about 20 to 24 pieces.) Layer in colander, salting each layer, and place a plate and weight on top. Let it drain 1 hour. Gently squeeze excess water from eggplant and dry with paper towels.

2. Put the olive oil into frying pan to depth of ½ inch. Turn heat to high. Fry the eggplant slices in hot oil until golden and cooked through. Drain on paper towels or brown paper bag.

3. Preheat the oven to 375°F. Combine the breadcrumbs, garlic, parsley, the grated mozzarella, and all but 2 tablespoons of the Parmesan. Add enough beaten egg to bind. Taste for seasoning and add salt and pepper.

4. Reserve 3 tablespoons tomato sauce and spoon the remainder into the bottom of a baking pan that will hold the eggplant rolls in one layer. Place 1 generous tablespoon filling on each slice of eggplant. Roll up and place in pan. Drizzle on remaining tomato sauce and sprinkle with reserved Parmesan. Bake for 20 minutes. *Serves 6 to 8.*

Eggplant in a Carriage

MELANZANE IN CARROZZA

Choose eggplants as similar in size as possible. Long narrow ones work best. Although the preparation may seem a bit time consuming, the "sandwiches" may be made and fried early in the day, reserved on a cookie sheet at room temperature, and reheated for 5 minutes in a 400°F oven. Decorate with a small bouquet of basil for a pretty presentation.

2 eggplants, 1½ to 2 pounds total weight	20 to 30 basil leaves
	Pepper
Salt	1 cup flour
Extra-virgin olive oil	3 eggs, beaten with 2
6 ounces fresh mozzarella cheese	teaspoons each water and oil
8 anchovy fillets	3 cups fresh breadcrumbs

1. Wash and trim the ends from the eggplant but do not peel. Cut into ¼-inch-thick round slices. Place in a colander, salt, weight, and let drain 1 hour. Pat dry.

2. Sauté the slices, a few at a time, in about ¼ cup olive oil until lightly browned (about 3 minutes per side). It may be necessary to add additional oil since eggplants absorb it as they cook. Or, brush both sides with olive oil and bake in a single layer in a 375°F oven for 12 to 15 minutes, turning once. The eggplant slices should be cooked through but not so soft that they do not hold their shape.

3. Cut the mozzarella into ⅛-inch-thick slices. Chop the basil and anchovies together. Season eggplant slices with pepper. They should not need salt because of the anchovies. Cover half the eggplant slices with mozzarella and sprinkle mozzarella with basil-anchovy mixture. Cover with remaining eggplant.

4. Dip eggplant "sandwiches" into flour, dust off excess, dip into beaten egg mixture, and finally coat with breadcrumbs. Be sure that each is coated well before shaking off excess crumbs. (This may be done hours ahead if desired.)

5. Put olive oil into a heavy skillet to ½ inch depth and heat to 375°F. Fry the eggplant sandwiches a few at a time in hot oil, turning

once, until golden on both sides. Drain on paper towels and serve with anchovy or marinara sauce if desired (pages 108 and 82). *Serves 6 to 8.*

Eggplant Fingers

MELANZANE A MANNELLA

These finger-length strips of fried, seasoned eggplant can be served warm or at room temperature. They make a great addition to an antipasto buffet since they can be made a day or two ahead. Vary the seasoning according to your whim or what is in your garden. Basil, mint, and parsley all work well.

2 small eggplants, about
   1½ pounds total weight
Salt
Olive oil for frying
3 medium garlic cloves,
   minced

3 tablespoons fresh oregano
   or 1 tablespoon dried
3 tablespoons red wine
   vinegar

1. Preheat oven to 350°F.
2. Wash and dry the eggplant. Trim tops and bottoms and cut each eggplant into ½-inch-thick slices. Cut each slice crosswise into ¾-inch-wide strips. Place the strips in colander, sprinkle with salt, weight, and allow to drain 1 hour.
3. Pat the eggplant dry. Put ¾ inch olive oil in a frying pan and heat until very hot. Add a few eggplant strips at a time so as not to crowd the pan and cook, turning, until golden on all sides (2 to 3 minutes). Remove with a slotted spoon to a baking dish. Continue with the remaining eggplant, seasoning each layer in the baking dish with garlic, oregano, vinegar, and salt as needed. When all the eggplant is added, bake 20 minutes. *Serves 4 to 6.*

Polenta Pizzas

PIZZETTE DI POLENTA

I created these appetizer "pizzette" based on the food memories of Italian friends. I have made them with various combinations of cheeses: Emmentaler, Fontina, and Parmesan; scamorza and pecorino. I sometimes serve them with a bit of marinara sauce (page 82).

4 ounces pancetta, finely chopped
4 cups water
1 tablespoon salt
1 cup Italian cornmeal, preferably coarse

3 ounces fresh mozzarella cheese, grated
3 ounces Fontina cheese, grated
½ cup grated Parmesan cheese

1. Put the pancetta in a small frying pan and slowly render until slightly crisped. Set aside with rendered fat.

2. Bring the water to a boil. Add salt and gradually stir in the cornmeal and cook, stirring frequently, until the mixture is thick and pulls away from the bottom and sides of pan, about 40 minutes. Stir in the reserved pancetta and fat and let mixture sit on heat 30 seconds without additional stirring. Immediately pour onto a buttered 12 x 16-inch baking sheet, spreading evenly. Smooth the top with a moistened spatula. Let polenta cool until firm.

3. Using a 3-inch-round cutter or a glass, cut out as many polenta rounds as possible. Invert rounds onto buttered baking sheet. (This may be done 2 days ahead and refrigerated.) Combine cheeses and sprinkle generously on top of each polenta round. (This can be prepared 8 hours ahead and refrigerated.)

4. Preheat the oven to 400°F. Bake until cheese melts and polenta is browned, about 8 minutes. Cool slightly before serving. *Serves 8.*

CORNMEAL

There are so few accounts of polenta in southern Italian cooking that many people are completely unaware that it was used at all. In fact, cornmeal was introduced to Naples from Spain at the end of the sixteenth century and enjoyed a long if not prolific history as part of "la cucina povera." Polenta was seldom eaten in the south as is but was used to thicken soups or as a substitute for pasta as in the Neapolitan Layered Polenta. Immigrants continued to cook with cornmeal in America as they had in the old country, but its use began to fade as their lives began to prosper. Italian-Americans were anxious to distance themselves from foods that were associated with hard times. Consequently, few southern recipes for polenta exist.

Italian cornmeal is usually available in two grades: fine and coarse. I prefer the coarser texture for savory recipes and the finer for baking, although one may be substituted for the other with acceptable results. Instant polenta may also be substituted with no loss of quality. Be sure to judge the cooking time by tasting to tell when the raw corn taste disappears; don't go by the time indicated on the box.

If you have trouble making a smooth, lump-free polenta, try stirring the cornmeal with enough cold water to make a smooth paste; then add this to the remaining water called for and bring to a boil, and cook until done.

Marinated Shrimp and Fennel

MARINATA DI GAMBERONI E FINOCCHIO

Marinated fish is a very popular southern Italian antipasto. Both in Italy and in the United States, Italians would take whatever fish was readily available, poach or fry it, and then dress it simply—usually with olive oil, lemon juice, and parsley. Conch, which the early Italians called "snail," was abundant in Rhode Island, and snail salad was the most common fish antipasto. May I never have to eat it again! Shrimp became part of the diet of Italian-Americans when they could afford it. This delicious shrimp antipasto is a more complex recipe than most simple marinated fish antipasti but it is well worth the extra effort. It can precede the most elegant of dinners or be the star attraction of a simple meal.

2 large heads fennel
¾ cup dry white wine
½ cup water
3 tablespoons olive oil
2 lemons
3 fresh thyme sprigs or
    ½ teaspoon dried

1 bay leaf
½ teaspoon salt
5 peppercorns
2 pounds medium shrimp
    in shells
1 stalk celery

SALSA VERDE

1 bunch parsley, chopped
    (about ½ cup)
1 teaspoon anchovy paste
    or 3 mashed anchovies
3 tablespoons minced red
    onion, soaked in cold
    water 1 hour (change
    water 3 times)

2 tablespoons capers
1 tablespoon minced garlic
¼ cup lemon juice
¾ cup extra-virgin olive oil
Salt and freshly ground
    black pepper

1. Trim tops and bruised outer layers from the fennel. Cut into ½-inch pieces lengthwise through the bulbs. Put into a noncorrosive pan with the white wine, water, olive oil, juice of 1 lemon, thyme, bay leaf, salt, and peppercorns. Bring to a boil, reduce heat, and

simmer until fennel is tender (12 to 15 minutes). Remove fennel with a slotted spoon and reduce cooking liquid to 3 tablespoons. Remove bay leaf, thyme sprigs, and peppercorns. Spoon the liquid over the fennel and let cool.

2. Put the shrimp, juice of 1 lemon, celery, and cold water to cover in a saucepan. Bring to a boil, turn off heat, and let shrimp cool. Peel shrimp when cool enough to handle. Combine shrimp and fennel.

3. Make the salsa. Stir together the parsley, anchovy, drained red onion, capers, garlic, and lemon juice. Beat in olive oil and season to taste with salt and pepper. Toss shrimp and fennel with sauce and let marinate at least 1 hour before serving. Serve at room temperature. *Serves 8.*

•   •   •

Note: For a very simple version of the above recipe, blanch the fennel in boiling salted water until just tender. Plunge into iced water, drain, and dry. Cook shrimp as in step 2. Combine shrimp and fennel and dress with the best quality extra-virgin olive oil, lemon juice, and chopped parsley.

White Bean and Tuna Salad

INSALATA DI FAGIOLI E TONNO

If there is an exception to the rule that the whole is only equal to the sum of its parts, this dish would be it. The combination of a few simple ingredients creates a dish so tasty that it is a long-standing favorite of Italians here and abroad. The early Italian-Americans were very suspicious of most canned foods and often discarded canned meats that were distributed by social workers. They had no qualms, however, about canned tuna, which was already an enormously successful industry in Sicily. Southern Italians in Italy used canned tuna often as a flavoring for pasta, bean, and rice dishes since it added saltiness and salt itself was a government-controlled product and hard to come by. Because salt was available in the United States, many of the canned tuna recipes disappeared.

1 cup dried white beans
   (Great Northern,
   cannellini)
1 celery stalk, with tops
1 small onion, peeled and
   cut in half
1 bay leaf
⅓ cup extra-virgin olive oil
1 7-ounce can tuna packed
   in oil (preferably Italian
   tuna in olive oil)

1 small red onion, finely
   minced and soaked 1 hour
   in cold water (change
   water 3 times)
⅓ cup black Gaeta olives
2 tablespoons red or white
   wine vinegar
Salt and freshly ground
   black pepper
½ cup fresh parsley leaves

1. Soak the washed and picked-over beans in cold water to cover overnight or at least 4 hours. Drain and rinse. Or use the quick soak method: place the washed and picked-over beans in a large saucepan. Cover with 2 inches of cold water and bring to a boil. Boil 2 minutes. Remove from heat and let soak covered 1 hour. Drain and rinse.

2. Put soaked beans in a large pot and cover with fresh cold water by 2 inches. Bring to a boil, reduce heat, and add the celery, onion, and bay leaf. Simmer 45 minutes to 1 hour, or until beans are tender. Drain and discard celery, onion, and bay leaf. Add olive oil to warm beans and toss gently, being careful not to break beans.

3. Break up the tuna and add to the warm beans. Drain and dry the red onion and add to the beans. Add olives, vinegar, salt, pepper, and parsley. Toss together gently and let sit an hour or so before serving. *Serves 6 to 8.*

. . .

Note: Dried beans should never be salted while they are soaking or being cooked: the salt toughens them. Canned beans are often used for this recipe but I really don't think that they are a satisfying substitute for those you cook yourself.

HERBS

Mother Nature was very generous to southern Italy where herbs grow wild and are available even to the poorest of families. The herbs are plentiful for most of the year and the Italian housewife dries what will not grow in winter.

The immigrants grew the herbs that they were used to —parsley, oregano, basil, marjoram—in their gardens and in pots on their windowsills or rooftops. They dried them in the sun or in attics when the climate permitted. Gradually, as urban families did less home gardening, they eliminated fresh herbs from recipes and authentic flavors disappeared from much Italian-American cooking. Eventually, as did many Americans, they began to rely—not always with restraint—on commercially dried herbs.

Today, it is possible to find fresh herbs in many markets. Choose them whenever possible. When it is necessary to substitute dried herbs for fresh, use a third as much. If the dried herb is added to anything other than a liquid, it should first be refreshed in a small amount of boiling or very hot water. If herbs have been added at the beginning of a long-cooking recipe, add a bit more a few minutes before the dish is finished, when correcting the seasonings.

Sausage and Pepper Appetizer

ANTIPASTO DI SALSICCIA E PEPERONI

I will always associate the aroma of sausages and peppers with Italian street fairs. The combination seems to have been made in heaven. The recipe below offers a new way to match them that makes a great appetizer which can be passed to guests. The pepper sauce can be made two to three days ahead and reheated when ready to serve.

6 red bell peppers
3 green bell peppers
6 tablespoons extra-virgin
  olive oil
3 garlic cloves, smashed
  and peeled
¾ pound peeled and seeded
  fresh tomatoes or well-
  drained canned Italian
  plum tomatoes (about
  1 cup)

¼ cup chopped parsley
Salt
8 Italian sausages, sweet or
  hot

Special equipment:
  40 wooden skewers
  soaked 1 hour in cold
  water

1. Wash the peppers. Remove stems, ribs, and seeds. Cut into 1-inch pieces.

2. Put the oil and garlic in a pot large enough to hold the peppers. Heat gently until the garlic is golden (about 3 minutes). If desired, remove the garlic for a more subtle flavor. Add the peppers, cover the pan, and continue to cook over gentle heat until peppers are slightly limp (8 minutes). Add the tomatoes, parsley, and salt to pot and put cover on slightly askew. Cook 30 minutes, or until peppers are soft. Puree contents in a food processor or blender and strain into a small pot. Cook gently until reduced and thick enough to coat a spoon.

3. Prick the sausages in 4 to 5 places with a small skewer. Parboil 8 minutes. Drain and when cool enough to handle, cut into 1-inch-long pieces. Place one piece on the end of a wooden skewer. Place on broiling rack over drip pan and broil 4 minutes, turning to cook evenly. Place on serving tray and serve with warm pepper sauce. *Makes 40 to 48.*

Baked Olives

OLIVE AL FORNO

Whether you cure your own olives (page 151) or purchase ready-cured ones, baking them with herbs and spices is a wonderful way to make them your own. The recipe below is one of my favorite combinations, but you can experiment with any number of herbs or spices. Once cooled, the olives can be put into glass jars and covered with oil, for long keeping. Use the oil from the olives for cooking or for dressing salads. I give jars of these olives as house gifts or Christmas presents. Giving gifts of homemade food was very much a part of the Italians' way of life both in this country and in Italy.

1 pound brine-cured black olives such as Gaeta	2 sprigs thyme, about 2 inches long
3 large garlic cloves, smashed and peeled	1 small dried hot pepper or ½ teaspoon flakes (optional)
3 sprigs rosemary, about 3 inches long, or 1 teaspoon fennel seeds	¾ cup extra-virgin olive oil

Drain the olives from the brine. Place in a shallow 9-inch round dish, preferably earthenware. Tuck the garlic and herbs in among the olives. Pour the olive oil over all. (Oil will not completely cover all olives.) Put into 325°F oven and cook 30 minutes, stirring from time to time. Serve at room temperature. To store, place in sterilized glass jars and add additional oil to cover completely. *Serves 8 to 10.*

Amalfi Coast–Style Artichokes

CARCIOFI AMALFITANA

The gardens of the Amalfi Coast are truly a wonder! On hillsides so steep that a goat would balk, Italians cultivate gardens as well as citrus and nut trees. It's no wonder that these same farmers were able to cultivate gardens in seemingly impossible places in the United States. The combination of lemon, mint, and walnuts is a delicious flavoring for artichokes.

6 medium to large artichokes, stems attached	6 tablespoons chopped fresh parsley
2 lemons	2 teaspoons grated lemon zest
5 garlic cloves, minced	Salt
¾ cup chopped walnuts	½ cup extra-virgin olive oil
¼ cup chopped fresh mint	

1. Peel the attached stems of the artichokes and immediately rub them with a cut lemon. Continually rub the artichoke with lemon half as you trim. Remove the small, tough row of leaves from the bottom. Turn artichokes on their sides and cut about 1 inch from their tops. Use a scissor to trim tops of other leaves. Turn trimmed artichokes upside down and press and roll to open and loosen the leaves. Remove the choke and purple top leaves with a grapefruit spoon or small curved knife.

2. Mix together the garlic, walnuts, mint, parsley, and lemon zest. Season with salt and moisten with about 2 tablespoons olive oil. Stuff the mixture well into the center of the artichoke and between the leaves.

3. Choose a casserole large enough to hold all the artichokes standing up in one layer. Heat half the remaining oil in the bottom of casserole and working with 1 or 2 artichokes at a time, lightly brown on all sides. Brown tops carefully so stuffing remains inside. When all the artichokes are browned, return them to the casserole with their stems facing up. Pour on the remaining oil and add enough water to come ¾ inch of the way up the sides. Cover with a double thickness of damp paper towels or a single layer of wax paper and the pan lid. Cook over medium heat until tender (about 45 minutes). If water evaporates while cooking, add more warm water to the pan.

4. Remove cooked artichokes from the pan to a serving plate. If necessary, reduce cooking juices to about ¾ cup. Squeeze the second lemon and add 3 tablespoons juice to pan. Heat briefly and pour over artichokes. Serve warm or at room temperature. *Serves 6.*

Nonna's Artichokes

CARCIOFI ALLA NONNA

This is the first way I ever remember eating artichokes. The preparation is simple and rustic. Nonna never cut away the tops of the leaves but opened them up by turning the artichokes upside down and pressing and rolling them on the counter. I still love the squeaking sound they make.

6 large artichokes	5 garlic cloves, minced
1 lemon	Salt
1 large bunch parsley, chopped	½ cup extra-virgin olive oil

1. Cut the stems from the artichokes, remove the small tough bottom leaves, and rub all over with lemon half. Turn artichoke upside down and press and roll to open up and loosen leaves.

2. Season the chopped parsley with garlic, salt, and enough of the olive oil to coat (about 3 tablespoons). Divide the parsley evenly among the artichokes, putting it in the centers and between the leaves.

3. Place the artichokes in a pot large enough to hold them in one layer. Salt and pour on remaining olive oil. Squeeze the juice of the lemon over artichokes. Pour enough water into pan to come 1 inch up the sides. Bring to a boil. Cover the pan with a double thickness of paper towel or single layer of wax paper and the pot lid. Reduce heat and simmer 45 minutes, or until tender. If water evaporates while cooking, add some warm water to the pan. Drain well before serving. *Serves 6.*

ROASTING PEPPERS

My grandmother only roasted red peppers because they were sweeter. She would lean them against a hot pot on the stove, turning them so that the heat of the pot and the flame of the burner would soften and char them. I use this more modern method.

Wash the peppers and place directly on an oven rack under a hot broiler. Broil and turn the peppers until they are charred on all sides. Remove from the oven and put into a paper bag for 20 minutes to steam. Remove the stems and peel the peppers. Cut in half and remove seeds. Cut as needed for recipe.

Roasted peppers have a particular flavor. If a recipe calls for peppers "peeled, if desired," you should use peppers that you peel with a vegetable peeler, not peppers that have been roasted and peeled.

Roasted Pepper Salad

INSALATA DI PEPERONI ARROSTITI

When I first ate this Sicilian salad many years ago in Boston's Italian North End, red and green peppers were the only varieties readily available. Now the markets have yellow and purple—an obvious sign of how popular Mediterranean flavors are today.

6 sweet green peppers, roasted and peeled (opposite page)
6 sweet red peppers, roasted and peeled (opposite page)
6 ripe salad tomatoes
1 egg yolk
1 teaspoon anchovy paste or 1 anchovy, rinsed and mashed
1 teaspoon red wine vinegar

1 cup extra-virgin olive oil
½ red onion, minced
3 tablespoons chopped parsley
3 tablespoons capers, rinsed, dried, and chopped
Salt
1 pound fresh mozzarella cheese, thinly sliced
½ cup fresh peas, blanched 5 minutes, or frozen peas, thawed

1. Cut the peppers into 1-inch strips. Dip the tomatoes into boiling water for 10 seconds. Run briefly under cold water. Peel. Cut into ¼-inch slices.

2. Put the egg yolk, anchovy paste, and vinegar into a bowl and stir together. Add olive oil in a steady stream while mixing well with a wooden spoon. The mixture should be fluid. Add the onion, parsley, and capers. Taste for salt.

3. Arrange peppers, alternating red and green, around the rim of a platter. Alternate cheese and tomatoes in the center. Sprinkle peas over entire salad and drizzle dressing on top. *Serves 8.*

Peppers Preserved in Vinegar

PEPERONI SOTT'ACETO

Preserving vegetables in vinegar is one of the many ways Italians have of putting up foods. Everyone seems to have her own little secret or superstition about the hows and whys. Carmella, an elderly Italian woman who spoke only her native dialect, owned a small fruit and vegetable store on "the Hill." There was a pot-bellied stove in the shop and during the winter Carmella kept it hot with pieces of orange or apple on top to fill the shop with wonderful aromas. Carmella was always there and was usually showing, not telling, customers how to prepare vegetables. When she showed me how to pickle peppers she insisted that there must always be four small onions in the jar—two for me and two for my husband.

Four 1-inch pickling onions	2 cups white wine vinegar
1¾ pounds sweet peppers, red or a combination of red and yellow	About ¾ cup water
	2 sprigs fresh oregano, marjoram, or thyme
1 teaspoon salt	(optional)

1. Cut 3 slashes ⅓ inch deep in both ends of the onions. Place in a 1½-quart glass jar.

2. Wash peppers and remove stems. Cut in half and remove ribs and seeds. Cut into 1-inch strips. Place in the jar with the onions. Sprinkle salt over peppers. Pour in vinegar and water, adding more water if necessary to cover peppers. Add herb if desired. Cover jar and let marinate at room temperature at least 2 weeks before using.

3. To use for an antipasto, remove the peppers from the vinegar, rinse if desired, and place on plate. Sprinkle with a little minced fresh garlic, salt, and extra-virgin olive oil. Garnish with anchovies and olives if desired. *Makes about 1¾ pounds.*

Calabrian Eggplant Salad

INSALATA DI MELANZANE CALABRESE

One winter's night, the artist Italo Scanga, a vibrant, energetic sculptor from Calabria who is working now in California, was visiting Providence. He had invited us to a dinner that he was preparing at a friend's house to introduce us to some of the robust food of Calabria. When Italo cooked, he simply made countless of his favorite dishes and placed them on the table at once. Most of the meal had been prepared by the time we arrived so the only help we could offer was putting it all out. He had made an eggplant salad late in the day and said he was chilling it to remove the warmth. He asked me to get it. I searched and searched through the refrigerator but could find nothing. When he realized what I was doing, he gave me a look of "don't you know anything" and pointed out the window. Nestled there in the snow, along with more than a few bottles of wine, was the eggplant. Italo was born in Calabria at a time when anything but natural refrigeration was unheard of. When Italo makes this salad he uses the entire eggplant—stems and all. He peels the stems and boils them separately since they take a little longer to become tender. He assured me that he wasn't just being frugal—the stems are considered a delicacy. After tasting them, I had to agree.

2 medium eggplants, about 1½ pounds total weight, unpeeled
1 small onion, sliced into rings
¾ pound red peppers preserved in vinegar, drained
¼ cup loosely packed whole fresh mint leaves

3 large garlic cloves, minced
1 teaspoon grated lemon zest
Salt and freshly ground black pepper
6 tablespoons extra-virgin olive oil
3 tablespoons red wine vinegar

1. Remove the stems from the eggplant and peel if using. Cut the eggplant lengthwise into ½-inch-thick slices and cut the slices in half lengthwise. Cook them in a large pot of boiling salted water until just tender but still holding shape, about 8 to 10 minutes. Cook

Calabrian Eggplant Salad (continued)

the stems in boiling salted water until just tender, about 8 minutes. Remove the eggplant and the stems with a slotted spoon and rinse with cold water. Drain well, squeezing gently to remove all excess water. Pat dry with a towel. Blanch the onion rings in the same water for 2 minutes. Drain and pat dry. Cut the peppers into 1-inch strips.

2. Alternate eggplant and preserved peppers in a single layer on a large platter. Top with the onion. Sprinkle with mint, garlic, lemon zest, salt, and pepper. Pour oil over vegetables; drizzle on vinegar. Let sit at room temperature 1 to 6 hours or overnight in refrigerator. Bring to room temperature, toss, and serve. *Serves 6 to 8.*

• • •

Note: Calabrians make this antipasto salad for long keeping. They put the finished eggplant, without the vinegar, in glass jars, being sure that the olive oil covers it completely. When ready to serve, they season it with vinegar and fresh garlic and herbs as needed.

Carmella Iacono in front of her fruit and vegetable store.

Baked Scamorza

SCAMORZA AL FORNO

Be sure to eat this antipasto while the cheese is still warm and runny. I place the still-hot baking dish in the center of the table and provide everyone with a small plate, knife, and plenty of small crostini. The recipe can be doubled for a buffet or large group, in which case it is best to keep it on a warming tray.

¾ pound scamorza cheese (page 100)	5 anchovy fillets, rinsed
½ cup extra-virgin olive oil	2 tablespoons fresh oregano or 2 teaspoons dried
3 ounces Gaeta olives	Freshly ground black pepper

1. Preheat the oven to 450°F.

2. Cut the cheese into ½-inch-thick slices. Put 2 tablespoons olive oil in the bottom of a shallow baking dish. Lay cheese slices in one layer or slightly overlapping in the dish. Sprinkle the olives over the cheese.

3. Mash the anchovies to a paste in a small bowl. Beat in the remaining olive oil and the oregano. Pour over the cheese and season with a generous grinding of black pepper. Place the cheese in the oven and bake until runny and slightly browned at the edges (6 to 8 minutes). Serve with plain or garlic Italian toasts (page 7). *Serves 6.*

WINE AND COFFEE

It was customary for Italian children to drink what their parents drank whether it was wine, coffee, or even a small dose of liquor. When we children ate with our grandparents, we were served homemade wine, mixed with water in proportion to our ages. In retrospect, I am grateful for the watering down of the rather potent home potable. Papa, like many of the Italian immigrants, made his own wine, at first using local grapes and eventually buying grapes from California. Making one's own wine was a common practice for the immigrants who settled in areas where they could grow grapes. It is not by accident that many of the premier names in the California wine industry are Italian.

My brothers and sister and I have also drunk coffee for breakfast for as long as I can remember. In Italy, southern Italians made "caffe" from a mixture of water and roasted grain such as barley. This "caffe" had no caffeine and was considered healthy for children to drink. My mother claims that I was a rather colicky baby and that it was only after giving me, at Nonna's suggestion, barley water that I was soothed. In the United States, the immigrants began to drink real coffee and social workers were horrified that even the children drank it. They were even more horrified that many families gave the children a small amount of liquor in their morning coffee to fortify them against colds and germs.

Marinated Zucchini

ZUCCHINE A SCAPECE

This is a popular way of preparing certain foods (fish, meat, vegetables, etc.) in many regions of Italy. The term "a scapece" means preserved under vinegar. It is of the same derivation as the Spanish "escabeche" and some claim it is derived from "esca Apicii," a reference to the Roman cookbook writer Apicius. In southern Italy, vegetables "a scapece" are almost always part of the restaurant antipasto assortment. This particular one would be made there with all green zucchini since I have never seen yellow summer squash as we know it. I like making it with the two colors. It makes a pretty summer presentation, the contrast of textures is good, and I have a lot of neighbors who grow summer squash.

3 medium zucchini,
   about 1 pound (see note
   next page)
3 medium yellow squash,
   about 1 pound
Olive oil for frying
½ cup basil leaves,
   left whole

¼ cup mint leaves,
   left whole
2 to 3 medium garlic cloves,
   minced
Salt and freshly ground
   pepper
3 tablespoons good red
   wine vinegar

Wash the squashes and trim the ends. Slice into ¼-inch-thick rounds. Heat ¼ inch oil in a large, heavy skillet until hot enough to brown a bread cube. Work with a few pieces of squash at a time; do not crowd pan. Add the pieces to the hot oil and fry until lightly browned on each side (about 3 minutes). Remove with a slotted spoon to a serving dish (do not drain), alternating green and yellow slices which should overlap slightly but will remain in one layer in concentric circles or ovals. Tuck basil and mint leaves alternately between slices and sprinkle with garlic, salt, pepper, and vinegar. Let stand 1 hour. The longer the finished dish sits, the better it is. If refrigerated, allow it to come to room temperature before serving. *Serves 6 to 8.*

· · ·

Marinated Zucchini (continued)

Note: When zucchini are small and young, they may simply be trimmed and cooked. If, however, you have reason to suspect their age, it is a good defense against excess water to salt, weight, and drain them 30 minutes before cooking.

Celery Salad

INSALATA DI SEDANO

Celery salad is a crisp addition to an antipasto plate. I use it mostly with wedges of Farmer's Frittata (page 201) or with marinated fish or shellfish. It is also delicious tossed with Bibb lettuce for a refreshing salad after the main course.

1 pound celery, without tops, peeled and ends trimmed
Salt
⅓ cup extra-virgin olive oil

2 tablespoons lemon juice or wine vinegar
1 teaspoon Dijon mustard
Freshly ground black pepper

1. Cut the trimmed celery into narrow sticks 2 inches long and ¼ inch wide. Blanch 1 minute in boiling salted water. Plunge into ice water, drain, and dry well. Cover celery with olive oil and let sit for ½ hour.
2. Mix the vinegar, mustard, salt, and pepper together. Toss together with celery. Correct seasonings. Serve at room temperature. This may be made a day ahead. *Serves 6.*

Salad from the Isle of Capri

INSALATA CAPRESE

The secret to this salad, named for the famous island off the coast of Naples, is to use the very best quality ingredients. That means waiting for native tomatoes and basil, hunting down fresh mozzarella, especially imported buffalo milk mozzarella, and stocking a top-grade extra-virgin olive oil. Although this salad has long been a favorite in Italy, it has only recently found its way into Italian-American cooking now that fresh mozzarella is available.

5 balls of buffalo milk or fresh cow's milk mozzarella	Salt and freshly ground black pepper
5 medium-size ripe tomatoes	About ¼ cup extra-virgin olive oil
½ cup snipped basil	

Slice the mozzarella into thin rounds. Slice the tomatoes into thin rounds. Alternate cheese and tomatoes on a serving dish or on individual salad plates. Scatter basil over top. Season with salt and pepper and drizzle on olive oil to taste. *Serves 8.*

Pushcart Row

Chapter Two

SOUPS

outhern Italians have a saying about soup: "Sette cose fa la zuppa." (Soup does seven things; it relieves your hunger, quenches your thirst, fills your stomach, cleans your teeth, makes you sleep, helps you digest, and colors your cheeks.) Italians felt that way about soup because it was a mainstay of "la cucina povera" diet both in Italy and in America. Many evening meals consisted solely of soup, bread, cheese, and fruit. Once the immigrants found that even a meager job allowed them to buy foods that had only been dreams in Italy, they began to replace soup meals with pasta, meat, and fish. Most families, however, maintained at least one night of the week as soup night. In Rhode Island it was usually Monday night because that was the day the butchers put out soup bones left from their weekend trimming of meat.

The Italian names for soup are almost as numerous as the beneficial claims. "Minestra," "brodo," "zuppa," and "minestrone" all refer to soup. "Minestra" literally translates to "soup" but is often used in Italy to mean a first course whether it be soup, pasta, risotto, and so on. In order to distinguish, Italians refer to the liquid food eaten with a spoon as "minestra in brodo" and to pasta, rice, and the like as "minestra asciutta" (literally "dry soup"). "Minestrone," one of the most recognizable of Italian soup names, indicates a big or important soup and is known as such because a well-made minestrone is a thick, substantial soup that may well meet all seven soup challenges.

"Brodo" means "broth" and may be made from meat, poultry, fish, vegetables, or a combination. Brodo is most always "ripieno," that is, filled with pasta, rice, or small pieces of meat or vegetables. Italians also use broth as the base of heartier soups, although poor families, especially in Italy, used water. Soup bones were available weekly in American butcher shops. Poor families in Italy might see the butcher only twice a year. I just about always use a meat or chicken broth to make soup.

What distinguishes a "zuppa" from other soups is that it is served over or with thick slices of toasted Italian bread. Using bread to thicken a soup was common practice in "cucina povera." So common in Italy, in fact, that it is responsible for the Italian expression equivalent to "six of one, half a dozen of another." In Italian, the expression is: "Se non é zuppa, é pan bagnata." (If it's not soup, it's wet bread.)

Many of the soups in this chapter are merely memories for Italian-Americans since families were anxious to leave these symbols of poorer times behind. Second- and third-generation Italian-Americans wouldn't think of eating just soup for dinner. Well, as the song goes, "Everything old is new again." I often serve my family a substantial soup, some bread, cheese, and fruit for a very satisfying meal.

Meat Broth

BRODO DI CARNE

Italian meat broth cooks a shorter time and is lighter than French stock. "Brodo" can be made totally from meaty bones, but the addition of a piece of beef neck, chicken neck, or veal breast will give it more flavor. Since the broth may be used as part of another soup which could be salty, do not salt it while cooking. The initial quick boil will clean the bones and save you from continuous skimming.

5 pounds meaty bones and
   pieces (combination
   chicken, beef, and veal)
2 medium onions, peeled
2 medium carrots, peeled

2 stalks celery with tops
5 sprigs parsley
2 canned Italian plum
   tomatoes or 1 large fresh
   tomato

1. Put the bones and meaty pieces in a large pot. Cover with warm water and bring quickly to a boil. Discard water and rinse the bones and meat. Return to the pot and cover with cold water by 2 inches. Bring to a boil.

2. Reduce heat, add the vegetables to the pot, and simmer gently, uncovered, for 3 to 4 hours. Skim top as necessary. Do not let the broth boil or it will be cloudy.

3. Strain the broth through washed cheesecloth and let cool. Refrigerate and when completely cold remove fat from the top.

4. The broth may be used immediately, stored 3 days in the refrigerator, or frozen. Reboil broth before using. *Makes about 6 quarts.*

• • •

Note: In order to extract as much flavor as possible for a broth, meats should be started in cold water. When meats are being cooked in a broth or liquid for the purpose of eating the meat, they should be covered with hot or boiling liquid.

Chicken Broth

BRODO DI POLLO

Many families in Italy raised their own chickens and the immigrants continued to do so in America. Those who didn't raise their own always bought live chickens from the poultry man, who would kill the chicken but not clean it or remove the feathers.

2½ pounds chicken in pieces
  with neck and giblets
4 quarts water
2 carrots, washed and cut
  in 2-inch pieces
2 onions, peeled and
  quartered

4 celery ribs, with tops,
  in 2-inch pieces
1 peeled plum tomato,
  canned or fresh
1 bay leaf
Small bunch parsley stems

1. Put the chicken in a 7- to 8-quart stockpot and add just enough water to cover the chicken. Bring to a boil and then immediately discard the water and rinse the chicken (this will clean the meat). Return the chicken to the pot, cover with 4 quarts fresh cold water. Bring to a boil and add the vegetables and seasonings, bring back to a boil, reduce heat, and simmer gently 2 hours.

2. Strain the broth through washed cheesecloth, allow to cool, and skim off the fat.

3. The broth may be used immediately, stored 3 days in the refrigerator, or frozen. Reboil the broth before using. *Makes 4 quarts*.

• • •

Note: Chicken meat may be minced and used for ravioli as in meat-filled ravioli, page 126.

Artichoke and Pea Soup

MINESTRA DI CARCIOFI E PISELLI

Among other things, spring in Sicily means tiny artichokes and peas. The early Sicilian-American cooks could not reproduce this soup as it had been in Italy. Today it is possible to make a delicious facsimile.

4 artichokes	Salt
1 lemon	4½ cups chicken broth
¼ cup olive oil	1 pound fresh peas, shelled
2 garlic cloves, minced	Freshly grated Parmesan
1 tablespoon chopped	cheese
parsley	

1. Remove the stems from the artichokes. Remove all outer green leaves, leaving only tender yellow leaves. As artichokes are trimmed, rub with a cut lemon or drop into cold water to which lemon juice has been added. Turn the artichokes on their sides and with a sharp knife cut about 1½ inches from the top. Quarter the artichoke hearts and remove the chokes. Cut into eighths.

2. Put the olive oil and garlic into a soup pot. Cook, watching carefully, over a low flame until the garlic is golden. Add the artichokes, parsley, and salt, toss, and sauté 5 minutes. Add the broth, bring to a boil, and simmer 25 minutes, or until the artichokes are tender. Add the peas and cook 5 minutes, or until the peas are cooked. Serve with a light sprinkling of Parmesan cheese. *Serves 4 to 6.*

• • •

Note: This soup may also be made with frozen artichoke hearts and tiny frozen peas. Many Italian-Americans prefer frozen artichoke hearts because they are closer in size to what was found in the "old country."

MEMORIES

"Nothing was wasted. . . . Their sense of hospitality always involved the breaking of bread."

My grandmother was a master cook. She did things that nobody else did in cooking, and she made dishes that nobody else even knew about. She did everything from scratch. She did her own pasta, she did her own gnocchi, she did her own ravioli, she did her own "struffoli" at Christmas.

My grandmother would never push us to learn how to cook. But as I was growing up, I would be there at her house a lot and I learned almost by osmosis. It wasn't like we had a formal cooking class, but you'd be there and you'd see her do it. I was always interested in cooking, so consequently I would be interested in what she was doing and watch it as much as I could.

My grandmother was not too easy to get recipes from. She was very subtle about it. She would never say no. She'd say, "All right, I'll give it to you," but it would never be that very moment; it would be maybe if you called her back two weeks later you'd get it. But she didn't really cook with recipes per se. I tried writing down how she would make things as she described the ingredients. I would say, "But Mama, how much?" And she'd say, "Well . . . about a handful." Well, my hand was larger than her hand, so my handful was different than her handful. So there was no accuracy in the description of these things. Even if there was a measured cup or a measured half cup, she'd say, "Well . . . about half a cup . . . maybe a little more." What does that mean? Does that mean three-quarters of a cup? But everything I've made that she's taught me how to make has come out. My test for what I do is the taste, because I remember how it tasted when she did it. So if it tastes like I know hers tasted, I know I got it.

I have some of my grandmother's work boards. She used to put a big board on the table. She had two sizes: she had a really big one where she would put the homemade pasta, and then she had a smaller one. She used the boards for making gnocchi or her pepper biscuits. She'd put the board right on the table and knead the dough there.

My grandfather's name was Joseph. Being that he was a Joseph, my grandmother would make him "zeppole" on St. Joseph's Day. After she died, we decided to make zeppole for him on St. Joseph's Day. Now Mama's process of doing these things was always the old-fashioned way. She didn't have the food processors, blenders, and so on. Everything was hand-mixed, hand-kneaded, hand-cut, and so on. So, my grandfather was at my house and we decided to make the "zeppole." We started to mix the ingredients and then we told him we could do some of this in the Cuisinart. He said, "What's this Cuisinart?" and we showed him the food processor. When he saw the steel blade he almost went into coronary arrest. He threw up his hands and said, "No, no, no—this is not how you do it. This has got to be done by hand." Now to make this batter, you had to add eggs one at a time and mix them well with your fingers. Well, the steel blade on the Cuisinart cut into the dough. Needless to say, they didn't come out like Mama's. Daddy Joe, as we called

Donna's grandmother as a young girl.

him, was so annoyed because he knew very well that this was not the proper way to make zeppole. Although he had not made them himself, he had watched her do it hundreds of times, so he knew.

We are nine grandchildren, living all over. Whenever we speak or get together we have this common ground of our grandparents and the things our grandmother used to make for us.

I remember one time when I was expecting my first child my grandfather asked me when the baby was due. At the time I think I had ten more weeks to go and so I told him. But he said "No, you're pregnant ten lunar months. The baby will come on the tenth lunar month." Till this day I don't understand what a lunar month is, but he was right.

My grandfather used to fish all the time. He'd go quahoging, he'd get snails, he'd get wild mushrooms. He used to hunt too and we'd have wild pheasant. He used to dress it and my grandmother would make the most incredible polenta with gravy sauce and my grandfather's wild mushrooms. It was wonderful.

I never knew where she got them, but my grandmother had these big long poles on which she would dry pasta and sausages. They were like thick dowels and she would just put them between chairs so the sheets of pasta would air-dry. She had a little entryway in the back of the house, like a pantry, and there was a window there. After she made the sausage, she would just drape it over the pole in the pantry. In the middle of winter she'd just crack the window so it would be cold in there. Then she would take the dry sausage and pack it in oil and that would preserve it.

My grandparents had this big wood-burning stove in the basement where my grandmother did all her preserving. She would do it all on this stove. Different types of tomatoes were grown for different purposes. Plum tomatoes were for preserving to be used in one dish; a big boy would be used for another type of cooking; another type she would put up, say, for pizza. And she knew exactly which one was used for each dish. My grandmother had this large walk-in closet in which she kept her preserves. Everything my grandfather planted, my grandmother preserved. String beans, peaches with the syrup—it would be preserved in glass jars.

Saturday night was steak night. My grandfather used to cut his own meat; he knew all the different parts such as what was good for ribs, what was good for "braciola," and so on. He'd buy a piece of meat and by the time he finished cutting it up, he'd have four or five different meals ready. Everything was used. He would go down to the wood-burning stove in the basement and start the wood fire about four o'clock. Dinner was at six o'clock. Some nights he would cook it pizziole, with the tomatoes. Mama would use one of her special jars of tomatoes.

Nothing was wasted. The fat from pork would be saved. It

would be rendered, put in a pan, and melted. When you melted the fat, you would have these little pieces of crispy, crunchy, pork fat. The fat that was melted would be strained through a fine strainer and put in containers. My grandmother would use maybe a table-spoon of it to make her gravy or to start a sauce, in pasta fagiole, escarole and bean soup, any kind of dish you wanted to add a little flavor to. The little pork bits were called giggoli (ciccioli) and they would be used sometimes in bread. I used to call it giggoli bread. You can either mix it in with the batter or make it like a jelly roll. We would also mix in black olives, pickled peppers, and pignoli nuts.

Donna's grandparents, Emily and Joseph Romano, on their wedding day.

I remember vividly on Friday nights it was such a treat to go into the Italian neighborhood and buy things from the pushcarts and the vendors. We'd buy our fish from the pushcarts on Friday. During Lent they were there every day of the week and on Christmas Eve. You'd buy your vegetables there. There were certain shops that my grandmother would go to. The vegetable lady had big bags of beans in burlap bags and it was wonderful.

Even though my grandmother was born in Italy, she was very Americanized. She had very American ideas and a sense of propriety. She was meticulous and always very elegantly dressed. She loved her grandchildren. The house was always open to all of us. It could be three o'clock in the morning, but this sweet little old lady would open the door, never complain, never say where have you been, why are you here, what's wrong. There was just always a bed there for you.

Holidays were big and my grandmother just loved preparing for them. The thing in her life was cooking and having her family to-

gether and being there. Christmas was especially her favorite. She'd start weeks ahead decorating the house and preparing little things. She'd make the "struffuli" a week before and put them in a very cool place in the house. She had different rooms for different things all over the house and we never knew what we were going to find in any room. When she would have people unexpectedly drop in on her, she would put three or four dishes on the table and suddenly disappear for a few moments. Then out would come some kind of dessert or a dish of something else, and we never knew where she was getting this stuff. She had it stashed somewhere. You'd look at something innocently and think it was just a basket, but all the while it was filled with "wandi."

The week of the holiday there would be feverish cooking. The yellow cream she used for her desserts would be made ahead and kept in the refrigerator. She made a sponge cake which she would fill with the yellow cream. It had seven layers and she would put what we called "conserva d'amarena," which is cherry preserved in a juice, on each layer.

At Easter she would make "pastiera" with rice, yellow cream, and ricotta. It was the most wonderful I have ever tasted.

When you went to my grandmother's, she always created a very safe, warm, cozy, wonderful atmosphere. It was home. And you'd walk in the house and smell food and cooking. You'd smell it all over the house. It's something I think is missing these days. I don't know if it can be duplicated. For Mama, though, this was her whole life. She would invite people over for dinner and be exuberant over preparations. For my grandparents, their sense of hospitality always involved the breaking of bread and eating at the table with friends. It made for a closeness. To be invited to the dinner table of a family was something not extended to just anyone. This was their way of letting people know that they thought a lot of them, and that they were welcome in their home, that they were taken into the family.

DONNA SCARPETTI RIZZO

Easter Soup

MINESTRA DI PASQUA

Although this soup was traditionally served at the beginning of an Easter meal, for many Italian-American families it began most any holiday meal. There are many variations of this light "minestra" but it is most important that the chicken broth be strong and flavorful. Easter Soup is one of the few exceptions to the Italian rule that soup and pasta are never served at the same meal since it often precedes lasagna, ravioli, or ziti at a festive occasion. If it is served before pasta, do not put any pasta in the soup.

1 head escarole,
    about 1½ pounds
Salt
1 slice stale bread,
    crust removed
¼ cup milk
½ pound ground beef
1 egg
3 quarts chicken broth
⅓ cup egg flake pasta
    (quadratini)
2 hard-boiled eggs,
    thinly sliced
½ cup freshly grated
    Parmesan cheese

The winners of an Easter egg hunt, Providence, Rhode Island, 1937.

1. Trim the escarole, wash, and cut in half. Cook in boiling salted water until just tender, about 4 minutes. Drain, plunge into ice water, drain, and squeeze dry. Cut into ¼-inch strips. Set aside.

2. Put the bread slice in a bowl and cover with milk. Let soften 10 minutes, then squeeze dry. Combine the bread with the ground beef, egg, and 1 teaspoon salt. Make tiny meatballs the size of marbles. There should be 48 to 50 meatballs.

3. Bring the chicken broth to a boil. Add the meatballs and simmer 5 minutes. Add the escarole and pasta. Cook 10 minutes. Divide the egg slices among the bottoms of wide soup dishes. Ladle on the soup and sprinkle with Parmesan cheese. *Serves 8 to 10.*

Celery Soup

ZUPPA DI ACCIA

"Accia" is the Calabrian dialect word for "celery." This soup was very much a part of "la cucina povera" in Italy and America since the ingredients were southern staples. Be very careful with the amount of salt, especially if using canned broth, since the cheese and dried sausage will add saltiness.

¼ cup extra-virgin olive oil
1 small onion, finely
  chopped
4 cups sliced celery (¼-inch
  slices)
¼ cup chopped celery tops
5 cups hot meat or chicken
  broth
Salt
6 Italian toasts (½-inch
  slices Italian bread lightly
  browned in 400°F oven
  until golden on both sides
  and brushed with olive oil
  on one side)

3 hard-boiled eggs, coarsely
  chopped
3 ounces sopressata or other
  dried sausage, chopped
4 ounces cacciocavallo or
  mild provolone cheese,
  chopped
Freshly grated pecorino
  cheese
Lovage leaves or chopped
  celery tops (optional)

1. Heat the olive oil in a soup pot, add the onion, celery, and celery tops, and cook over low heat until softened (8 minutes). Add the hot broth and salt and bring to a boil, then simmer, partially covered, 20 minutes.

2. Place the bread slices in 6 soup bowls. Divide the eggs, sausage, and cacciocavallo cheese evenly among the 6 servings and put on top of the bread. Bring the soup to a boil and ladle while hot into the bowls. Sprinkle with grated cheese and lovage leaves or chopped celery tops. *Serves 6.*

Asparagus Soup

ZUPPA DI ASPARAGI

Here is an absolutely delicious Calabrian recipe to prepare with no effort and little time.

2 tablespoons extra-virgin olive oil
2 garlic cloves, minced
2 pounds asparagus, trimmed, peeled, and cut in 1-inch pieces
Salt and pepper

1 quart chicken broth
4 eggs
½ cup freshly grated Parmesan or pecorino cheese
6 slices Italian bread, toasted

1. Heat the oil and garlic in a soup pot until the garlic is golden. Add the asparagus and cook until they begin to color. Season with salt and pepper. Add the broth, bring to a boil, reduce the heat, and simmer 15 minutes, or until the asparagus are tender.

2. Beat the eggs and cheese together. When the asparagus are tender, reduce the heat so the soup is no longer simmering. Very slowly ladle some of the hot soup into the beaten eggs, stirring continuously. After adding about 2 cups of the hot soup to the eggs, reverse the process and gradually stir the eggs back into the soup pot. The soup must not boil or the eggs will scramble. Heat until thickened.

3. Put 1 slice of toasted bread in each soup dish. Ladle the hot soup on top and pass additional grated cheese. *Serves 6.*

• • •

Note: To trim asparagus, hold the tip in one hand and the base of the stalk in the other. Bend gently. The asparagus will snap, leaving the tender part with the tip.

Farmer's Fresh Tomato Soup

PASSATO DI POMODORO ALLA CONTADINA

In Italy and later in America, fall was alive with the bustle of whole families harvesting and putting up tomatoes. This Italian farmer's soup is one delicious way of making use of a bumper crop. Tomatoes in Italy were sweeter than the ones the immigrants could grow in New England. I know many Italian-Americans who always add a pinch of sugar to tomato recipes. As with all tomato recipes, the cook really has to be the judge as to whether or not the tomatoes are sweet enough. It's really a matter of balancing the natural acidity in the tomato. The soup should by no means be sweet in terms of sugary. Serve toasted garlic bread alongside if desired.

¼ cup plus 2 tablespoons extra-virgin olive oil
2 medium onions, coarsely chopped
3 garlic cloves, minced
2 ribs celery, coarsely chopped
3 pounds plum tomatoes, washed, stemmed, and coarsely chopped
Salt
Pinch of sugar (optional)

3 pieces day-old Italian bread, crusts removed
4 cups hot meat broth
½ cup basil leaves, torn in strips
2 tablespoons chopped parsley
2 tablespoons chopped fresh marjoram
6 small fresh marjoram sprigs

1. Heat the oil, onions, garlic, and celery in a soup pot over medium-low heat, stirring occasionally, until golden (about 20 minutes). Add the tomatoes and salt, and cook, partially covered, until the tomatoes are softened (20 minutes). If necessary, add a pinch of sugar to balance acidity.

2. Put the bread in a small bowl and add 1 cup of hot broth to soften. Mash it well with a wooden spoon. Add the softened bread and remaining broth to tomatoes, stirring well to completely dissolve the bread. Simmer 30 minutes. Add the herbs during the last 5 minutes of cooking. Pass the soup through the fine blade of a food mill or puree in a food processor and strain.

3. Put the soup back in the soup pot and correct seasoning. Simmer 10 minutes. Ladle into heated soup bowls and pour 1 teaspoon olive oil over each serving. Garnish with sprigs of fresh marjoram. *Serves 6 to 8.*

Cauliflower Soup

MINESTRA DI CAVOLFIORE

There's probably no sense in making this soup if you don't like cauliflower. As with so much of Italian food, this recipe uses a few basic ingredients to showcase the star vegetable. A purist would even shudder at the cheese! Make this soup as garlicky and spicy as you like but be sure to serve lots of crusty Italian bread or bruschetta (toasted Italian bread brushed with olive oil). When I want a soup with a bit more texture, I remove 1 cup of the cooked cauliflower, puree it, and return it to the remaining soup.

1 large head cauliflower, about 2 pounds
2 tablespoons white or cider vinegar
¼ cup olive oil
4 to 6 garlic cloves
¼ to ½ teaspoon hot pepper flakes

3 cups hot meat broth
Salt
⅓ cup parsley, chopped
6 ounces freshly grated pecorino cheese

1. Break the cauliflower flowerets into small (½ inch) pieces. Trim the stem end and cut into ½-inch pieces. Wash the cauliflower in 2 quarts cold water blended with 2 tablespoons vinegar. Drain and drop into a large pot of boiling salted water. Boil 4 minutes, drain, and dry well.
2. Heat ¼ cup olive oil in a soup pot, add garlic and hot pepper, and cook gently until the garlic is golden. Add the cauliflower and cook 5 minutes, stirring to prevent it from browning. Add the hot broth, salt, and parsley and cook until the cauliflower is tender. Ladle into soup bowls and sprinkle with a generous amount of cheese. *Serves 6.*

TOMATOES

Tomatoes were introduced to Italy from South America in the sixteenth century, but it was not until the eighteenth century that someone bravely tasted them and decided that they were fit for consumption. Those first tomatoes were yellow, which accounts for their Italian name, "pomodoro," meaning "golden apple." Once the word on tomatoes was out, southern Italians lost no time in growing a number of varieties and adding them to their cooking.

Tomatoes must have presented one of the greatest challenges to the early immigrants. In Italy they had been used to two to three long growing seasons a year. In America, they had to rely on what they could preserve from the summer to last them through the year.

Here is a list of ways southern Italians use tomatoes.

Pomodori per sugo (tomatoes for sauce): Small, pear-shaped tomatoes, also called plum or Roma, now found fresh in many American markets but grown at home by Italian-Americans. Best tomato for sauce because of greater proportion of pulp to juices. Buy large quantities in season and preserve—either whole peeled or as sauce. A very easy way to preserve plum tomatoes is to wash, dry, and put them in freezer bags. Freeze and when ready to use, place in warm water until skin peels away easily. Seed, juice, and chop as required.

Pelati: Canned, peeled, plum tomatoes. Southern Italians are never without a supply of pelati and use them interchangeably with fresh plum tomatoes. Early immigrants relied only on their own canned tomatoes. Good commercial brands are available today. Look for genuine "San Marzano" tomatoes on the can—not a brand name but the area near Naples which produces the most consistently sweet, meaty canned tomato. Use juices with tomatoes when the recipe calls for cooking for a long time and drain well when a short cooking time would not allow juices to evaporate. Save some of the juices when draining tomatoes so if the dish reduces too rapidly, you can add tomato juices in place of water.

Conserva: Tomato paste made from a long, slow reduction of fresh tomatoes resulting in a concentrated tomato flavor. In many areas of Italy, conserva is reconstituted with water for quick tomato sauce. Made at home in Italy either by cooking fresh tomatoes to paste or, by leaving chopped tomatoes out in the strong sun, stirring often until all water is evaporated. Italian-Americans originally cooked and preserved their own but gradually began to rely on the canned commercial product which, used sparingly, is acceptable but in large quantities is glaringly unlike the homemade.

Piennoli or Pomodori d'Inverno: Sun-dried tomatoes. Southern Italians in Italy string cherry tomatoes, dry them briefly in the sun, then hang them in the house to have for the winter. They also cut plum tomatoes in half, dry them thoroughly in the sun, and store them, usually in oil. The northeast climate prevented immigrants from drying tomatoes successfully but they are now available commercially and add a rich flavor to cooked dishes.

Pomodori per insalata: Red salad tomatoes, eaten fresh in salads and used for stuffing and baking. Unlike the salad tomato in Italy, which is partially green and eaten underripe. When good summer tomatoes are abundant, I use them also for cooking, being sure to squeeze them well to remove all juices. Some Italian-American families grew only salad tomatoes and used them as plum tomatoes.

Fennel Soup

ZUPPA DI FINOCCHI

I must admit that I don't recall eating much cooked fennel while I was growing up. We always ate it raw in salads and since I was so fond of its clean, crisp taste I wasn't in much of a hurry to experiment with it cooked. Little did I know what delights awaited me! Cooked fennel takes on a mellow—shall I say "comforting?"—taste. Often called "anise" in the American market, its wonderful, licorice-type flavor makes this simple soup special. For a richer soup, beat 2 eggs with the cheese, gradually add about a cup of soup to the mixture to heat, and then gradually stir the eggs into the hot soup. Heat but do not boil.

3 medium to large heads fennel, about 2½ pounds
3 garlic cloves, minced
¼ cup olive oil
4 cups meat or vegetable broth or water

Salt and pepper
6 slices day-old Italian bread, ½ inch thick, lightly toasted
1½ cups grated pecorino cheese

1. Trim away any bruised outer part of the fennel. Remove the tough cores and coarsely chop the bulbs. Chop the feathery green fennel tops and reserve ½ cup.

2. Put the garlic and olive oil into a soup pot and cook gently until the garlic is golden. Add the chopped fennel pieces and cook until they begin to soften, about 10 minutes. Stir in the reserved fennel greens, salt, and pepper. Add the broth and bring to a boil. Reduce the heat and simmer 30 minutes.

3. Put 1 slice of toasted bread in the bottom of each of 6 soup bowls. Divide the cheese evenly, sprinkling it on each piece of bread. Bring the soup to a rolling boil and immediately ladle over the bread and serve. *Serves 6.*

Neapolitan Mushroom Soup

ZUPPA DI FUNGHI NAPOLETANA

If my family had to choose just one favorite soup, it would be this Neapolitan one.

1 ounce dried porcini
   mushrooms
3 tablespoons unsalted
   butter
3 tablespoons extra-virgin
   olive oil
1 small onion, minced
3 garlic cloves, minced
1½ pounds mushrooms,
   wiped clean, stems
   trimmed, sliced
4 fresh plum tomatoes,
   peeled, seeded, and
   chopped, or 4 canned
   Italian plum tomatoes,
   drained and chopped
1 teaspoon salt

Freshly ground pepper
1 tablespoon minced fresh
   marjoram or 1 teaspoon
   dried
1 tablespoon minced fresh
   thyme or 1 teaspoon dried
5 cups meat broth
8 slices Italian bread, ½ inch
   thick
3 egg yolks
⅓ cup grated Parmesan
   cheese
2 tablespoons pecorino
   romano cheese
3 tablespoons chopped
   parsley, plus about ¼ cup
   chopped for garnish

1. Soak the porcini mushrooms in ½ cup warm water for 30 minutes. Drain, reserving the liquid. Rinse, dry, and chop the porcini mushrooms. Strain the soaking liquid through washed cheesecloth, paper towels, or a coffee filter. Set aside.

2. Melt the butter and 1 tablespoon olive oil in a large pot over low heat. Add the onion and garlic. Cook, stirring frequently, until the onion is wilted but not browned, about 5 minutes.

3. Add the porcini mushrooms and cook for 8 minutes. Increase the heat to medium and add the fresh mushrooms. Cook until the juices run, about 10 minutes. Add the reserved porcini soaking liquid and continue to cook until reduced by half, about 5 minutes. Add the tomatoes, salt, pepper, marjoram, and thyme and cook 5 minutes. Add the broth and simmer 15 minutes.

4. While the soup is cooking, toast the bread on both sides in a

Neapolitan Mushroom Soup (continued)

400°F oven until lightly browned on both sides. Remove and brush one side with the remaining olive oil. Use more oil if necessary.

5. In a small bowl, beat the egg yolks with ⅓ cup Parmesan cheese, the pecorino romano cheese, and 3 tablespoons parsley. Gradually whisk 1 cup of the hot soup into the eggs to warm them. Reverse and slowly whisk the eggs into the soup. Cook, stirring constantly, over medium-low heat until the soup thickens. (Do not boil or the soup will curdle.)

6. Place a slice of toast in each of 8 bowls. Ladle in the hot soup and sprinkle with Parmesan cheese and parsley. *Serves 8.*

Zucchini Rice Soup

MINESTRA DI ZUCCHINE E RISO

Italians often serve soups at room temperature, allowing them to sit so their flavors blend. If you let this soup sit, the rice will absorb the broth and the soup will be thick.

1½ pounds zucchini (3 medium), trimmed	6 cups meat or vegetable broth
1 medium onion, minced	1 cup Arborio rice
1 garlic clove, minced	3 tablespoons chopped parsley
¼ cup extra-virgin olive oil	2 tablespoons snipped basil
Salt and pepper	Freshly grated Parmesan cheese
Freshly grated nutmeg	
1 pound tomatoes, peeled, seeded, and chopped (about 1½ cups)	

1. Cut the zucchini into ½-inch pieces.
2. Cook the onion and garlic in olive oil in a large soup pot until softened but not browned. Add the zucchini, season with salt, pepper, and nutmeg to taste, and cook, stirring occasionally, until the zucchini is softened (about 10 minutes). Add the tomatoes, raise heat, and cook 3 minutes. Add the broth, rice, parsley, and basil.

Bring to a boil, reduce heat, and simmer until the rice is tender (20 minutes). Let cool slightly before serving with grated cheese. *Serves 6.*

Vegetable Soup

ZUPPA DI VERDURE

This hearty vegetable soup will benefit from sitting. Don't cut the vegetables too small since the finished soup should have a chunky look.

¼ cup extra-virgin olive oil
1 large onion, coarsely
  chopped
2 celery stalks, trimmed and
  coarsely chopped
2 carrots, peeled and
  coarsely chopped
1 pound savoy cabbage,
  shredded
Salt and pepper
2 cups shredded romaine or
  escarole lettuce
1 pound potatoes (3 small),
  peeled and cubed

¾ pound tomatoes
  (2 medium), peeled,
  seeded, and coarsely
  chopped
1 quart meat broth
1 cup peas
⅓ cup minced parsley
2 garlic cloves, minced
6 to 8 slices Italian bread,
  toasted
Freshly grated Parmesan
  cheese

1. Heat the olive oil with the onion, celery, and carrots until the vegetables are softened. Add the cabbage, salt, and pepper and cook, stirring often, until the cabbage is wilted. Add the lettuce, season, and stir until wilted. Stir in the potatoes and tomatoes, season, and cook 3 minutes. Add the broth, bring to a boil, reduce the heat, cover pan, and simmer 30 minutes. Add the peas and cook 5 minutes, covered. Mix the parsley and garlic together and stir into the pot. Cook 5 minutes.

2. Put a piece of toasted bread in each soup bowl. Ladle on hot soup and sprinkle with Parmesan cheese. Serve immediately. *Serves 6 to 8.*

LA CUCINA POVERA

For the most part, the cooking of the immigrants was "la cucina povera"—poor or working-class cooking. It was not the food prepared in wealthy homes or elegant restaurants but the food made by frugal housewives who relied on ingredients that could be grown or produced at home or nearby. Although many of the dishes showed ingenuity, meals were often repetitive. Recipes and skills were handed down from generation to generation by demonstrating. Recipes were rarely written down.

With the better life they found in America, the immigrants began to change their style of eating. In many cases their dream had been to live like their Italian bosses, "i padroni," and they imitated many of the eating styles they remembered or imagined they remembered from the wealthy homes. Consequently, many of the simple, rustic dishes became more elaborate than they had ever been. Other dishes were abandoned completely because they were too obviously related to their impoverished condition in the "old country." Fortunately, these rustic dishes are once again appreciated, not only for their frugality, but their simple pleasure.

Italian girls being taught to eat like Americans.

Pasta and Bean Soup

PASTA E FAGIOLI

I must admit that when I was growing up I was seldom overjoyed to discover that dinner at Nonna's would include "pasta fazool"! In fact, it wasn't until I was pregnant with Brad, our firstborn, that I inexplicably began to crave this soup. I can remember many quick trips to restaurants in "Little Italy" looking for a bowl of this soothing soup to go! The use of the pancetta is optional. I often omit it, which results in a lighter, vegetarian version. I especially like to make this soup when fresh cranberry beans are in season, although any dried or canned white bean works perfectly well. Cranberry beans are similar to pinto beans except the skin color is beige on pink skin rather than vice versa. They are popular with Italians. Pinto beans may be used in their place.

2 ounces pancetta, minced (optional)
2 tablespoons extra-virgin olive oil
½ small hot red pepper or ⅛ teaspoon hot pepper flakes
1 small onion, finely chopped
1 small rib celery, finely chopped
1 carrot, finely chopped
2 garlic cloves, minced
1¼ pounds fresh tomatoes, peeled, seeded, and finely chopped

Salt
1½ pounds (before shelling) fresh cranberry beans, or ¾ cup dried cranberry beans, precooked, or 2½ cups canned beans, drained
4 cups meat broth or water
¾ cup assorted short macaroni
Freshly grated pecorino cheese

1. Put the pancetta, if using, and olive oil in a soup pot and cook over gentle heat until the pancetta renders fat but does not brown (about 4 minutes). Add the hot pepper, onion, celery, carrot, and garlic to the olive oil and cook gently 10 minutes, or until the vegetables are soft. Add the tomatoes and salt and cook 10 minutes.

Pasta and Bean Soup (continued)

2. If using fresh beans, shell, rinse, add to the tomatoes, and cook together 3 minutes. Add the hot broth and cook until the beans are tender (45 minutes to 1 hour). If using precooked dried beans or canned beans, add to the tomatoes, cook 3 minutes, add the broth, and cook 15 minutes.

3. Add the macaroni to the soup and continue cooking until the pasta is al dente. Remove the soup from heat and let rest 10 minutes before serving. Serve with freshly grated pecorino cheese. *Serves 6.*

HOT PEPPER

At one time in Italy, imported black pepper was an exotic spice and not available to everyone. Southern Italians relied on hot red pepper (peperoncino) which they grew and dried themselves. A prudent housewife from Calabria was sure to hang a dried red pepper in the doorway to keep away evil spirits. Italian-Americans continued this practice and eventually jewelry makers reproduced the pepper in gold and silver so everyone could carry their protection with them.

Many southern Italians still prefer to cook with hot pepper, which they use either fresh or dried in a quantity just enough to add a bit of zip. Hot pepper may be purchased fresh, or in flakes, or in dried whole pods. To substitute, one small fresh hot pepper equals approximately ½ teaspoon dried flakes or 1 dried pod.

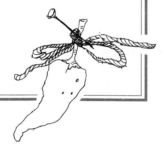

Dried Fava Bean Soup

MACCO DI FAVE SECCHE

Why do we see so few recipes for fava beans? Is it because they have to be peeled? Actually, it is only necessary when the beans are no longer very young and tender. And then, it really is not much of a job and the results, such as in this hearty Calabrian soup, are well worth the bit of effort. Fava beans were very much a part of southern Italian cooking in Italy, and the early immigrants planted them in their gardens. Once the Italian-Americans began to rely on markets for their vegetables, the use of fava beans began to dwindle, since they were never grown commercially in abundance.

½ pound dried fava beans (broad beans)

4 tablespoons extra-virgin olive oil

⅓ pound fatty prosciutto end pieces, chopped

1 large onion, coarsely chopped

½ small, fresh, hot red pepper, ½ dried hot pepper, or ¼ teaspoon dried flakes

2 ripe plum tomatoes, peeled, seeded, and chopped, or canned and drained (⅔ cup)

1½ quarts water or vegetable broth

Salt

¼ pound wide flat noodles, such as pappardelle

Freshly grated pecorino cheese (optional)

1. Soak the beans overnight in a large amount of cold water. Drain the beans. Plunge into a pot of rapidly boiling water and boil 5 minutes. Drain and plunge into a bowl of cold water. Peel.

2. Put 2 tablespoons of the olive oil, the prosciutto pieces, and onion into a soup pot. Cook over medium-low heat until the onion is softened and prosciutto fat has been rendered. Stir in the hot pepper and tomatoes and cook 3 minutes. Add the beans and water or broth, bring to a boil, reduce heat, and simmer until the beans are tender and falling apart (about 1 hour). The soup should be thick. If it is too watery, turn up the heat and reduce. Taste for seasonings and add salt as needed. (The soup may be made ahead, 3 days if desired, to this point.)

Dried Fava Bean Soup (continued)

3. Cook the noodles in a large amount of boiling salted water until tender. Drain and add to the hot soup. Stir in the remaining 2 tablespoons olive oil and serve. If desired, pass freshly grated pecorino cheese. *Serves 6.*

Soup of a Thousand Little Things

MILLECOSEDDE

A "thousand" is perhaps a bit of an exaggeration, but this Calabrian version of pasta and bean soup ("pasta e fagioli") is plentiful indeed. No less than four different types of dried beans will suffice for its making. There is nothing magical about the particular beans suggested below. You may substitute your favorites or what you can find. I have written this as a winter recipe with dried beans and canned tomatoes. It is equally good in summer or fall when fresh beans and fresh tomatoes are available. Peel, seed, and chop the fresh tomatoes and add the fresh beans directly to the pot at the same stage as you would add the soaked dried beans.

¼ pound dried ceci beans	Salt and pepper
¼ pound dried shell beans (cranberry beans)	½ small head savoy cabbage (5 cups shredded)
½ pound dried cannellini beans (Great Northern whites)	1 cup drained canned Italian plum tomatoes, chopped
4 tablespoons extra-virgin olive oil	1½ quarts boiling water
	¼ pound dried lentils
2 carrots, peeled and coarsely chopped	½ pound tubetti or other short macaroni
1 small onion (¾ cup diced)	Freshly grated pecorino cheese
1 celery rib (⅓ cup diced)	
½ pound mushrooms, wiped clean and diced	

1. Soak the ceci, shell, and cannellini beans in cold water to cover by 2 inches overnight. Or use the quick soak method: put all

the beans in a pot with 6 cups water. Bring to a boil, boil 2 minutes, remove from the heat, and let stand covered 1 hour.

2. Heat the olive oil in a 5-quart pot. Add the carrots, onion, and celery and cook until softened but not browned (10 to 12 minutes). Add the mushrooms, salt, and pepper and cook until the mushrooms lose their juice and begin to brown. Add the cabbage, salt, and pepper and cook until wilted. Add the tomatoes and cook 5 minutes. Add the drained beans, boiling water, salt, and pepper and cook 45 minutes.

3. Wash and drain the lentils. Pick over to remove any particles. Add to the soup and cook until all the beans are tender. If the soup becomes too thick while cooking, add more boiling water.

4. Add the macaroni to the boiling soup and cook until "al dente." Let rest 10 minutes and serve while hot with a generous grating of pecorino cheese. *Serves 8.*

Married Soup

MINESTRA MARITATA

This is a Neapolitan version of the substantial southern soup which "marries" pork with the vegetables of the season for a one-dish meal. It is a hearty, cold weather soup to find simmering on the stove when you come in from outdoor activities. Married Soup was more readily available to Italian-Americans than their poor relatives in Italy who seldom saw meat.

1 small piece prosciutto bone	Pinch of hot pepper flakes
1 piece prosciutto rind (about 6 inches square)	1 medium onion, coarsely chopped
¾ pound boneless pork shoulder, trimmed and cut into ½-inch cubes	1 stalk celery, coarsely chopped
	7 cups boiling water or broth (approximately)
6 ounces Genoa salami, cut into ¼-inch dice	¾ pound broccoli rabe
	¾ pound escarole, washed
3-inch-square piece of cheese rind, Parmesan or romano	¾ pound savoy cabbage
	Grated pecorino cheese

1. Blanch the prosciutto bone and rind in boiling water 10 minutes. Discard the water and rinse the bone and rind. With a sharp knife, remove excess fat from rind. Cut the remaining rind into narrow strips.

2. Put the rind pieces, bone, stew meat, salami, cheese rind, hot pepper, onion, carrot, and celery into a soup pot. Cover with boiling water, adding more if necessary to cover ingredients. Return to a boil, reduce the heat, and simmer 1½ hours.

3. Wash the greens. Peel the stems of the broccoli rabe. Remove the tough centers of the escarole leaves. Discard the tough outside leaves of cabbage. Coarsely chop all greens. Blanch 5 minutes in boiling salted water. Drain and cool.

4. When the soup has cooked 1½ hours, add the greens to the pot. Cook 45 minutes. Remove and discard the bone and the ham and cheese rinds. Serve with grated pecorino cheese. *Serves 6 to 8.*

Bread Soup in the Style of Foggia

PANCOTTO COME A FOGGIA

There is obviously a lot more than cooked bread (pancotto) in this splendid soup. Pancotto is a great way to use up stale bread but I'm so fond of it that I let bread get stale just to make the soup! This particular recipe is a specialty of Foggia in Puglia, but similar versions were made by all southern Italians in Italy and America. They were part of the rustic cooking of the poor and are seldom seen today.

¼ pound pancetta, diced
2 medium onions, coarsely chopped
3 garlic cloves, chopped
3 tablespoons extra-virgin olive oil
3 medium all-purpose potatoes, peeled, cut into 1-inch dice
⅓ pound spinach or arugula, washed and trimmed, torn into bite-size pieces
1 medium head chicory (about ½ pound), washed and trimmed, torn into bite-size pieces
½ cup leafy fennel tops, chopped (optional)
¼ teaspoon hot pepper flakes
Salt
5 cups hot meat broth
2 cups stale Italian bread, cut into 1-inch cubes

1. Combine the pancetta, onions, garlic, and olive oil in a 5-quart soup pot. Cook over low heat 15 minutes, or until the vegetables are wilted but not browned.

2. Add the potatoes and toss to coat. Add the spinach, chicory, fennel tops, hot pepper, and salt and cook, covered, until the greens begin to wilt (about 3 minutes).

3. Add the hot broth, bring to a boil, reduce the heat, and simmer with the cover ajar, 45 minutes.

4. Toast the bread cubes in a single layer on a baking sheet in a 450°F oven for 5 minutes. Add bread to the pot after the soup has cooked 45 minutes. Stir bread in gently. Cook 15 minutes.

5. Ladle the soup into bowls and drizzle about 1 teaspoon olive oil on top of each serving. *Serves 8.*

Clam Soup

ZUPPA DI VONGOLE

Neapolitans never had to skip a beat in making this soup since they found that the waters of the East Coast provided clams much as they knew them in Italy. Consequently, this soup along with spaghetti with clam sauce was a regular part of the immigrants' diet and both were found in all the Italian-American restaurants. The pancetta topping is my own addition to the recipe. It adds extra zip but you may omit it for a simpler recipe.

2 dozen littleneck or
   cherrystone clams
⅓ cup extra-virgin olive oil
4 garlic cloves, minced
1 medium onion, chopped
2 cups chopped Italian plum
   tomatoes with juice

1 cup dry white wine
½ cup chopped parsley
¼ cup chopped fresh
   oregano or ½ teaspoon
   dried
¼ teaspoon hot pepper
   flakes

––––––––

TOPPING

½ cup minced pancetta
2 garlic cloves, minced

2 tablespoons olive oil
⅓ cup chopped parsley

––––––––

8 slices garlic crostini
   (page 7)

1. Scrub the clams well and wash in several changes of cold water. Be sure not to skimp on the washing of the clams or the resulting dish will be too salty.

2. Put the ⅓ cup olive oil, 4 cloves minced garlic, and chopped onion into wide soup pot. Cook over low heat until the onion is softened but not browned (6 to 7 minutes). Add the tomatoes and white wine, bring to a boil, then reduce the heat and add ½ cup parsley, the oregano, and hot pepper and simmer 15 minutes.

3. To make the topping, put the pancetta, 2 cloves minced garlic, and 2 tablespoons olive oil in a small sauté pan. Cook over low heat until the pancetta is slightly crisped (about 8 minutes). Add the parsley and continue to cook over low heat 3 minutes. Set aside.

4. Add the clams to tomato base. Increase the heat to high, cover the pan, and cook until clams open. Taste the soup for salt and hot pepper and season to taste.

5. Divide the clams and broth among 4 soup bowls. Sprinkle the pancetta topping over each and serve with garlic crostini.
Serves 4.

. . .

Variation: The clams may also be served over ¾ pound cooked vermicelli. In that case, eliminate the bread.

Rhode Island, the Ocean State, was popular with the many immigrants who came from the coastal areas of Italy.

PASTA
PASTA
PASTAS
CHEESE RAVIOLI
MEAT RAVIOLI
RAVIOLETTE
EGG NOODLES
MANICOTTI
JUMBO STUFFED SHELLS
SPINACH NOODLES
CAVATELLI - GNOCCHI
TORTELLINI - LASAGNA
GRATED CHEESE
MOZZARELLA
ASSORTED ITALIAN SPECIALTIES
MAMA'S FRESH PASTA
VENDA RAVIOLI

Chapter Three

PASTA

I can hardly imagine a world without pasta! Whether it is a simple plate of "spaghetti aglio olio" or an intricately layered Calabrian lasagne, pasta is among the most satisfying of foods. Italians seem to know this well because there is seemingly no end to their pasta inventiveness.

There also seems to be no end to today's confusion about fresh and dried pasta. Fresh pasta, made at home or in specialty shops with all-purpose flour and eggs, is not a superior product to dried pasta made with semolina and water and sold in boxes or cellophane packages; it is a different product, just as rice is different from pasta. Southern Italians rely mainly on commercially made dried pasta which has the body to stand up to their sauces.

Southern Italians also make fresh egg pasta for such dishes as ravioli, lasagna, or cannelloni and occasionally noodles, which are thicker than the northern variety. When they make pasta at home, they use regular all-purpose flour, which is the same as our all-purpose flour, or the soft-milled Italian "tipo 00." There are some classic southern recipes which call for homemade pasta made with semolina, such as the Calabrian "sagne chine." In that case, semolina is mixed with water only, not eggs. Perhaps it happens, but I have never run across semolina and egg pasta in southern Italy. I have seen it in the United States, however, and can only surmise that it was a result of a generation of Italian-Americans who, unlike their ancestors, could afford such a use of eggs.

Almost as soon as the Italians had settled in America, pasta factories were opened. The quality of the American-made pasta varied greatly. Some was made, as it had been in Italy, with semolina; others were made with soft flour; some added artificial coloring to make the pasta golden. Spaghetti was sold loose, not boxed, in very long strands that the buyer had to break apart himself before weighing out the amount he wanted. Short macaroni was sold in colorful packages that usually bore pictures of Italy and professed to be "Qualita extra sublime" and "Napoli style." Eventually those American pastas were manufactured to satisfy a general American market rather than the Italian-American one. They were no longer made with the hard durum semolina so they became very soft when they were cooked. A better choice today is to select from the large variety of pastas imported from Italy. The dried pasta (pasta secca) from southern Italy is justly famous. Made with hard durum wheat semolina and water, it not only has a slightly nutty flavor but, better yet, the ability to hold its firm texture when cooked.

Most southern Italians, in Italy and America, referred to all hollow or pierced dried pasta (pasta secca), whether it is long spaghetti or short round rigatoni, as "maccheroni" (macaroni). Some Italians, in fact, called all pasta, even fresh egg pasta, macaroni. My family identified homemade pasta by its name such as "ravioli," "lasagne," "cannelloni"—everything else was "macaroni." "Pasta," today's sophisticated term, was not part of our vocabulary. One of the explanations of the derivation of the word "maccheroni" is that it comes from the Greek word, "makar" meaning "divine." I have no reason to doubt this because in my mind that is exactly what macaroni is!

There are a number of sauces in this chapter which are matched with a particular pasta shape for a specific recipe. As you find favorites, you will no doubt do as I do and use the sauce for a different pasta. The early Italian-Americans did not have the same selection of macaroni shapes that we do today and they combined the sauce with the pasta shape that was available. Cooking should not be rigid but should reflect your taste. However, you will be most successful if you try to give some thought to the reasoning behind saucing. Thinner sauces, such as clam sauce or anchovy sauce, work well with narrow spaghetti that will twirl and capture the flavors. Regular spaghetti and short narrow macaroni work well with tomato sauces. Larger hollow shapes such as rigatoni will catch chunky pieces of meat or vegetables. The fillings of stuffed pasta should marry well with the sauce that is used.

Nonna's Meat Sauce

RAGU ALLA NONNA

I don't remember a visit to my grandmother's house when there was not a meat sauce cooking on the stove waiting to be used for macaroni, eggs, eggplant, peppers, and the like. My mother said that she only made it twice a week, but I cannot picture her kitchen without the familiar sauce pot sitting on the stove. Often referred to as "gravy" by many Italian-Americans, the ragu is a southern Italian staple. It was unthinkable to exclude macaroni with ragu from a holiday meal. No matter how elegant a wedding dinner, for example, it always began with ziti (which means "bridegrooms" in Neapolitan dialect) and ragu.

I should not put that in the past, because the practice continues today with very Americanized families of southern Italian heritage.

Wedding photo of Loretta d'Ambra Verde and Tomasso Verde—Nonna and Papa.

The importance of ragu is a given; the way to make it is as varied as the number of families who do. Some make it with canned tomatoes, others with tomato paste and water; some add lots of meat, others little. Some cook theirs for two hours, others for six or more. Garlic, onion, herbs, and wine are all requirements for some and blasphemies for others. It was quite common for an Italian wife to learn how to make a ragu from her mother-in-law so she could please her new husband. My Irish mother had a surprise for my father when they were married. Long before my mother met my father, her mother did her meat marketing at my father's family meat market on "the Hill." My maternal grandmother wanted to make sauce for spaghetti just like the Italians did and asked the butcher's wife, my Nonna, to share her recipe. Hence, long before she met or

Nonna's Meat Sauce (continued)

married my father, my mother was eating and making her future husband's sauce just like Mama made.

I completely understand the aversion to having to adjust to a new ragu. Of all I've tasted, I like Nonna's best. It is familiar and comforting. No other tastes "right." Because it was available to her from the family market, she used a good bit of meat, often adding braciola to those below. She shunned garlic because it didn't "age well" in the sauce. If she used the ragu for a recipe that needed garlic, she added it fresh. Tomato paste didn't give the flavor she wanted and she didn't cook her sauce for hours because she said it was finished before. She insisted that the seeds must be removed from the tomatoes or the sauce would be bitter. She held a strainer over the pot and poured and pushed the tomatoes through. This not only seeded them, but broke them up to the proper consistency. (I chop them up first in a food processor and then pour them through a sieve into the pot). She also decided that browning meatballs before adding them made them unagreeably firm and instead began to put them directly into the simmering sauce. The only other rule about which she was unbending was that when she served the pasta, we had better be at our places!

I'm sure that if you have a family ragu, you will skip right over this recipe and stick with your own. But for those of you who have yet to be Italianized—then, from Nonna to you.

(About ⅓ pound) beef, such as eye of the round, in one piece	¼ cup extra-virgin olive oil
	1 small onion, sliced
	3 large (35-ounce) cans Italian plum tomatoes, with juices
(About ⅓ pound) pork, in one piece	
Small piece (about ⅓ pound) chicken on the bone (necks and wings are fine)	Salt and freshly ground black pepper
	1 recipe meatballs (optional) (page 154)

Heat the oil in a large saucepan (5 to 6 quarts). Pat the meats dry and working with a few pieces at a time, brown in hot oil. Turn the meat to brown evenly and well. Do not rush this, but make sure that all are a rich brown color. Add the onion and cook until translucent. Whir the tomatoes in a blender or food processor and strain to remove seeds. (The tomatoes may also be put through a vegetable mill or pushed through a strainer, which will break them up as well as strain.) Add to the browned meats with salt and pepper. Bring to a boil and cook briskly for 15 minutes. Lower the heat to a simmer and partially cover the pan. Cook, stirring occasionally, about 2 to 2½ hours. If desired, add meatballs after the first hour. Add a little warm water if the sauce becomes too thick. Remove the meats from the sauce and serve or store separately. *Makes about 2 quarts.*

• • •

Note: Chicken should be discarded, but beef and pork may be eaten for another meal.

Meat Sauce with Pork

SUGO DI CARNE DI MAIALE

Not all southern Italians make a ragu as rich as Nonna's. Meat was a rarity for many families, in Italy and in the early days of life in the United States. Many people made a meat sauce only in winter when the family pig was slaughtered. Calabrians make this simple ragu. When it is finished, they remove the meat, shred it, and return it to the sauce, which they then serve over rigatoni with freshly grated pecorino cheese.

2½ pounds inexpensive pork meat from neck or shoulder
¼ cup olive oil
1 small onion, coarsely chopped

Two 28-ounce cans Italian tomatoes, with juices, chopped
Salt

1. Rinse the meat and cut into pieces about 4 inches square. Heat the oil in a deep pot. Add the onion and cook until translucent. Add the pork pieces and brown on all sides. Add the tomatoes, a 28-ounce can of water, and salt to the pork. Bring to a boil, reduce the heat, and cook with the cover slightly ajar, until the pork is falling from the bones (2½ to 3 hours).

Meat Sauce with Pork (continued)

2. Remove the pork from the sauce, trim away fatty parts, and shred the meat into small pieces. Discard bones. Return the meat to the sauce and heat uncovered. Serve over cooked macaroni and pass pecorino cheese. *Serves 6.*

Quick Tomato Sauce

SALSA MARINARA

Many southern Italians, my family included, refer to a quick tomato sauce as "marinara" sauce because the fisherman's wife was able to make it quickly at the moment of her husband's unscheduled return. Some people claim that it was so named because the fisherman himself could make it easily at the end of a long day of fishing, but I have my own ideas about who did all the cooking! Some Néapolitans call this sauce by the dialect name for tomato "pummarola." This is by far the most often used tomato sauce. It is tossed with spaghetti, served over breaded, fried foods, or mixed into baked dishes. Italians make marinara sauce as often with canned plum tomatoes (pelati) as with fresh. In the old days that meant only tomatoes that were canned at home. The variations of this sauce could fill a book. Many people sauté chopped onion with the garlic. Seasonings range from salt and pepper to oregano, basil, parsley, marjoram, rosemary. It may be made hot with the addition of peperoncino. I make a simple version which I can later doctor to suit whatever dish it accompanies. Some people add a pinch of sugar to any tomato sauce to combat the acidity of the tomatoes. I taste first and if it needs it, I add it.

¼ cup extra-virgin olive oil
2 small garlic cloves, minced
   or crushed and peeled
4½ cups peeled and seeded
   fresh, or canned and
   drained, Italian plum
   tomatoes, finely chopped
   or whirred in a processor
   or blender

Salt and pepper
2 tablespoons snipped fresh
   basil or other herb

Heat the oil and minced or crushed garlic gently in a small sauce pan until the garlic is golden. If desired, discard the garlic. Add the tomatoes, salt, and pepper and cook gently for 30 minutes, or until the juices are reduced and the oil separates from tomatoes. The sauce should be thick enough to hold its shape on a spoon. Stir in the basil or other herb and stir over heat 5 minutes. *Makes about 3½ cups.*

•   •   •

Note: More often than not I use minced garlic and leave it in. The whole cloves can be discarded after browning for a very subtle flavor, or left in and discarded at the end for a slightly more pronounced flavor. (See Garlic, page 147.)

•   •   •

Note: This sauce may be made even faster by using a wide frying pan. The juices will reduce more quickly and the flavor will not be as intense. If you are using farm-fresh ripe tomatoes, it makes a particularly delicious, quick "marinara" sauce.

Raking macaroni at the Atlantic factory, New York, 1943.

COOKING PASTA

My rules for cooking pasta are simple but they make the difference between divine food and disaster. For dried pasta (pasta secca), buy only imported semolina pasta. Cook all types of pasta, fresh or dried, in an abundant amount of rapidly boiling salted water, at least 4 to 5 quarts for a pound, in a pot large enough for the pasta to move around. Stir the pasta into the water so it does not stick together and never cover the pot. When the pasta is al dente, tender but firm to the bite, drain it either in a colander or by removing it from the water with a strainer. Allow a little of the cooking water to remain to prevent sticking and help bind the pasta with the sauce. NEVER rinse. Put in a warm pasta bowl and add cheese and sauce. When I have made a sauce in a wide pan I often toss the pasta directly into the pan. The final rule is one that is broken so often it brings tears to my eyes: Don't oversauce the pasta. The idea is pasta with sauce, not sauce with pasta. Ideally the last bite should be the last bite of both. If pasta is indeed so delicious—and it is—we should taste it as well as the sauce.

Christmas Eve Vermicelli

VERMICELLI DI VIGILIA

The tradition of a meatless Christmas Eve meal is one that Italian-Americans maintained long after they had blended into the "melting pot." Originally, this meal consisted of seven fish courses which might have signified the seven sacraments or the seven gifts of the Holy Ghost or some other religious commemoration. The fish was served with any number of other meatless dishes such as this pasta. Gradually, the immigrants altered their ancestors' menu, adding or eliminating fish dishes as their environment dictated. The meal was one of the most steadfast of Italian traditions and many Italian-Americans continue today to gather the night before Christmas for the "great fish feast." This delicious recipe is often part of that meal.

1 pound vermicelli or thin
   spaghetti
½ cup extra-virgin olive oil
2 garlic cloves, minced
½ cup dark or light raisins

⅓ cup pinoli nuts
2 tablespoons minced
   parsley
Salt and pepper

Stir the vermicelli or spaghetti into 5 quarts rapidly boiling salted water. Heat the olive oil, garlic, raisins, and pinolis until the garlic is golden and the raisins are plumped. Stir in the parsley, salt, and pepper. Drain the spaghetti when cooked al dente and toss into the warm oil. Serve immediately. *Serves 4 to 6.*

MEMORIES

"You learn to cook like the mother-in-law."

I come from a family of ten children. My uncle lived with us so there were thirteen at the table and we always set up the dining room table for our Sunday meal and it was always a big spread. We had soup, and then we had macaroni and we had the meat in the sauce also. And we had a roast, either a lamb or a roasting chicken, with roasted potatoes and vegetables and salad and fruit. In the summertime we would make homemade ice cream.

My mother did all the cooking and we set up the table and cleared the table. She always washed the dishes. My mother was always in the kitchen. She never had time to do anything else.

We came home from school at 11:30 and the second session, the afternoon, began at 1 o'clock. We always sat down to a dinner. I didn't know what it was to have a sandwich. We had a full meal and then we'd go back to school.

My father had a big garden. He had two of them, one at the house and then they had a lot that the cotton mills owned and let anyone use who wanted to. And we used to have everything. It was so fresh and tasty. My mother would put on the water and we'd go pick the corn. It was so sweet.

Lucy's mother, Teresa Campobiano.

The boys worked in the garden. And my uncle who lived with us helped. They had to carry pails to water the second garden. They would catch the rainwater in barrels.

I cook like my mother and his (my husband's) mother which is the same because they came from about the same area in the hills around Naples. My sister married an Italian boy from another area of Italy and she learned to cook his way. Basically this is what happens, you learn to cook like the mother-in-law. My sister's sauce is altogether different from mine. They don't use tomatoes when they make macaroni sauce; they use paste. I don't know how they do it.

My father loved to come to our house for holidays because I stayed with the tradition: Christmas, Christmas Eve fish dinner, lamb at Easter. My brothers married different nationalities and they had, maybe, ham for Easter. My father would say, "No, no, that's not right."

At Easter we all had to go to Mass and then promptly at 9 o'clock we had our Easter breakfast, which was beautiful. It was a huge spread. All the best china would come out. We would have a special big omelet with asparagus, Italian sausage, lots of parsley, ricotta cheese, and some scamorza. We would have boiled eggs, three or four different types of cheese, Easter bread, the "special cake," rice pie. That afternoon we would have a huge Easter dinner also.

Dad used to make his own wine. A produce man would deliver cases of red and white grapes and Dad used to make his wine. I never touched it! To this day I don't like wine. My oldest sister helped my mother with the preserving. She wasted nothing. She could preserve anything.

Dad did all the shopping but there were also a lot of peddlers who came to the house. My mother had a poultry man who delivered live poultry. She had to strangle the neck. And the feathers. That's where the girls came in. We had to pluck them.

Everything was always fresh. In the summer the farmers would come to the house. They had such varieties of lettuce. I loved the bitter greens.

My father was a good cook too. He never actually cooked but he had an aunt in Italy who cooked for royalty and he knew how to cook. In fact, I think he taught my mother how to cook. He would say that his aunt used to do it this way or that.

My father would give me little hints. For example, he told me not to put oregano in my marinara sauce until it was cooked or it would be too bitter. He also told me to always break up dried herbs before adding them to bring out more flavor.

My father was very fussy with his food. Very. That's why I suspect that he taught my mother to cook. Even though I never saw him in the kitchen cooking.

Spaghetti had to be al dente. He couldn't stand it if it was over-cooked. He would get so mad if it was overcooked. My poor mother had a hard time because she had to cook three pounds at a time. Sometimes we ate pasta every night. But back then we called it macaroni.

Lucy's mother with Lucy.

A meal to my parents was very important. It was marvelous. We would be an hour, hour and a half at the table. Just sitting there and not rushing anything.

People had large families back then and in many ways it was easier. We never expected too much from our parents. We accepted hand-me-downs.

Another thing that was so marvelous was that you visited your aunts whether you wanted to or not. Holidays, you went down, wished them a happy holiday. Families were very close.

Sundays in the summer when it was hot we would sometimes go to the beach. My mother would spend all day Saturday cooking a Sunday dinner and then pack it up so we would have a meal. What a job! My father bought big cars secondhand from the funeral parlor so we could all ride together.

LUCY ROSSI
(family from area around Naples)

Linguine with Shellfish

LINGUINE CON FRUTTI DI MARE

In the old days in Italian neighborhoods, seafood was always sold from pushcarts. Early in the morning on "fish day," the fishmonger would push his cart, lined with ice, down to the dock to select the fish and shellfish that he would sell. Wednesdays and Fridays were the usual days for selling seafood.

1 pound littleneck clams	¼ cup dry white wine
1 pound mussels	¾ pound fresh plum
¾ pound shrimp	tomatoes, peeled and
½ cup extra-virgin olive oil	seeded, or ¾ pound
3 large garlic cloves, minced	drained canned tomatoes,
1 small hot red pepper,	cut in strips
seeded and chopped, or	¼ cup minced parsley
¼ teaspoon dried hot	Salt, if necessary
pepper flakes	1 pound linguine

1. Wash the clams and mussels in several changes of cold water, scrubbing well. Remove the beards from the mussels. Peel the shrimp and rinse.

2. Put the oil in a frying pan with the garlic and hot pepper. When garlic is just golden add the clams and mussels. Cover the pan and cook until the shellfish are opened (mussels will open in about 5 minutes; clams will take from 8 to 12 minutes). Using a slotted spoon, remove shellfish to a bowl as they open. Remove the meat from the shells. (If desired, leave a few in the shells for decoration.) Cut the clams in half or in quarters. Save any juices that collect in the bowl. Strain juices from the bowl and from the pan through a coffee filter or a washed cheesecloth.

3. Stir the linguine into 5 quarts of rapidly boiling salted water and cook until al dente.

4. While the linguine cooks, return the strained juices to the pan. Add the white wine and boil 3 minutes. Add the tomatoes and cook 5 minutes. Add shrimp and just as they begin to turn pink add the clams, mussels, and parsley and taste for salt. When the shrimp are all pink and all is hot, pour over the drained hot linguine. *Serves 6.*

Spaghetti with Oil and Garlic Neapolitan Style

SPAGHETTI AGLIO E OGLIO (OLIO)

It's amazing that such a simple recipe has ever been written down and yet I have often seen many versions of it. The variations are always simple, hot pepper or not, parsley or not, garlic crushed or minced. The recipe that follows is how Nonna made it. It was always a comforting welcome at the table and is today for my family.

1 pound spaghetti	Salt
½ cup olive oil	Pinch of hot pepper flakes
3 garlic cloves, minced	or to taste

Stir the spaghetti into 5 quarts boiling salted water. Heat the olive oil and garlic until the garlic is golden. Add the salt and hot pepper flakes. Drain the spaghetti when cooked al dente. Toss with the warm oil and serve immediately. *Serves 4 to 6.*

• • •

Note: Neapolitans are much more apt to use hot red pepper flakes (peperoncini) than ground black pepper. It is a matter of preference, but don't make the mistake of using both!

GRATING CHEESE

In order to maintain their moisture, keep grating cheeses wrapped in plastic and foil in the refrigerator and only grate as much as you need at a time. I grate hard cheeses by hand because a food processor makes hard little grains that have none of the melting or blending capacity of the hand-produced flakes.

Parmigiano Reggiano (Parmesan):   Made from cow's milk. To be called "parmigiano" this cheese must be produced by required methods in a designated area of Italy. You will know it because its name "parmigiano reggiano" is unmistakably stamped on the rind. Be particularly aware of this, not because Parmesan is the only good grating cheese available, but because you should receive exactly what it is you want. Many people sell a number of look-alikes in the name of parmigiano. They will not have that distinctive mellow, nutty flavor. Parmesan should be golden colored and slightly moist.

Grana padano: Made from cow's milk. A common substitute for Parmesan, this was the cheese most often found in American markets before Parmesan became more available. It is less expensive than Parmesan and less mellow. Its flavor varies from mild to piquant depending on its age. The light, buff-colored cheese has a grainy texture with tiny eyes. Look for its name, which is stamped conspicuously all over the rind.

Pecorino: Sheep's milk cheese aged for grating. Most commonly found are pecorino romano and pecorino sardo. Sharp, tangy, and slightly salty, pecorino is a favorite with southern Italians since its flavor stands up well to olive oil–based dishes.

Ricotta salata: Briefly aged sheep's milk cheese imported from Italy. Mild but distinctly flavored, it is used to grate or crumble onto cooked pasta or for antipasto.

Spaghetti with Red Clam Sauce

SPAGHETTI ALLE VONGOLE CON POMODORI

Spaghetti with clam sauce was a regular standby for meatless Friday nights, as well as a traditional part of the Christmas Eve fish celebration. Whether it was a white, tomatoless clam sauce or this red one depended on the area of Italy from which the family had emigrated. Some areas of southern Italy held to the tradition that the Christmas Eve meal should be all white, hence the absence of tomato.

2 to 2½ pounds littleneck
  or cherrystone clams
2 tablespoons plus ½ cup
  extra-virgin olive oil
3 garlic cloves, minced
¼ teaspoon hot pepper,
  if desired
2 cups drained canned
  tomatoes, chopped

½ cup dry white wine
2 tablespoons chopped
  parsley
1 pound linguine or
  vermicelli

1. Wash the clams in several changes of cold water, scrubbing well. Put into a heavy pot with 2 tablespoons olive oil, cover, and cook until the clams are opened (about 8 to 12 minutes depending on size). Remove the clams with a slotted spoon. Strain the juices through a washed cheesecloth or a coffee filter and set aside. Remove the clams from shells and coarsely chop.

2. Heat ½ cup olive oil, garlic, and hot pepper in a 12-inch frying pan. When the garlic is golden, add the tomatoes, white wine, and reserved clam juices. Bring to a boil, reduce the heat, and simmer 30 minutes, or until reduced so the oil separates from the tomatoes. Add the clams and parsley to tomatoes to reheat just before the spaghetti is cooked. Check the seasonings. No salt should be needed.

3. Cook the spaghetti in 5 quarts rapidly boiling salted water until al dente. Drain and toss with the sauce. *Serves 6.*

. . .

Variation: I make a fresh tomato version of this recipe which has a less concentrated tomato flavor. In place of the canned tomatoes, add 2 cups of peeled, seeded, juiced fresh tomatoes cut in narrow strips. Sauté on high heat 3 to 5 minutes only to evaporate water. Toss in fresh oregano or basil and serve as above.

Spaghetti with Tuna Fish and Swiss Chard

SPAGHETTI CON TONNO E BIETOLINI

It is unfortunate that so few of the southern Italian pasta recipes that used canned tuna became part of Italian-American food. This recipe from Basilicata is a particularly appealing combination of flavors.

1 pound Swiss chard
 (or substitute beet greens)
⅓ cup extra-virgin olive oil
 plus extra for finished
 pasta
1 small onion, finely
 chopped

¼ cup flat-leaf parsley,
 coarsely chopped
One 7½-ounce can Italian
 tuna packed in olive oil,
 drained
Salt
1 pound spaghetti

1. Wash the chard, separate ribs and leaves, and string ribs if necessary. Cut the ribs into 2-inch pieces and put in a large pot of boiling salted water to blanch. After 7 minutes, add the leaves and continue to boil for 3 minutes. Drain, rinse with cold water, and dry. Finely chop the ribs and leaves together.

2. Heat the olive oil in a sauté pan and cook the onion over medium-low heat until softened but not browned. Add the chard and parsley and toss together. Crumble in the tuna fish and taste for salt. Set aside.

3. Cook the spaghetti in 5 quarts boiling salted water until al dente. Drain and toss with the sauce. Top each serving with a teaspoon extra-virgin olive oil. *Serves 6 to 8.*

BREADCRUMBS

Southern Italians often substitute toasted or fried breadcrumbs for grated cheese in pasta recipes and just about
always use them in fish dishes. The original church laws
that governed fast days forbade the use of meat in any
form, including cheese. Furthermore, in the often lean
times for the southern Italians, breadcrumbs were cheaper
and more readily available.

Delivering bread in Providence, Rhode Island, circa 1920.

To make breadcrumbs, grate stale Italian bread. I use
a hand-held grater and rub the bread on the next-to-small-
est hole. Remove the crust only if you want a perfectly
white breadcrumb, otherwise leave it on. Breadcrumbs
may also be made in a blender or food processor. Store in
a cool place in a plastic bag until needed.

Piquant Linguine with Onions

LINGUINE CON CIPOLLE PICCANTE

Calabrians claim that onions strengthen the voice and send away bad moods. Maybe, maybe not, but this recipe is a great example of cooking from the cupboard if the cupboard happens to have an Italian heritage. The ingredients are ones that I always have on hand. You may substitute pecorino cheese for the breadcrumbs, if desired.

3 medium onions (¾ pound), thinly sliced

½ cup plus 3 tablespoons extra-virgin olive oil

2 tablespoons fresh oregano or 2 teaspoons dried

½ cup sun-dried tomatoes

½ cup Gaeta or similar black olives

Salt and freshly ground black pepper

½ cup dry breadcrumbs

¾ pound linguine

1. Put the onions and ½ cup oil into a 10-inch sauté pan with a cover. Cover and cook over medium-low heat until the onions are completely softened (30 minutes). Do not allow to brown.

2. While the onions are cooking, cut the sun-dried tomatoes into ¼-inch-wide strips. Coarsely chop the fresh oregano leaves. Pit the olives and slice lengthwise into quarters.

3. When the onions are ready, add the sun-dried tomatoes, oregano, olives, salt, and pepper to the onions. Cook gently, uncovered, 10 minutes.

4. Heat 3 tablespoons oil in a frying pan. Add the breadcrumbs and toss over high heat until colored and toasted (about 4 minutes). Set aside.

5. Cook the linguine in 4 quarts rapidly boiling salted water until al dente. Drain and place in a warmed pasta dish. Pour on the onion sauce and mix well. Sprinkle on the toasted breadcrumbs and serve. *Serves 4 to 6.*

Linguine with Paprika Sauce

LINGUINE CON SALSA DI PAPRICA

This is one of the most unusual uses of paprika I have found. I fell in love with it the first time I tasted it, but I warn you that it is unusual! Italo Scanga introduced me to this dish, which is a wonderful Calabrian example of the frugal and creative use of food. The flat-sided linguine is particularly good for this sauce.

4 garlic cloves, crushed
   and peeled
½ cup extra-virgin olive oil
4 tablespoons paprika
½ cup dry white wine
¾ cup drained canned
   tomatoes

Salt
Additional extra-virgin olive
   oil for coating platter
1 pound linguine di passeri
¼ pound pecorino romano
   cheese, freshly grated

1. In a 10-inch sauté pan, over low heat, cook the garlic cloves in oil until browned. Discard the garlic. Add the paprika to the oil and stir to make a paste. Add the wine and reduce by half. Put the tomatoes in a blender or food processor or chop by hand until very fine. Add to the pan with the salt and cook 10 minutes.

2. Warm a serving platter and coat it with 2 to 3 tablespoons olive oil. Cook the linguine in a large amount of boiling salted water until al dente. Drain and put on the warm platter coated with olive oil. Pour on the hot sauce. Sprinkle on all the cheese. Toss and serve. Pass additional cheese and olive oil if desired. *Serves 6.*

PAPRIKA

In Calabria cooks preserve sweet or hot peppers by drying them in the sun and crushing them or by making a "conservata," which is a pepper paste made with sweet and hot peppers. They use either product to flavor pasta sauces, soups, and stews. Drying peppers was close to impossible for the immigrants because the climate in most of the United States, particularly the Northeast, did not provide the necessary long, dry sunny days. Making a "conservata" was possible and was often done but it required a minimum of five days and a good deal of labor to make. It eventually disappeared in all but a few households. Calabrian-Americans began to substitute sweet or hot paprika for the homemade products. They often combine paprika with tomato paste to simulate a "conservata." You will find paprika in some of the recipes in this book. I think the ones imported from Hungary are the best.

Buying macaroni by the pound.

Spaghetti Harlot's Style

SPAGHETTI ALLA PUTTANESCA

Although many recipes for this popular dish have been printed, it is a dish that should not be restricted by a single recipe. Add more or less anchovies or olives or capers depending on your taste. Supposedly named because ladies of the night were able to fix it quickly between "tricks," it combines almost all the tasty staples of the southern Italian kitchen.

½ cup extra-virgin olive oil
1 large onion, minced
3 garlic cloves, minced
4 anchovy fillets, minced
1½ pounds tomatoes
  (about 2 cups), peeled
  and seeded, or same
  amount canned, drained,
  and chopped
1 cup black brine-cured
  olives (such as Gaeta),
  halved and pitted

2 tablespoons capers, rinsed
2 teaspoons red wine vinegar
2 tablespoons minced fresh
  oregano, basil, or
  marjoram
Salt and freshly ground
  black pepper or hot
  pepper, if desired
Pinch of sugar, if needed
1 pound spaghetti
¼ cup fresh flat parsley
  leaves

1. Put the oil, onion, and garlic in a large skillet or flameproof casserole. Cook over gentle heat until the onion is softened but not browned. Mash in the anchovy fillets.

2. Add the tomatoes, olives, capers, vinegar, herb, salt, pepper, and pinch of sugar, if needed. Simmer 15 minutes.

3. Add the spaghetti to 5 quarts rapidly boiling salted water and cook until just tender to the bite, al dente. Drain and toss with the sauce and fresh parsley leaves. *Serves 6.*

Spaghetti Vesuvius

SPAGHETTI AL VESUVIO

When I was a young girl, the two most popular Italian songs were "O Sole Mio" and "Return to Sorrento." Both songs reflected the longing the Italians felt for the beauty of the landscapes they had left behind. There are many things about this dish that must have reminded Italians everywhere of their beautiful Naples. The name alone brings to mind that city's famous volcano which stands guard over the bay. Moreover, the long, slow cooking of the tomatoes gives them a very special, sweet flavor that resembles the tomatoes of San Marzano near Naples. The addition of hot pepper, of course, alludes to the fires of the now-dormant volcano.

½ cup extra-virgin olive oil
3 garlic cloves, minced
1 small onion, minced
1 tablespoon chopped hot
    red pepper or ½ teaspoon
    dried
10 fresh plum tomatoes
    (about 2 pounds), peeled,
    left whole, stems removed

Salt
Pinch of sugar
¼ cup chopped parsley
¼ cup chopped basil
1 pound spaghetti

1. Put the olive oil, garlic, onion, and hot pepper in a large sauté pan. Cook until the onion is completely softened but not browned. Cut the tomatoes in half from top to bottom. Do not remove the seeds or juice. Put in the pan, cut side up, and cook over medium-low heat 5 minutes. Sprinkle with salt and a pinch of sugar. Carefully, so as not to break the tomatoes, turn them over. Place in a 225°F oven 2½ hours. (The tomatoes may also be cooked slowly on top of the stove.)

2. Sprinkle the tomatoes with parsley and basil and continue to cook 30 minutes, basting with pan juices from time to time.

3. Cook the spaghetti in 5 quarts boiling salted water until al dente. Drain and put into a pasta dish. Pour the tomatoes over. Toss together before serving. *Serves 6.*

LAYERED CHEESE

Layered cheeses are kneaded, stretched and then shaped. They are sold fresh or aged and often smoked, and play an important role in southern Italian cooking.

Mozzarella: Made in Italy originally from the milk of water buffalo. Its name comes from "mozzare," "to cut off," since small pieces are cut off the large curd to form small egg-shaped cheeses. Buffalo milk mozzarella is imported to the United States and is a delicious eating cheese, as in the "Insalata Caprese" (page 43). I never cook with it. It is costly and its subtle flavor is masked by other ingredients. Excellent fresh cow's milk mozzarella is now made in the United States. (In Italy cow's milk mozzarella is usually called "fior di latte.") It has a soft, melting texture that in no way resembles the rubberized, mass-produced supermarket product. Fresh mozzarella is sold in its own whey and has a shelf life of about one week. I pour out the whey after a few days and replace it with fresh water which keeps the mozzarella fresher a little longer. Fresh mozzarella was not available to the early immigrants and they substituted imported scamorza or provolone.

Scamorza: Made from cow's milk and molded into pear shapes. After it is made it is immersed in a brine solution to intensify the flavor and prolong its shelf life. The smoked variety has a brown rind. Used for eating and cooking, it has a soft slightly dry texture.

Provolone: Primarily made from cow's milk and seen hanging from ceilings in Italian markets. Brine-cured to intensify the flavor and prolong shelf life, it may be mild or pungent depending on age, and is often smoked.

Caciocavallo: Made from cow's milk. Caciocavallo is formed into large pear-shaped cheeses that are tied together by red string bags. Brine cured, its flavor and texture change with age. Young, it is a mild eating or cooking cheese; aged, it is grated.

Thin Spaghetti Syracuse Style

VERMICELLI ALLA SIRACUSANA

This Sicilian recipe is brimming with the flavors of southern Italy: eggplant, tomato, peppers, and olives. I'm sure that no two Sicilians or Sicilian-Americans ever make it the same. So feel free to adjust it to your taste with more or less anchovies or capers or herbs. One aspect that seems to be constant, however, is the size of the pasta. It should be spaghetti and should be thin. This dish is hearty enough to make a meal in itself.

2 medium eggplants, about 2 pounds total weight
Salt
½ cup plus 3 tablespoons olive oil
3 large garlic cloves, smashed and peeled
2 pounds tomatoes, peeled, seeded, and chopped
2 sweet peppers, yellow or green, roasted (page 34) and cut into 1-inch squares
6 to 8 anchovy fillets (rinsed if packed in salt)

20 brine-cured black olives (Gaeta or Calamata), pitted
1 to 1½ tablespoons capers, rinsed
Freshly ground black pepper
¼ cup chopped basil (about 14 leaves)
1½ pounds vermicelli or thin spaghetti (spaghettini)
¼ pound freshly grated caciocavallo or pecorino cheese

1. Wash the eggplant and trim the tops but do not peel. Cut into cubes approximately ⅜ inch. Place in a colander and salt the layers. Put a plate on top and weight the plate. Let sit over a bowl or in a sink 1 hour to drain.

2. Squeeze the eggplant gently with paper towels to dry. Put ½ cup olive oil and garlic in a large sauté pan and cook over low heat until the garlic is browned. Discard the garlic. Add the eggplant to the pan and cook over medium-high heat until the eggplant is golden. Add the remaining 3 tablespoons oil to the pan. Add the tomatoes and salt and bring to a boil. Reduce the heat to simmer, cover the pan, and simmer for 10 minutes. Add the peppers to the pan, cover again, and cook 5 minutes.

Thin Spaghetti Syracuse Style (continued)

3. Chop the anchovy fillets and slice the olives into strips. Add the anchovies, olives, and capers to the pan. Season with salt and a generous grinding of black pepper. Add the basil, return cover and simmer 15 minutes.

4. Cook the vermicelli in 5 quarts rapidly boiling salted water until al dente. Drain and toss into the hot sauce along with the grated cheese. Serve immediately. *Serves 6.*

HOT PEPPER OIL

Hot pepper oil (olio al peperoncino or peperolio) is olive oil steeped with hot pepper (peperoncino). In Apulia, where it is most often found, it is known as "olio santé," holy oil, a term which reflects its ancient use for anointing priests, kings, and athletes. Hot pepper oil is added to a finished dish to give it zest. This is no doubt the tradition that led to the bottle of hot pepper flakes that sits on many tables in Italian-American restaurants and pizzerias.

You can make your own hot pepper oil, which will blend into a finished dish better than the flakes. Vary the amount of hot pepper to your liking. To 2 cups extra-virgin olive oil, add 1 hot red pepper, ½ teaspoon crushed red flakes, or 1 dried hot red pepper. Let steep 1 week before using. No recipes in this book call specifically for hot pepper oil, but if you wish to add a bit of "fire," or as the Apulians say, "a tear or two," to any dish that does or does not already contain hot pepper, add some olio al peperoncino to the finished dish. It is a good way for each diner to adjust the amount of "heat" in the dish to his or her own liking.

Macaroni with Mushrooms

MACCHERONI AI FUNGHI

The majority of southern Italians who emigrated to the East Coast of the United States settled in urban areas, even though most of them had led rural lives in Italy. Some people, however, did seek out the country and there they continued to hunt game and pick wild greens and mushrooms as they had done in the "old country." This hearty recipe, which often preceded a meal of wild game, was made with wild mushrooms and not with the milder cultivated type. Since it is not always easy to find wild mushrooms in the market—or in the woods—this recipe combines dried wild mushrooms with fresh market ones. A very small amount of dried mushrooms will flavor an entire pound of cultivated ones so that they taste more like their woodsy cousins.

½ ounce dried porcini mushrooms
3 tablespoons extra-virgin olive oil
1 onion, coarsely chopped
2 garlic cloves, coarsely chopped
1 small hot red pepper, seeded and chopped, or ½ teaspoon hot red pepper flakes
¾ pound mushrooms, wiped clean and cut into ½-inch pieces

Salt
2 cups chopped, peeled, and seeded fresh tomatoes, or 2 cups drained, canned
¼ cup chopped parsley
2 tablespoons fresh oregano or 2 teaspoons dried
1 pound penne or similar macaroni
4 ounces freshly grated pecorino cheese

1. Cover the dried porcini mushrooms with ½ cup warm water and let soak at least 30 minutes. Drain and reserve the juices. Rinse the mushrooms under warm running water to remove all dirt, discard any tough pieces, dry them, and coarsely chop. Filter the mushroom juices through some washed cheesecloth or a coffee filter and set aside.

2. Heat the oil, onion, and garlic in a sauté pan over medium-

Macaroni with Mushrooms (continued)

low heat until the vegetables are translucent. Add the hot pepper and porcini mushrooms and cook 3 to 4 minutes. Add the fresh mushrooms and salt to taste and cook until mushroom juices run. Add the reserved porcini mushroom juices, turn the heat to high, and reduce liquid to about ¼ cup.

3. Add the tomatoes to the pan and simmer 25 minutes. Stir the herbs into the sauce during the last 5 minutes of cooking.

4. Cook the macaroni in 5 quarts boiling salted water until al dente. Drain and toss with the sauce in a pasta serving dish. Sprinkle on the cheese and serve. *Serves 6.*

MEMORIES

"The restaurant was home . . ."

The cooking here (in my restaurant) is regional cooking of the Abruzzi region. My father learned the way that his people cooked, and my mother lived in more or less the same paesa. It's simple. Plain simple cooking. When my father opened the restaurant his idea was to help the working people. His restaurant was small and for these people. He'd come in at 5 o'clock in the morning and make all the lunches for all the Italian workers in the neighborhood. He'd make peppers and eggs or zucchini and eggs—peasant-type cooking. He bought all these ingredients from the pushcarts in the neighborhood.

My mother and my father both did the cooking in the restaurant. My mother used to make the homemade macaroni. Then my father got a man to come and help when he got a bigger place, but he made sure that he did things his way. Then I had an uncle, my mother's brother, and he came in to work and my father taught him. Then he started to do the cooking for my father and it stayed the same— everything stayed the same and it still is.

Even though my mother and father lived in a tenement house, they always had pots on the windowsill where they grew the basil and the mint and oregano. In the winter they would dry up all of it so they wouldn't have to go in search of it. As long as my mother and father lived we always had fresh herbs in the yard or in pots. Everybody did.

The neighborhood was beautiful. Mostly Italian. We lived in two- and three-family tenement houses. Everybody was friendly, everybody was helping each other, we didn't lock doors—it was a beautiful atmosphere. There was no violence, no stealing.

There was a lot of poverty but the women were all home, they brought up the kids, the fathers went to work. I can remember with the Depression we did without a lot of stuff but we prospered because we saved, we didn't waste, and we paid cash for everything.

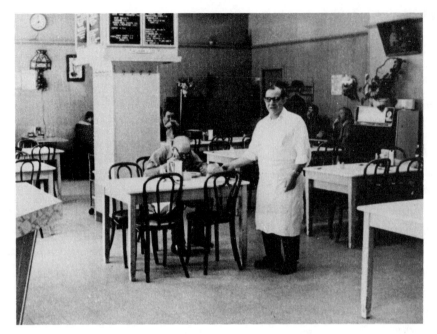

Interior of Angelo's restaurant on "The Hill."

*It's mostly families that come here [to the restaurant]. We had
some customers of ours that used to come when they were courting,
and then they got married and they had children and so three or four
generations would come here.*

*My sisters and I were here so much, we'd eat here more than at
home. Even when we were in school, we used to come here for lunch.
We'd do the cashier for an hour, have a sandwich or some soup, and
then go back to school. We worked all our lives in here. The restaurant was home—we only went home to sleep.*

VERA MASTRODICASA MUOIO
*(operates Angelo's Civita Farnese restaurant;
family from Abruzzi region)*

Macaroni with Broccoli

MACCHERONI CON BROCCOLI

Broccoli lovers, rejoice! Here is a recipe in which nothing interferes with the flavor of the vegetable. So often this distinctive vegetable is present in a one-floweret here, one-there fashion just for its color and the true fan cannot get enough of it. Purists can even eliminate the cheese.

1 large bunch broccoli,
    about 2 pounds
4 tablespoons butter
4 garlic cloves, peeled
4 tablespoons extra-virgin
    olive oil

Salt and pepper
1 pound cut ziti, penne, or
    similar-size macaroni
1 cup grated pecorino or
    Parmesan cheese

1. Divide the flowerets from the broccoli stems. Peel the stems, cut into 2-inch pieces, and cook in boiling salted water for 2 minutes. Add the flowerets to the pan with the stems and cook together until all is tender (about 4 minutes). Drain, plunge into cold water, dry, and chop into ½-inch pieces. Set aside.
2. Melt the butter and keep warm. Sauté the garlic in the olive oil until lightly colored. Discard the garlic. Add the broccoli and heat. Season with salt and pepper.
3. Cook the pasta in 5 quarts boiling salted water until al dente. Drain and mix with the broccoli. Pour on the cheese and butter and serve immediately. *Serves 6.*

· · ·

Variation: If broccoli rabe is your passion, use 1½ pounds and ½ cup olive oil in place of oil and butter. Add hot pepper if you like or adorn with "a tear or two" of olio al peperoncini.

ANCHOVIES

Southern Italians often use anchovies as a seasoning—an outgrowth of the days when salt taxes were so steep that fish products were used to replace salt. Now anchovies are an essential part of many recipes for their flavor alone.

Anchovies are sold packed in oil or in salt. Always taste those packed in oil because the oil is rarely a good grade; it's best to rinse and dry the anchovies before using. Anchovies in salt, "acciughe sotto sale," are better if you can find them. You can reduce the saltiness, if it troubles you, by soaking the rinsed anchovies in water or milk for 1 hour, changing the water often. You will probably have to debone salt-packed anchovies. If you find a good source, store salted anchovies at home. Rinse, pat dry, debone, and put in a small dish. Cover with olive oil, capers, and garlic (optional), seal with plastic wrap, and refrigerate. Be careful when you cook anchovies not to let them burn or they will become bitter.

Anchovy Sauce

Anchovy sauce is delicious over spaghetti (this recipe makes enough for one pound), or with plain vegetables, or breaded, fried foods.

½ cup best-quality olive oil	4 to 6 anchovies, salted or packed in oil, rinsed
4 garlic cloves, minced	Pepper

Put the olive oil and garlic in a small pot and cook over gentle heat until the garlic is softened but not browned. Add the anchovies to the oil, choosing the amount according to taste. Season with pepper and mash well. Cook gently a few minutes to blend the flavors.

Macaroni with Cauliflower

MACCHERONI CON CAVOLFIORE

Italian cooking at its best is always the perfect marriage of a few well-chosen ingredients. Macaroni with cauliflower is a great case in point. If it is a first course, be sure to follow it with a full-flavored second course. This recipe does not call for grated cheese but bread-crumbs lightly browned in olive oil are a nice topping. You could use pecorino cheese instead, if desired.

1 large head cauliflower, about 2 pounds	Salt
½ cup extra-virgin olive oil	1 pound short macaroni, such as cut ziti or penne
5 large garlic cloves, minced	½ cup fresh breadcrumbs sautéed in 3 tablespoons olive oil (optional)
½ teaspoon hot pepper flakes	
6 anchovy fillets, rinsed, patted dry, and minced	

1. Remove the green leaves from the cauliflower. Trim the stem close to the head and cut a cross deep into the core of the cauliflower to hasten cooking. Wash, upside down, in cold water. Place in a pot of boiling salted water and cook until tender (about 20 minutes). Drain well and chop very fine.

2. Put the olive oil, garlic, and hot pepper into a sauté pan. Cook gently until the garlic is golden. Add the anchovies and stir 1 minute to blend the flavors. Add the cauliflower and mix together well. Taste for salt. Let cook 2 to 3 minutes.

3. Cook the pasta in 5 quarts boiling salted water until al dente. Drain and put into a warm pasta bowl. Toss in the warm sauce and sprinkle with breadcrumbs if desired. *Serves 6.*

• • •

Note: As wonderful as cauliflower tastes, it does not smell particularly wonderful when it cooks. Adding half a lemon or half a glass of milk to the cooking water helps not only reduce odors but keeps the vegetable white. A Neapolitan friend soaks a piece of bread in vinegar, lays it on the edge of the cooking pot, and keeps it in place by placing the cover slightly askew over it.

OLIVES

In a bookshop in a small town in southern Italy, I found a charming Calabrian cookbook that had a number of recipes that included olives. I was eager to translate the text to see how they compared to their American versions. I was surprised to find that many recipes began by telling the cook when to pick the olives. It reminded me of what the author Luigi Barzini meant when he said, "Italians live close to their food," and I wondered at how much the immigrants must have missed those olive trees.

The Italians who settled in the East were not able to pick their own olives but they did not have to go without. Merchants sold fresh olives from Italy and California then and still do today. The produce stands hold bins full of both small green underripe olives and small ripe black ones waiting to be cured. Southern Italians cook with cured olives to add piquancy and saltiness that are characteristic of much of their food. And they love to nibble on them between meals and before as an antipasto.

Early Italian-American markets did sell imported cured olives but the selection was small and they were expensive. Many Italian-Americans turned to commercially cured California olives and the bland substitution robbed many dishes of their original flavor.

Olives may be stored for a few weeks out of the refrigerator if they are covered with a brine solution or olive oil. If the vendor does not cover your olives with a brine, make your own solution by mixing one tablespoon of salt to one quart of water.

It would be impossible to list all the varieties of cured olives available today but here are some of the more common ones.

Gaeta olives: Imported from the coastal town near Naples, renowned for their remarkable flavor. Sold either brine-cured or salt-cured and rubbed with oil. I prefer the brine-cured and use them for cooking and snacking. I use the salt-cured for snacking only.

Calabrese olives: Tiny, green olives, brine-cured with herbs and hot pepper that reflect the piquant cooking of Calabria. I use these only for snacking.

Large green Sicilian olives: Usually cracked before being cured in brine sometimes with the addition of vinegar. Often sold mixed with other olives for what Italians call "Insalata di Olive" (Olive Salad.) Particularly good when cooked with chicken or fish.

Kalamata: Brine- and vinegar-cured Greek olives often substituted for Italian black olives because they are more readily available and economical. I only buy them when I cannot get Gaeta olives. If very vinegary, blanch 30 seconds in boiling water before cooking with them.

Macaroni with Olives

MACCHERONI CON LE OLIVE

The short, corkscrew-shaped fusilli is a particularly good pasta for this recipe because bits of the wonderful piquant flavors are caught in the twists. Early Italian-Americans did not have the same abundance of pasta shapes available to them as we do today and many of the traditional Italian combinations disappeared.

½ cup extra-virgin olive oil
1 medium onion, minced
1 medium garlic clove
　minced
1 pound fresh tomatoes,
　peeled, seeded, and
　chopped, or 1 pound
　drained canned tomatoes,
　chopped
1 cup brine-cured black
　olives (or ½ cup each
　black and green), halved
　and pitted

2 tablespoons capers, rinsed
　and drained
2 teaspoons red wine vinegar
2 tablespoons fresh oregano
　or 2 teaspoons dried
Pinch of sugar
Salt and pepper
1 pound short fusilli or other
　short macaroni
1 cup freshly grated
　pecorino cheese

1. Heat the oil, onion, and garlic in a large skillet and cook over moderately low heat until softened but not browned, 6 to 8 minutes.

2. Add the tomatoes, olives, capers, vinegar, oregano, sugar, salt, and pepper and simmer for 15 minutes over low heat. Be careful with the salt since olives and capers are salty.

3. Cook the macaroni in a large pot of boiling salted water until al dente. Drain and mix with the sauce. Sprinkle on the cheese and serve immediately with additional cheese on the side if desired. *Serves 6.*

Ziti with Minted Summer Squash

ZITI CON ZUCCHINI GIALLI E MENTA

The Italian-Americans who started their own gardens must have quickly learned that there is no stopping the growth of summer squashes! Fortunately, mint does the same thing and this combination is worth the planting of both.

2 pounds yellow squash, about 4 medium, washed and ends trimmed
½ cup extra-virgin olive oil
3 large garlic cloves, smashed and peeled
¼ cup thinly sliced scallions, white part only
Salt
½ small hot red pepper, seeded and diced, or ¼ teaspoon hot pepper flakes

1 pound cut ziti, penne, or similar short tubular macaroni
½ cup coarsely chopped flat-leafed parsley
½ cup coarsely chopped fresh mint

1. Cut the squash into small dice no larger than ¼ inch.
2. Cook the oil and garlic in a large sauté pan until the garlic is well browned. Discard the garlic. Add the scallions to the oil and cook until tender but not browned. Add the squash, salt, and the hot pepper. Cover and cook over medium-low heat, stirring occasionally, until the squash is completely softened, about 15 minutes. (If the squash becomes dry during cooking, add 1 to 2 tablespoons hot water.)
3. Stir the macaroni into 5 quarts boiling salted water and cook until al dente. Drain. Mix with the squash and the parsley and mint. Serve immediately. *Serves 6.*

Ziti in the Manner of San Giovanni

ZITI ALLA SAN GIOVANNI

I really have no idea why this recipe is associated with either St. John or with his namesake town west of Naples. I can only say that I am grateful that someone found it worthy of creation. It is an unusual, delicious combination of flavors. Unusual because nuts are rarely used in southern Italian pasta dishes, although they were just about always present in southern Italian and Italian-American homes, mostly for cracking open and eating as is.

¼ cup extra-virgin olive oil
3 medium garlic cloves, smashed and peeled
6 ounces thinly sliced prosciutto, cut into fine strips
⅔ cup walnuts (about 3 ounces), coarsely chopped
1 pound ziti or similar short tubular macaroni

4 tablespoons unsalted butter, melted
1 cup freshly grated Parmesan cheese (about 4 ounces)
30 small fresh sage leaves
Salt and freshly ground black pepper

1. In a large skillet or flameproof casserole, heat the oil and the garlic cloves over low heat until the garlic is browned, about 6 to 8 minutes. Remove and discard the garlic.

2. Add the prosciutto and walnuts to the oil and cook, stirring occasionally, until the walnuts are lightly toasted and the prosciutto fat is translucent (about 8 to 10 minutes). Remove from the heat and set aside.

3. Stir the macaroni into 5 quarts rapidly boiling salted water and cook until just tender to the bite, al dente. Drain the macaroni and toss into the prosciutto and walnuts. Add the cheese, melted butter, sage leaves, salt, and pepper. Toss well and serve. *Serves 6.*

Shepherds' Macaroni

MACCHERONI ALLA PASTORE

This Calabrian dish is simplicity itself—fresh cheese and lots of black pepper! It is said to be named for the shepherds who created the dish as a way of using sheep's milk ricotta cheese, which was plentiful to them. If you can find a fresh sheep's milk cheese, by all means use it; it is not an impossible task since today there are a number of people raising sheep to make cheeses. If you cannot find sheep's milk cheese, cow's milk ricotta makes an equally delicious dish.

1 pound short macaroni, such as cut ziti or penne	8 tablespoons soft butter, cut in small pieces
Salt	2 teaspoons or more freshly ground black pepper
½ pound fresh ricotta cheese	

1. Cook the macaroni in 5 quarts rapidly boiling salted water until al dente.

2. While the macaroni is cooking, strain the ricotta into a warmed pasta serving dish. Mix in the softened butter. When the macaroni is almost tender, remove 3 tablespoons of the boiling cooking water and stir it into the ricotta. Stir well to make a smooth sauce. Add salt and black pepper. The sauce should be quite peppery, so season it to your liking.

3. Drain the cooked pasta but leave a bit of cooking water clinging to the macaroni to help it blend with the sauce. Add to the ricotta and toss well. Serve immediately. *Serves 6.*

• • •

Variation: For a delicious variation, toss ¼ cup fresh basil leaves and 2 ounces grated dry ricotta (ricotta salata) into the finished pasta. The imported dry ricotta is made from sheep's milk, so even if you have used cow's milk cheese in the recipe the finished dish gives a hint of the traditional Calabrian recipe.

Shepherd-Style Macaroni with Sausage

MACCHERONI ALLA PASTORA CON SALSICCIA

Happy were the shepherds who had a bit of sausage to add to their sheep's milk for this variation of the preceding recipe. I like to use rigatoni for this Calabrian specialty because the macaroni's wide openings trap the sausage and cheese inside.

½ pound fresh Italian sausage	Salt
1 pound rigatoni or similar large macaroni	Freshly ground black pepper
¾ pound fresh ricotta cheese	2 ounces freshly grated pecorino cheese

1. Peel the sausages and crumble into a sauté pan. Cover with ½ cup water, bring to a boil, reduce the heat, and simmer covered, a few minutes, until the fat is rendered and the sausage is cooked. Remove the sausage pieces with a slotted spoon and reserve both cooking juices and sausage.

2. Cook the macaroni in a large pot of boiling salted water. While the pasta is cooking, strain the ricotta into a pasta dish. When the macaroni is almost cooked, add the hot reserved sausage juices to the ricotta cheese and stir well. Drain the macaroni when al dente and add to the cheese. Mix in the sausage pieces, salt, pepper, and pecorino cheese. Serve immediately and pass extra pecorino cheese. *Serves 6.*

Lasagne Noodles with Pancetta Sauce

LASAGNE CON SALSA DI PANCETTA

Some sauces just seem best with big wide noodles and this is one of them. You can use a packaged noodle or make your own according to the recipe for homemade semolina lasagna (pages 133–35). The finished dish should be full of color and texture, so do not chop the vegetables too small.

⅓ cup extra-virgin olive oil
½ pound pancetta, coarsely chopped
2 small onions, coarsely chopped
¾ pound mushrooms, wiped clean, stems trimmed, cut in large pieces
Salt and pepper
1½ pounds plum tomatoes, peeled and seeded, or same amount canned, drained, and coarsely chopped (about 2½ cups)

⅓ cup coarsely chopped flat-leaf parsley
2 tablespoons fresh oregano or 2 teaspoons dried
1 tablespoon fresh thyme or 1 teaspoon dried
1 pound lasagne noodles, broken in half
3 ounces dry ricotta cheese (ricotta salata), grated

1. Put the olive oil, pancetta, and onions into a sauté pan. Cook over medium-low heat until the onion is translucent and the pancetta has rendered its fat (about 12 minutes). Add the mushrooms, salt, and pepper and cook, tossing occasionally, until the mushroom juices run (about 4 minutes). Add the tomatoes, salt, and pepper, bring to a boil, reduce the heat, and simmer 15 minutes. Add parsley, oregano, and thyme and cook 5 minutes.

2. Cook the lasagne noodles in 5 quarts boiling salted water until al dente. Fresh noodles will cook very quickly. Drain and immediately toss with the sauce and grated cheese. *Serves 6 to 8.*

FRESH CHEESE

On both sides of the Atlantic, the southern Italians used whatever animal's milk was plentiful to make fresh cheese and ricotta. In Italy it was usually sheep's milk and in America goat, then cow's milk. In the early days of immigration the Italians made cheese at home or got it from a neighbor who did. After a while "latticini" shops opened which only sold dairy products. The "latticini" shops disappeared when Italian cheeses woefully went into mass commercial production.

Today there is an effort among Italians to bring us closer to our food. Most Italian neighborhoods have shops that carry fresh cheese and fresh ricotta. Ricotta is actually a by-product of cheesemaking. After the milk is heated and the curds are separated, the whey is reheated (hence ricotta, "recooked") until a cheese forms. Fresh cheese has a shelf life of about one week.

Signor Basso of Providence Cheese Shop on Atwells Avenue serving his fresh cheese.

"*Cavatelli*" *with Arugula*

CAVATIEDDI CON LA RUCA

"Cavatelli" ("cavatieddi" in dialect) are very small, shell-shaped pastas made from flour and water. They are a specialty of the region of Apulia where they are usually made at home. Italian-Americans from that region of Italy continued to make this specialty in the United States, teaching each new generation this delicate art. Today, it is possible to buy fresh "cavatelli" in some Italian neighborhoods or frozen ones in some markets. Sometimes the fresh or frozen ones are made with ricotta cheese and these may be used in the same way. Dried "cavatelli" are imported from Italy and they may also be used. Apulians especially like to mix their homemade "cavatelli" with bitter, wild greens.

½ pound arugula
1 pound fresh, frozen, or
   dried "cavatelli"
Salt
½ cup extra-virgin olive oil
½ hot pepper, seeded and
   chopped, or ¼ teaspoon
   hot pepper flakes

4 ounces freshly grated
   pecorino cheese
   (about 1 cup)

1. Wash the arugula in several changes of cold water. Drain and dry well. Discard any tough stems and tear the leaves into bite-size pieces.
2. Add the "cavatelli" to 5 quarts boiling salted water and cook until tender: about 3 minutes for fresh, 10 minutes for dried, and up to 15 minutes for frozen.
3. While the "cavatelli" are cooking, heat the oil and hot pepper in a large sauté pan. Add the arugula and salt and cook until the greens are wilted (1 to 2 minutes).
4. Drain the "cavatelli" and add to the arugula. Mix in the pecorino cheese and serve immediately. *Serves 4 to 6.*

"Orecchiette" with Broccoli Rabe

ORECCHIETTE CON BROCCOLI DI RABE

"Orecchiette," which means "little ears," is the name given to the small disc-shaped pasta made from semolina and water. They are a specialty of Apulia where they are often homemade. Dried imported "orecchiette" are available in Italian groceries and they are very good. If you have trouble finding them, the same sauce works well on "cavatelli" or any narrow short macaroni.

1 pound broccoli rabe	¼ teaspoon hot pepper
Salt	flakes
1 pound "orecchiette"	⅓ cup extra-virgin olive oil
2 ounces flat anchovy fillets	4 ounces freshly grated
(about 10), drained and	pecorino cheese
rinsed	(about 1 cup)
4 large garlic cloves, minced	

1. Wash the broccoli rabe and peel the stems. Cut into inch-long pieces. Bring 5 quarts water to a boil and add 2 tablespoons salt. Add the broccoli rabe and cook until almost tender, about 3 minutes. Remove with a strainer or slotted spoon and rinse with cold water. Return water to a boil and add the "orecchiette." Cook until tender, 10 minutes.

2. While the "orecchiette" are cooking, put the anchovies, garlic, hot pepper, and olive oil into a sauté pan over medium-low heat. Mash the anchovies and garlic to a paste with the back of a wooden spoon. Cook 2 to 3 minutes, or until the garlic is slightly softened, and remove from heat.

3. When the "orecchiette" are just about tender, return the broccoli rabe to the pot with the pasta to reheat. Boil together about 30 seconds and then drain. Mix the pasta and rabe with the sauce, taste for salt, and serve. Pass a bowl of the grated pecorino cheese on the side. *Serves 6.*

Spinach-Filled Ravioli

RAVIOLI DI SPINACI

Many Italian-American families set aside Sunday morning after church for making pasta such as ravioli. Very often the whole family would be involved. Spinach ravioli have become such standard restaurant or supermarket food that it is easy to forget how special they were when made at those family gatherings.

1 recipe homemade pasta with 3 eggs
  (page 122)

FILLING

1¼ cups cooked spinach,
  squeezed dry, finely
  chopped
1¼ cups ricotta cheese,
  drained 30 minutes
¾ cup freshly grated
  Parmesan cheese

1 egg, beaten
Salt and freshly ground
  black pepper
Pinch of freshly grated
  nutmeg

About 2 cups heated ragu or marinara sauce
  (pages 79–81 or page 82)
Grated cheese

1. Make the pasta according to the directions for homemade pasta and roll to ¹⁄₁₆-inch thickness by hand or on the next to the last setting on a pasta machine.
2. Mix the filling ingredients together. Fill and cut the ravioli according to the directions on pages 130–31.
3. Add 2 tablespoons oil and the ravioli to 5 quarts rapidly boiling salted water and cook until tender. Drain and toss gently with the tomato sauce. Sprinkle with cheese and serve. *Serves 6 to 8.*

Homemade Pasta

2 to 2¼ cups all-
    purpose flour

½ teaspoon salt
3 large eggs

Making the dough: Sift the flour and salt in a mound
onto a counter. Make a well in the center and break the
eggs into it. Beat the eggs with a fork or fingers until
blended. Gradually incorporate the flour into the eggs to
make a soft, nonsticky dough. Test by pressing your finger
into the dough. Your finger should release from the dough
without sticking. When as much flour as possible has been
added, clean your hands and the counter. Knead the dough
8 to 10 minutes until smooth. Let rest ½ hour under a
bowl or wrapped in plastic. Dough may also be made in a
food processor.

Food Processor: To make dough in the food processor, beat the eggs in the machine first. Then add 1 cup of
flour and the salt and blend 10 seconds. Add the remaining
flour gradually through the feed tube or ½ cup at a time.
When a dough forms, knead in the machine 45 seconds.

Resting: Pasta dough rests so that the gluten relaxes,
allowing you to roll it out without its snapping back. To
relax pasta dough more quickly, put it under a metal bowl
which has first been warmed on the stove. The warmth
relaxes the dough well.

Green Pasta: Southern Italians are very fond of green
pasta. To make green (spinach) pasta, beat 2 tablespoons
cooked well-dried minced spinach with the eggs. Continue
as above, increasing the flour by ¼ cup until the dough is
no longer sticky.

Rolling the dough: Divide the dough into egg-size pieces. Work with one piece at a time and keep the remaining dough covered. Set a pasta machine at its widest setting and run the dough through 4 or 5 times to knead, folding the dough in 3 after each run through. Then, without folding, run the dough through the rollers, gradually reducing the setting until the dough is as thin as desired. Cut according to recipe directions.

• • •

Note: The amount of flour needed for the dough can vary depending on a number of conditions such as the weather or how quickly it is incorporated. It is always possible to add more flour to a sticky dough but impossible to correct a tight, dry dough. When you work on a counter rather than a bowl, you can control the amount of flour pulled into the liquid.

MEMORIES

"Cooking cannot be done quickly. There has to be love and care and patience . . ."

My mother is a fantastic cook. She knows real family-style cooking. No schooling, just natural talent. It's the way with most Italian women. They're just born with it, it's their heritage, it's in their culture to be good cooks. We can benefit from this culinary expertise that these people carry in their genes.

It seems a shame that in the society we live in today everything is quick, everything is fast. That's one thing my mother always mentioned—cooking cannot be done quickly. There has to be love and care and patience and time to do it well. When my mother made a gravy it was a four-hour chore. She used to make her own macaroni by hand. A lot of Italian people did. So when they came to this country they carried on that kind of tradition.

These people (the Italian immigrants), their main priority in life, the main reason they existed really was to make sure that their families were happy and well fed. No matter how they had to do it, they did it. If they had to grow their own, they would.

We are so happy that we have these kinds of memories of the way our parents and grandparents did things. Today's society is so push-buttoned, so microwave that it's been lost along the way.

When my mother was cooking, she never used recipes. She knew what she was doing. She didn't look in a book or at index cards. Everything came out of her memory, out of her mind, out of her feel and her touch. People would come in (the meat market) and buy a veal roast and then go up and ask her how to cook it. She'd tell them how to stuff it, the timing it took to cook it, the seasoning. She's not selfish with her knowledge, she gives it freely.

The neighborhood was one big family, every family was yours. There was no such thing as locks on doors, everybody socialized with each other, everybody borrowed from each other, everybody paid back what they borrowed.

(Left to right) Father and mother, Giuseppe and Maria De Giulio, and their son, Joseph, holding a portrait of his grandmother, Consiglia De Giulio, who died in 1963, age 108.

My father had a market and he did very well. He worked very hard, like all the immigrants did. Each one did their own thing and brought up their families with dignity and imparted to them the natural tendency Italians have of being honorable people. Pride in your name was big. My father always told us that you do not dishonor your name, because your name is what you are, it is your heritage. It isn't a financial thing as much as a whole line of generations you had behind you that you had to be proud of.

My parents worked hard to see that their children had it easier, especially in education. That was their primary reason for working hard—to make sure that the children who followed them had the opportunity to better themselves. And that's probably the biggest reason they came here from Italy.

Christmas Eve, la Vigilia, was 100 percent fish. That was a fish dinner. No matter where you were, you had to make it your business to be at your matriarch's and patriarch's home wherever they were. Children, grandchildren had to be there. That was the tradition.

JOE DE GIULIO, JR.,
Son of Guiseppe, owner of Acorn Market

Meat-Filled Ravioli

RAVIOLI CON CARNE

Serve these ravioli with two cups of any one of the tomato sauces (pages 79–83). They are also delicious boiled and then added to hot chicken broth (page 48) and sprinkled with grated Parmesan cheese.

1 recipe homemade pasta with 3 eggs (page 122)

FILLING

½ pound escarole, washed and tough ends removed
2 tablespoons butter
1 garlic clove, minced
¼ pound ground pork
¼ pound ground chicken
2 ounces finely chopped prosciutto

1 egg, lightly beaten
2 tablespoons fresh marjoram or 2 teaspoons dried
Salt and freshly ground black pepper

Freshly grated Parmesan cheese

1. Make the pasta according to the directions for homemade pasta and roll to ¹⁄₁₆ inch thickness by hand or on the next to last setting on a pasta machine.

2. Blanch the escarole 2 minutes in a large amount of rapidly boiling salted water. Drain, rinse with cold water, and squeeze dry. Finely chop. Melt the butter in a 10-inch skillet. Add the garlic and cook until golden. Add the pork and chicken and cook until the meats are no longer pink. Stir in the escarole and cook until completely dry. Remove from heat and add the prosciutto, beaten egg, and seasonings.

3. Fill with the escarole filling and cut the ravioli according to the directions on pages 130–31.

4. Add 2 tablespoons oil and the ravioli to 5 quarts rapidly boiling salted water and cook until tender. Drain and sauce as desired. Sprinkle with parmesan cheese. *Serves 6 to 8.*

• • •

Variation: When I serve these in soup, I make half the dough green (spinach pasta) and half plain egg pasta for a pretty presentation.

Ravioli Aquilana

RAVIOLI ALL'AQUILANA (GRAVIOLI)

Here is a good reason to grow your own sage! Regardless of my heritage, I can't claim to be able to grow an entire herb garden in windowsill pots, but I am able to keep a sage bush alive from year to year and encourage all fans of this dish to do the same. Aquilana is a town in Abruzzo justly famous for this dish. The ravioli should be as thin and light as possible so oil is added to the dough to help roll it.

1 recipe homemade pasta with 3 eggs and
    1 teaspoon olive oil (page 122)

FILLING

½ pound fresh ricotta
    cheese, drained in a sieve
    30 minutes
¼ pound fresh mozzarella
    cheese, minced or
    shredded
¼ cup freshly grated
    Parmesan cheese
1 egg, lightly beaten
Salt, pepper, and freshly
    ground nutmeg

SAUCE

6 tablespoons butter
About 30 to 40 small fresh
    sage leaves (cut large
    leaves in half; pieces
    should be about 1½ inches
    long)
Salt and pepper

¼ cup freshly grated
    Parmesan cheese

1. Make the pasta according to the directions for homemade pasta, beating the oil with the eggs and rolling as thin as possible (last setting on the pasta machine).

Ravioli Aquilana (continued)

2. Make the filling: push the ricotta through the sieve into a bowl. Stir in the remaining ingredients and mix until well blended. Fill and cut the ravioli according to the directions on pages 130–31.

3. Make the sauce: melt the butter in a small saucepan. Add the sage leaves, salt, and pepper. Keep warm.

4. Add 2 tablespoons oil and the ravioli to 5 quarts rapidly boiling salted water. Stir gently until water returns to a boil. Cook until tender (4 to 5 minutes). Drain and place in a warm serving dish. Sprinkle on the Parmesan cheese. Pour on the sauce and serve immediately with extra cheese on the side if desired. *Serves 6 to 8.*

Sausage Ravioli

RAVIOLI CON SALSICCIA

Here is a rather modern way of enjoying sausages and peppers—a combination that brings to mind East Coast Italian street fairs.

SAUCE

3 tablespoons extra-virgin olive oil

2 garlic cloves, peeled and minced

4 red peppers, quartered, stems, seeds, and ribs removed

1 cup chopped peeled tomatoes, fresh or 1 cup drained canned

Salt and freshly ground black pepper

———

1 recipe homemade pasta with 3 eggs (page 122)

———

FILLING

½ pound sweet Italian sausage

1 tablespoon extra-virgin olive oil

½ pound ground veal

1 egg, lightly beaten

2 tablespoons grated Parmesan cheese

Salt and freshly ground black pepper

1. Heat the oil and garlic in a 10-inch skillet until the garlic is golden. Add the peppers, cover the pan, and cook over medium-low heat for 10 minutes. Add the tomatoes, salt, and pepper. Partially cover the pan and cook until the peppers are soft (about 40 minutes). Puree in a food processor or blender and strain, pushing well on solids to squeeze out all the moisture. Adjust the seasonings and keep warm until ready to use.

2. Make the pasta according to the directions for homemade pasta (page 122) and roll to 1/16 inch by hand or on the next to the last setting on a pasta machine.

3. Make the filling: remove the casing from the sausage. Break the sausage meat up and cook in olive oil in a 10-inch skillet over medium-high heat until its color begins to fade (about 5 minutes). Add the veal and cook until the meats are no longer pink. Remove from heat and drain off fat. Cool slightly, then add egg, cheese, and seasoning.

4. Fill and cut the ravioli according to the directions on pages 130–31.

5. Add 2 tablespoons oil and the ravioli to 5 quarts rapidly boiling salted water and cook until tender. Drain and mix with heated pepper sauce. Serve immediately. *Serves 6 to 8.*

SHAPING RAVIOLI

There are many tools on the market for shaping ravioli. Two of the most useful are the ravioli tray and the ravioli wheel.

Making ravioli in a shop in the Italian section of Providence.

Ravioli Tray: The ravioli tray consists of two pieces: a metal tray with twelve evenly placed holes about 1½ inches in diameter, surrounded by raised, fluted 2-inch squares, and a plastic tray with twelve 1-inch-round depressions. To make ravioli in a tray, lightly flour the metal tray and lay the thin strip of rolled pasta dough on top so that it completely covers the tray. Gently press the plastic tray on top of the pasta until small depressions form in the dough. Remove the plastic tray and put a generous teaspoon of filling in the depression. With fingers or pastry brush dipped in water, draw lines between rows of filling lengthwise and across. Lay the second sheet of pasta dough over fillings. Run a heavy rolling pin over the top of the dough until the raised, fluted edge has cut all the pieces into squares.

Ravioli Wheel: A ravioli wheel is a small tool with a revolving head that is fluted. Some ravioli wheels are made so that they cut and seal the dough at the same time and these are the most useful. To use either wheel, lay the strip of pasta dough on a lightly floured counter. Place generous teaspoons of filling evenly placed ½ inch from the edges and 1½ inches apart along the pasta strip. With your fingers or a pastry brush dipped in water, draw lines between the rows of filling lengthwise and across. Cover with a second sheet of pasta dough and gently press with your fingers along the water lines to seal. Run the ravioli wheel along the same lines to cut pasta into squares.

Drying: As soon as the ravioli squares are cut, put them in one layer, not touching, on a lightly floured towel to dry. Turn to dry the second side. They may be made several hours ahead.

Freezing: Ravioli freeze beautifully. Put the dried pasta squares on a cookie sheet, not touching, and put in the freezer until the pieces are completely frozen. Put the frozen pasta in plastic freezer bags in the freezer until ready to use. Do not thaw ravioli to cook but drop the frozen pieces directly into boiling water.

Square-Cut Pasta with Herb Sauce

TONNARELLI CON SALSA DI ERBE

Usually when people think of Italy they see red—sauce, that is. It is easy to overlook some of the lesser known green sauces. The people who came from Liguria have made basil pesto popular, but this flavorful southern Italian parsley and walnut sauce is seldom seen outside the home. The sauce is particularly delicious with these homemade square-cut noodles, but you can also use a packaged thick spaghetti such as perciatelli. Semolina flour, not the granular semolina, if you can find it, makes a wonderful tonnarelli noodle. Otherwise all-purpose flour works perfectly well. You may have to adjust the amount of flour used depending on which type you choose.

HOMEMADE PASTA

3 to 3½ cups flour
½ teaspoon salt

4 large eggs

———————

SAUCE

1 cup parsley, stems
  removed
⅔ cup walnut pieces
  (3 ounces)
1 medium garlic clove
Salt and pepper

¾ cup olive oil
½ cup freshly grated
  Parmesan cheese
  (2 ounces)
2 tablespoons butter,
  melted

1. Make the pasta according to the directions for homemade pasta (page 122) and roll to ⅛-inch thickness. Lay strips of dough on a lightly floured kitchen towel and let dry until the surface is still pliable but slightly leathery. Turn and dry the other side. Do not allow to become brittle or the pasta will break when cut.

2. Using a pasta attachment with a narrow or spaghetti cutter, cut the sheets of dough to form square-cut noodles. These may be used immediately or stored for later use.

3. To make the sauce: Wash the parsley and dry very well. Put in the bowl of a food processor or in a blender and process 30 seconds. Add the walnuts to the parsley in a bowl and process until very fine. Smash the garlic on a counter and peel. Chop coarsely and add to the processor bowl with salt and pepper. With the machine running, add the olive oil in a steady stream until well incorporated.

4. Add the noodles to 5 quarts rapidly boiling salted water and cook until tender but al dente. Place a few tablespoons of the herb sauce in the bottom of a warmed pasta bowl. Drain the pasta, leaving a small amount of water clinging to the noodles, and immediately add to the sauce in the bowl. Toss in the remaining herb sauce. Sprinkle on the cheese, pour on the butter, toss again, and serve. Pass extra grated cheese and a cruet of olive oil if desired. *Serves 6 to 8.*

Calabrian Lasagne with Artichokes and Tiny Meatballs

LASAGNE CHINE

This is without a doubt one of my favorite lasagne recipes. It is possible to make it with a commercial noodle, but I know you will find that the homemade ones make this a tender dish worthy of any elegant dinner. I roll my noodles in a pasta machine, but when I do, I can't help but think of my grandmother who rolled hers so skillfully on her large wooden board set on her kitchen table and cut them swiftly with her great butcher's knife. Though the recipe may seem like many steps, the entire dish can be assembled the day before baking.

SEMOLINA PASTA

3¼ cups semolina
1 teaspoon salt

1 cup or more lukewarm
water

Calabrian Lasagne (continued)

MUSHROOM-TOMATO SAUCE

¼ cup extra-virgin olive oil
1 small onion (½ cup, minced)
1 carrot (¼ cup, minced)
1 celery rib (¼ cup, minced)
One 28-ounce can Italian plum tomatoes, drained and chopped
Salt and freshly ground pepper
1 ounce dried porcini mushrooms, soaked 30 minutes in warm water

MEATBALLS

½ pound ground pork
1 egg, beaten
3 tablespoons freshly grated pecorino cheese
Salt and pepper
Flour
3 tablespoons extra-virgin olive oil
¾ cup meat broth

VEGETABLE FILLING

3 tablespoons extra-virgin olive oil
1 small onion, minced
2½ pounds fresh peas, shelled, or one and one-half 10-ounce packages frozen peas, thawed
Two 9-ounce packages frozen artichoke hearts, thawed and thinly sliced
Salt and pepper

ADDITIONAL FILLING

4 hard-boiled eggs, coarsely chopped
1 pound fresh mozzarella, shredded

TOPPING

1½ cups freshly grated pecorino cheese

1. Put the flour and salt into the bowl of a food processor. Pulsate to blend. Gradually pour enough water through the feed tube to form a dough. Knead 45 seconds. The dough will be stiff. Put aside to rest for 30 minutes, covered with an upturned bowl.

2. Divide the dough into large egg-size pieces and knead 10 to 12 times in the widest setting of the pasta machine. The dough may break apart at first but will eventually roll out into a smooth sheet. (Keep the remaining dough well covered until ready to roll.) Pass the dough through the rollers, turning the rollers down one notch at a time until reaching the next to last thinnest setting. Cut the strips into 8-inch lengths and leave the width that of pasta machine.

3. Bring 5 quarts of water to a boil. Add a heaping tablespoon salt and a few tablespoons olive oil. Have ready a bowl of cold water with 2 tablespoons oil mixed in. Put pasta pieces, 2 or 3 at a time, into the boiling water. Boil 1 minute. Remove with a slotted spoon and put immediately in a bowl of cold water mixed with oil to stop cooking. Remove the pasta and lay in a single layer on a dampened towel and cover with a second damp towel. Continue with the remaining pasta until all is used up.

4. For the sauce: put the olive oil, onion, carrot, and celery into a small pot. Cook until softened but not brown. Add drained tomatoes, salt, and pepper. Cook over gentle heat for 30 minutes, stirring frequently. Puree through a food mill or push through a strainer. Return to the pot.

5. Drain the mushrooms and save the juices. Wash the mushrooms under warm water, dry, and chop into small pieces. Strain the juices through a coffee filter or washed cheesecloth to remove all traces of sand. Put the mushroom pieces and 1 cup strained juices into the pot with the tomatoes. Cook 20 minutes, adding more mushroom juices or tomato liquid if mixture begins to stick. The resulting sauce should hold its shape on a spoon. (Can be prepared 1 day ahead and refrigerated.)

6. For the meatballs: mix the ground pork, egg, pecorino, salt, and pepper together mixing well. Make tiny meatballs about the size of marbles. Dust lightly with flour and fry in hot oil until browned and cooked through (6 to 8 minutes). Remove with a slotted spoon. Discard all but 2 tablespoons of oil from the skillet. Add the broth and boil 30 seconds, scraping up any browned bits. Strain and set aside. (Can be prepared 1 day ahead. Refrigerate meatballs and broth separately.)

7. For the vegetables: put the olive oil and minced onion in a sauté pan. Cook gently until golden. Add the fresh peas, artichokes, salt, and pepper and cook until the vegetables are tender, stirring frequently, about 5 minutes. (If using frozen thawed peas, mix in at this point.) Cool to room temperature.

8. To assemble: generously coat a 9 x 13-inch baking pan with olive oil. Lay strips of pasta in the bottom of the pan so that at least half of their length hangs out of the pan. Lay more strips on the bottom of the pan to completely cover the space. Spread ¼ of the sauce over the pasta in the bottom of the dish. Layer with ¼ of the vegetable mixture, ¼ of the chopped eggs, ¼ of the meatballs,

Calabrian Lasagne (continued)

and ¼ of the mozzarella. Cover the filling with the strips of pasta. Repeat the layering 3 times. Fold in the pasta overhang. Cover the center of the lasagna with additional pasta strips if necessary. (Can be prepared 1 day ahead to this point. Brush with olive oil, cover, and refrigerate. Bring to room temperature before continuing.)

9. Preheat the oven to 350°F. Sprinkle the pecorino evenly over the top layer of pasta. Ladle the reserved meat juices from step 6 evenly over the cheese. Bake 40 minutes, or until the top is browned and the center is hot. Cool slightly before cutting. *Serves 8 to 10.*

"Nonna's Lasagne"

LASAGNE ALLA NONNA

It could be argued that this typical Neapolitan lasagne, often called "lasagne di carnevale," is one of the most recognizable of southern Italian foods. In Italy, lasagne made with meat had always been associated with special occasions. In America, the Italians found that meat was not so difficult to come by and a meat lasagne was no longer reserved for festive meals. Because it was so popular, it wasn't necessarily regarded as the special dish it was meant to be. The following recipe is a true "lasagne di carnevale" that celebrates a festive occasion and a full pantry. Simpler versions can be made by eliminating the sausage, the meatballs, and/or the hard-boiled eggs.

1 recipe for semolina lasagne
(pages 133–35)
or ¾ pound commercial
lasagne noodles
Olive oil
Salt
½ pound ground beef
½ cup fresh breadcrumbs
1 egg, lightly beaten
Freshly ground black pepper
3 to 3½ cups meat sauce
(pages 79–81)

½ pound Italian sausage,
removed from casing,
crumbled and sautéed
until browned
2 hard-boiled eggs, in thin
slices
1 pound ricotta cheese
¾ pound fresh mozzarella
cheese, grated
½ cup freshly grated
Parmesan cheese

1. Bring 5 quarts of water to a boil. Add a heaping tablespoon salt and 2 tablespoons olive oil. Have ready a bowl of cold water with 2 tablespoons oil mixed in. Put the lasagne noodles, 2 or 3 at a time into the boiling water. Boil 1 minute. Remove with a slotted spoon and put immediately in the bowl of cold water to stop cooking. Remove the noodles from the water and lay in a single layer on a dampened kitchen towel and cover with a second damp towel. Continue with remaining noodles.

2. Combine the ground beef with the breadcrumbs, the beaten egg, salt and pepper and blend well. Make small meatballs the size of a walnut shell and fry in 2 tablespoons olive oil until browned. Drain and set aside.

3. Preheat the oven to 375°F. Brush a rectangular baking pan, 9 x 13 inches, with olive oil. Lay the lasagne noodles on the bottom of the pan, overlapping them slightly so they completely cover the bottom of the pan. Cover the noodles with a layer of sauce. Cover the sauce with some of the sausage, meatballs, and hard-boiled egg slices. Dot the filling with large spoonfuls of ricotta cheese and spread it slightly. Sprinkle on mozzarella and Parmesan cheeses. Put on another layer of noodles and continue to build the lasagne until all the ingredients are used. The top layer of the lasagne should be only sauce, mozzarella and Parmesan cheeses. Bake 45 minutes or until browned and bubbly. Let rest 10 minutes before serving. *Serves 10.*

Loretta d'Ambra Verde—Nonna.

Oven-Baked Rigatoni

RIGATONI AL FORNO

Oven-baked pasta dishes such as this and the following recipe are meals in themselves for my family. In the old days they were usually part of a holiday meal or celebration when there would be many people to feed. Both recipes can be doubled.

¼ pound Italian sausage, casing removed, crumbled
1 medium yellow onion, coarsely chopped
2 garlic cloves, minced
⅓ cup plus 3 tablespoons extra-virgin olive oil
¼ cup chopped sun-dried tomatoes
¼ teaspoon hot pepper flakes, or more to taste
1 teaspoon sweet paprika

2 cups drained canned Italian plum tomatoes, chopped
Salt
¼ cup coarsely chopped flat-leaf parsley
1 cup ricotta cheese
¾ pound rigatoni or similar fat macaroni
½ cup freshly grated pecorino cheese

1. Put the sausage, onion, garlic, and ⅓ cup olive oil into a sauté pan. Place over medium heat and cook until the onion is softened but not browned. Add the sun-dried tomatoes, hot pepper flakes, and paprika and cook 5 minutes. Add the canned tomatoes, salt, and parsley, bring to a boil, reduce the heat, and simmer gently 20 minutes.

2. Preheat the oven to 350°F. With 1 tablespoon of the remaining olive oil, coat the bottom and sides of an ovenproof pasta dish and strain the ricotta cheese into the dish.

3. Cook the rigatoni in 5 quarts boiling salted water. Add 2 tablespoons boiling water from the pasta to the ricotta cheese and stir to blend. Drain the pasta when it is still slightly undercooked (after about 7 minutes) and pour over the ricotta cheese in the pasta dish. Immediately mix in the sauce. Sprinkle the pecorino cheese on top and drizzle on the remaining olive oil. Bake 20 minutes, or until the pasta is cooked and the cheese is lightly browned. *Serves 6.*

Oven-Baked Macaroni with Eggplant

MACCHERONI E MELANZANE AL GRATIN

2 medium eggplants,
  2 pounds total weight
Salt
Olive oil for frying eggplant
¼ cup extra-virgin olive oil
1 small onion, chopped
2 garlic cloves, minced
3 pounds fresh tomatoes,
  peeled, seeded, and
  chopped, or 3 pounds
  drained canned tomatoes
  (about 4½ cups), chopped

Salt
3 tablespoons snipped basil
Pinch of sugar, if necessary
1 pound short macaroni,
  such as ziti or penne
2 ounces butter
  (4 tablespoons)
4 ounces freshly grated
  Parmesan cheese
  (about 1 cup)
8 ounces fresh mozzarella,
  finely chopped or grated

1. Wash the eggplant but do not peel. Cut into ⅛-inch slices and place in a colander, salting each layer. Place a plate and a weight on top and let drain 1 hour. Pat dry and squeeze gently to remove excess liquid.

2. Put ¼ inch olive oil into a frying pan and heat to very hot. Fry one layer of eggplant at a time, turning to brown both sides. Drain on paper towels, layering the eggplant and towels as necessary.

3. Put ¼ cup olive oil, onion, and garlic in a 2-quart pot. Sauté until softened but not browned. Add the tomatoes and salt. Cook until the water has evaporated, about 30 minutes. Add the basil 5 minutes before cooking is finished. Taste for seasonings and add a pinch of sugar if necessary.

4. Cook the macaroni in 5 quarts boiling salted water. Drain when the macaroni is still quite firm, about 7 minutes. Mix with the butter and half of the Parmesan cheese and salt if necessary.

5. Preheat the oven to 350°F. Spread a little of the tomato sauce on the bottom of an ovenproof dish. (I use a 10 x 16 x 3-inch terracotta dish, but any similar size will do.) Layer the pasta, the eggplant, the mozzarella, and the sauce until all the ingredients are used up, ending with one thin layer of eggplant. Sprinkle with the remaining Parmesan cheese and bake 40 minutes, or until lightly browned. *Serves 6 to 8.*

Neapolitan Layered Polenta

MIGLIACCIO NAPOLETANO

This is one of the rare cornmeal recipes of southern Italy (page 25). The recipe itself is quite old and was originally made without the tomato sauce. Some good things can be made better and the addition of the sauce did just that. The recipe may appear long, but it is not difficult and it has the advantage of being able to be assembled well beforehand and baked when needed. If you already have marinara sauce on hand you can use that and begin with step 2.

TOMATO SAUCE

3 tablespoons extra-virgin olive oil

1 small onion, finely chopped

1 can (28 ounces) Italian peeled tomatoes, drained and coarsely chopped

Salt and freshly ground black pepper

½ teaspoon sugar if necessary to sweeten sauce

2 tablespoons snipped basil

———

¼ pound pancetta, minced

1 tablespoon salt

¾ pound coarse Italian cornmeal

1 cup freshly grated Parmesan cheese (about 4 ounces)

1 pound sweet Italian sausages

½ pound whole milk mozzarella cheese, finely diced

½ cup freshly grated pecorino romano cheese (2 ounces)

3 tablespoons unsalted butter

1. In a large noncorrosive saucepan, heat the oil and the onion and cook over moderate heat until softened and translucent, 3 to 5 minutes. Add the tomatoes, salt, pepper, and sugar if necessary. Bring to a boil, reduce the heat, and simmer, stirring occasionally, until the sauce thickens to a coating consistency, about 30 minutes. Stir in the basil 5 minutes before cooking is finished. (The tomato

sauce can be made up to 2 days ahead. Refrigerate, covered; reheat before step 5.)

2. In a small skillet, cook the pancetta over moderately low heat until brown and crisp, about 8 minutes. Set aside with 2 tablespoons of the rendered fat.

3. In a large saucepan, bring 2 quarts water to a boil, add the 1 tablespoon salt and gradually stir in the cornmeal in a slow stream, stirring constantly to avoid lumps. Cook over moderate heat, stirring, until the polenta masses together and begins to pull away from the sides of the pan and has lost the raw corn taste (about 40 minutes). Remove from the heat and stir in the reserved pancetta and fat and ½ cup Parmesan cheese. Pour into a 17 x 12-inch jellyroll pan or onto a cutting board. Smooth the surface with a wet spatula. Let cool until set. Cut into 3-inch squares. (The polenta can be made up to 2 days ahead. Cover and refrigerate. Let return to room temperature before proceeding.)

4. Remove the sausage from its casing and coarsely chop. Put into a medium skillet over medium heat and sauté until no longer pink. Drain on paper towels.

5. Generously butter a large shallow baking dish, preferably earthenware. Spread a thin layer of the tomato sauce over the bottom of the dish. Arrange ⅓ of the polenta squares on the tomato sauce in a single layer. Sprinkle half the mozzarella and chopped sausage over the polenta. Spoon on ⅓ of the tomato sauce. Mix the remaining Parmesan cheese and the pecorino cheese and sprinkle ⅓ over the sauce. Dot with 1 tablespoon butter. Repeat with half the remaining polenta, all the remaining mozzarella and sausage, half the remaining sauce and grated cheeses, and 1 tablespoon butter. Top with the remaining polenta, tomato sauce, and cheese. Dot with the remaining 1 tablespoon butter. (The dish can be assembled up to 1 day ahead. Let return to room temperature before baking.)

6. Preheat the oven to 375°F. Bake the polenta for 30 minutes, or until the cheese is bubbling and the dish is piping hot throughout. *Serves 8 to 10.*

The original Camille's Roman Gardens, Providence, Rhode Island, in 1914 when it was called Marconi's (named for the man who invented the wireless). It has been a favorite dining spot for Italians ever since.

Chapter Four

MAIN COURSES

F or a truly Italian meal, the second and first courses should be balanced so that they equal one meal. It is simply a lovely way to savor different dishes. Too often each course arrives, a meal in itself, making it impossible to enjoy without overindulging. Keep this in mind when creating a menu. Fortunately, most Italian restaurants are now willing to divide courses among patrons who wish to eat in an honest Italian fashion. The idea of huge plates of pasta followed by large cuts of meat was an unfortunate stage in the development of Italian-American restaurants adjusting to a land of plenty.

Perhaps no other aspect of the Italian-American diet showed as many changes as did the consumption of meat. In southern Italy, the diet relies very little on meat. Pasta, vegetables, and fish are the mainstays. When there is meat it is usually a small serving of simply grilled veal or sausages, or a roasted chicken. Mostly, meat is reserved for celebrations. Consequently, many of these recipes that I have collected here are rather elaborate—for Italian cooking, that is. Meat found its way into the Italian-American diet mostly at the insistence of the United States government. Groups of social workers were sent out to convince the early immigrants that their diets were deficient unless they included meat regularly with their meals. These well-meaning government representatives preached the prevailing belief that too many vegetables in a diet were a detriment to the digestive system. Modern nutrition has proved the government wrong and we now know that the Italian diet, lean in meats, is indeed a healthy one. Be that as it may, as the immigrant was able to afford more, he started to consume a greater amount of meat. Steaks and roasts replaced simpler suppers of soup or pasta. Roasted chicken was part of every Sunday meal. The Neapolitan ragu, usually made with a small piece of meat, soon contained beef, pork, sausages, braciola, and meatballs, all of which might be consumed at the same meal. It's interesting to note that many people will say that spaghetti and meatballs is an Italian-American invention and not truly Italian. Serving them together is indeed not Italian. The sauce is served first over pasta, then the meatballs, along with whatever other meat was cooked in the ragu, are served as the second course or, more commonly, at another meal. Serving them together or serving spaghetti as a side dish (perish the thought!) was in response to the government's insistence that protein and starch (meat and potatoes) should be served together.

Although the agreeable Italian immigrants were anxious to adapt the new American ways, eating habits were an important part of their culture and they were never eager to abandon their own meal concepts. Consequently, many meals began to take on a rather unusual format. Thanksgiving, for example, would include all the traditional American foods such as turkey, stuffing, and potatoes. To begin with, however, there would be a holiday soup, pasta with meat sauce followed by the meat from the ragu, and then the turkey. And most Americans consider themselves full when they eat the usual Thanksgiving spread! This is how it was with almost all the people I talked to. Their families never gave up their own eating habits but simply incorporated new ideas. No wonder that Italian cooking, of all the ethnic cuisines, has had such staying power.

Because so many of the early Italian-Americans settled in coastal regions, they had little trouble maintaining fish in their diets. Fish pushcarts were a regular feature of most neighborhoods. Cooks simply used the methods they knew with what they could find. Eels and squid could be bought. Octopus was available for holiday times and, when it was not, conch became a favorite for making fish salad. Smelts were a staple. Clams were abundant. Because such a variety was available, Italian-Americans were able to maintain the very old tradition of serving an all-fish Christmas Eve dinner.

The egg recipes in this chapter are among my most favorite. My grandmother did wonders with eggs and perhaps it is this association that makes these dishes so special to me. I always looked forward to one of Nonna's suppers of eggs. Many of these recipes can be used as appetizers, luncheon dishes, or simple supper entrées.

Chicken Breasts with Sliced Tomatoes

PETTI DI POLLO AL POMODORI

Some of southern Italy's finest treasures—mozzarella, black olive paste, and tomatoes—are combined in this recipe. For the prettiest presentation, choose a broiling dish that can go from the oven to the table.

3 whole chicken breasts, boned (6 cutlets)	Salt and pepper
	Olive oil for frying
2 eggs, beaten	2 tablespoons olivada
1½ cups dried breadcrumbs	(black olive paste)
¼ pound mozzarella cheese, grated	3 medium tomatoes, sliced into ⅛-inch-thick
3 tablespoons extra-virgin olive oil	slices

1. Detach the small fillets from the underside of each cutlet. Cut the remaining cutlet horizontally into 2 pieces. Pound all the pieces lightly just to even out. Dip the pieces into the beaten eggs and coat with the breadcrumbs.

2. Toss the grated mozzarella cheese with 1 tablespoon olive oil, salt, and pepper and set aside. Heat the olive oil to ¼ inch deep in a frying pan. Working with a few pieces at a time, fry the chicken on both sides until cooked (about 2 minutes per side). Drain on paper towels, place on a broiler dish, and keep warm while cooking the remaining chicken.

3. Spread the olivada on the top side of each piece of cooked chicken. Cover with the tomato slices and drizzle the remaining 2 tablespoons olive oil over the tomatoes. Sprinkle the cheese over the tomatoes and broil until the cheese melts. *Serves 6 to 8.*

• • •

Note: Olivada is available in specialty food shops. You can make your own by pitting brine-cured olives and mincing them to a paste.

Chicken in Lemon

POLLO AL LIMONE

A wonderful combination of sunny tastes!

8 fresh plum tomatoes
  (1½ pounds), peeled,
  seeded, and coarsely
  chopped
3 tablespoons extra-virgin
  olive oil
Salt and pepper
1 pound small white boiling
  onions

½ pound pancetta, diced
One 3- to 4-pound chicken,
  cut in 8 serving pieces
5 garlic cloves, peeled but
  left whole
1 tablespoon chopped fresh
  rosemary or 1 teaspoon
  dried
Grated rind of 1 lemon

1. Put the tomatoes and 2 tablespoons olive oil in a small non-aluminum frying pan. Season with salt and pepper and cook over medium-low heat until the water evaporates (about 20 minutes). Set aside. Blanch the onions in boiling water for 1 minute, plunge into cold water, drain, and peel. Cut a cross in the root end and set aside.

2. Put the pancetta and remaining 1 tablespoon olive oil in a sauté pan over medium-low heat. When the pancetta has crisped slightly, remove from the pan with a slotted spoon. Wash the chicken and pat dry. In the same sauté pan, brown the chicken on all sides (about 15 minutes) and remove to a side dish. Season with salt and pepper.

3. Add the onions and garlic to the same pan and cook until the onions are softened. Discard all but 2 tablespoons fat from the pan and return the dark meat chicken pieces to the pan. Add the rosemary and lemon rind, cover, and cook 15 minutes, adding a few tablespoons hot water if the pan becomes dry.

4. Return the white meat chicken to the pan, cover, and cook 15 minutes, or until the chicken is cooked. Add the tomatoes and reserved pancetta to the pan and heat together 5 minutes. *Serves 6.*

GARLIC

The most common flavorings of southern Italian cooking are garlic, oil, and parsley. Many dishes call for nothing more. And yet garlic is never the overwhelming, pungent flavor that many pseudo-Italian restaurants or recipes would have us believe. Properly handled, it should never overpower a dish.

Always buy fresh garlic. It is easy to peel if you first smash the clove with the side of a chef's knife. Remove any green sprout from the center of the clove since this new growth will be bitter. Chop garlic by hand on a board so the milky juices will escape. When garlic is chopped in a machine or put through a garlic press, these bitter juices go into the dish. If garlic is to be part of something to be mixed in a food processor, chop it coarsely on the counter first and then put the pieces in the processor.

Since garlic will burn if it is heated too fast, it is best to put it into a cool pan at the same time as the oil and allow it to heat gently. The intensity of garlic in a dish depends less on how much is used than on how it is handled. Smashed cloves that are removed once they are browned will produce a more subtle flavor than ones that are minced and allowed to remain in the finished dish. I think of garlic as a personal thing. Adjust the amounts to your own taste.

Piquant Chicken

POLLO PICCANTE

One of the surprises I discovered traveling in southern Italy is the use of pickled vegetables in dishes. I knew that my grandmother and all our relatives put up their own vegetables in brine, but I hadn't remembered finding them cooked in a dish. They add a marvelous contrast of flavors.

¼ cup extra-virgin olive oil
2 large garlic cloves, smashed and peeled
One 3-pound chicken fryer, butterflied and backbone removed
½ cup dry white wine

Salt
1 cup pickled sweet red peppers, cut in 1-inch strips
One 9-ounce package frozen artichoke hearts, thawed

1. Put the olive oil and garlic into a 12-inch sauté pan. Cook over gentle heat until the garlic is browned. Discard the garlic.

2. Pat the chicken dry and tuck the wings back on themselves. Put the chicken, skin side down, in the sauté pan with the hot oil. Cook over medium-high heat until browned (8 to 10 minutes). Turn and brown the other side for 8 to 10 minutes.

3. Turn the chicken, skin side up, and drain off all but 2 tablespoons fat from the pan. Add the wine and reduce to ¼ cup on high heat. Reduce the heat to medium, salt the chicken, cover the pan, and cook 15 minutes.

4. Uncover the pan and add the peppers and artichoke hearts. Salt the vegetables. Cover again and cook 15 to 20 minutes, or until the chicken is cooked through.

5. Remove the chicken, cut in quarters, and put on a serving dish. Boil the pan juices on high heat until they are reduced to almost a glaze consistency, pour over the chicken, and serve. *Serves 4.*

Chicken with Green Olives

POLLO CON OLIVE VERDE

Judging from the way olives and anchovies are served in most Italian-American restaurants, the diner would be led to believe that they only belonged on an antipasto plate. The truth is that southern Italians use them, alone or in combination, in a great many dishes. This flavorful recipe is a great case in point. Simple chicken achieves new heights. Double this recipe for a flavorful country party dish. The combination of ingredients will be even better if the dish is made ahead and left to rest for a day.

3 tablespoons extra-virgin olive oil
One 3- to 3½-pound chicken, cut in 8 serving pieces
Salt and pepper
1 onion, chopped
2 garlic cloves, minced
½ cup red wine vinegar
1 tablespoon chopped fresh oregano or 1 teaspoon dried

1 bay leaf
⅔ cup pitted and quartered green olives (¼ pound), preferably Sicilian but any brine-cured olive will do
6 anchovy fillets, rinsed and chopped
3 tablespoons chopped fresh parsley

1. Heat the oil in a sauté pan. Pat the chicken pieces dry and add to the pan. Brown on all sides (about 15 minutes). Season with salt and pepper and remove from the pan. Discard all but 3 tablespoons of fat from pan. Add the onion and garlic to the pan and cook until softened. Return dark chicken meat to the pan, add the vinegar, and reduce on high heat 1 minute. Turn the heat to medium-low, add herbs, cover, and simmer 15 minutes, adding a few tablespoons warm water if the pan becomes too dry.

2. Return the chicken breasts to the pan. Gently fold in the olives, cover, and cook 15 minutes. Fold in the anchovies and parsley and heat 5 minutes. *Serves 6.*

Braised Duck with Olives

ANITRA IN UMIDO CON OLIVE

Duck is not eaten often in Italy, and when it is, a leaner wild duck is usually what's available. The early Italian-Americans found a fattier bird in the poultry shops and broiled, fried, or poached it first to get rid of the excess fat.

5-pound duckling
1 small onion, chopped
1 medium carrot, chopped
1 stalk celery, chopped
¼ pound prosciutto, chopped
3 tablespoons extra-virgin olive oil

Salt and freshly ground black pepper
1 cup dry white wine
1 cup pitted and halved brine-cured black olives (such as Gaeta)
½ cup chopped parsley
1 bay leaf

1. Preheat the broiler.
2. Remove the excess fat from the cavity of the duck. Trim off the neck skin. Chop off the wing tips and reserve with the neck and gizzards for another use. To quarter the duck, place the duck, breast side up, on a cutting surface and cut through the breastbone. Turn the duck over, push down on the breast halves, and cut the backbone in half. Turn each half skin side up, and feeling for the end of the rib cage, cut the pieces in half just below the ribs. Trim away the excess skin and fat.
3. Put the duck, skin side up, on a rack in a broiler pan and broil 6 inches away from the heat 5 minutes. Prick the skin all over with a skewer or the tip of a paring knife to release the fat, being careful not to pierce the meat. Broil another 5 minutes, pricking the skin once more. Turn and broil 5 minutes. Remove from the oven and keep warm.
4. While the duck is broiling, put the onion, carrot, celery, and prosciutto in a large sauté pan with the olive oil and cook over moderate heat until the onion is golden, about 10 minutes.
5. Transfer the broiled duck to the pan with the onions. Season with salt and pepper and add the wine to the pan. Bring to a boil, reduce the heat, cover the pan, and simmer over medium heat 15

minutes. Add the olives, parsley, and bay leaf, cover the pan again, and cook another 20 minutes, or until the duck is cooked. Remove the duck to a serving platter. If there is excess liquid in the pan, turn the heat to high to reduce. Check the seasonings and pour the vegetables over the duck. *Serves 4.*

CURING FRESH OLIVES

If you have ever bitten into a fresh, uncured olive you understand the miracle of curing; it turns a bitter, inedible fruit into a delicious food. The first step in curing olives is to remove the bitterness, which is commonly done with either a lye or a simple water process. Italian-Americans have never been fans of lye processing because they felt that the chemical operation removed too much of the olive flavor. They use a simple water system instead. Once the bitterness is removed, the olives must be further cured by resting in either a brine solution or salt or oil. Curing in brine is the most common home method.

The process is the same regardless of whether you are curing a pint or a bushel of olives. Try to select olives without any bruised spots. Put the olives in a large non-metal container and completely cover with cold water. Cover and weight the container so the olives are entirely submerged. Change the water daily for 10 days. Drain the olives. Rinse the olives and the container with water. Return the olives to the container and completely cover them with a brine solution made in the proportion of 1 tablespoon of salt per quart of water. Cover and weight the olives and let them cure for at least 1 month before using. It is best to crack very large olives before curing.

Stewed Rabbit

CONIGLIO IN UMIDO

This same recipe can be made with chicken if you can't find rabbit. It is a simple, straightforward recipe with a wonderful combination of flavors. Be sure to brown the pieces of meat well and do not undercook it. No pink areas around the bones!

1 rabbit (about 5 pounds), with liver and kidneys	3 small hot red peppers, washed, seeded, and sliced
¼ cup extra-virgin olive oil	Salt
3 medium onions, coarsely chopped	⅓ cup capers, rinsed
1 cup dry white wine	4 sprigs fresh thyme
3 garlic cloves, smashed and peeled	2 sprigs fresh oregano

1. Remove the excess pockets of fat from the rabbit. Cut into 11 pieces: cut the hind legs into leg and thigh; cut the loin crosswise into 3 pieces; cut the rib section in half crosswise; and leave the front legs whole. Put the pieces into cold, salted water to cover for 15 minutes. Drain and dry well.

2. Put the oil and onions into a wide pan large enough to hold the rabbit. Heat until the onions are golden. Remove the onions from the pan with a slotted spoon and reserve. Add the rabbit to the pan in batches (do not crowd) and brown on all sides. Transfer to a plate. Add the wine to the pan and boil to reduce to ¼ cup, scraping up any browned bits. Return the onion and the rabbit to the pan. Sprinkle with salt and turn to coat with the juices. Add the garlic and hot pepper. Cover and simmer until the rabbit is almost tender when pierced with a knife, turning occasionally, about 40 minutes.

3. Meanwhile, remove the membrane from the kidneys and trim the liver. Pat dry. Cut into ⅛-inch dice. Mix into the pan with the rabbit. Stir in the capers, thyme, and oregano. Simmer, uncovered, until the kidney and livers are cooked (6 to 10 minutes). *Serves 4.*

THE CHICKEN MAN

The early Italian-Americans refused to buy slaughtered poultry or rabbits. They preferred to raise their own chickens and rabbits even when they lived in the city. When ordinances made this impossible, Italians bought their animals live from "the chicken man" who had indoor coops to choose from. He would slaughter them only after they were sold and housewives often took them home to clean themselves. Since animal innards were an important part of their diet, they didn't want to risk being cheated out of any part.

When I was very young, we lived in the country and my grandparents lived in the city, where they were no longer allowed to have chickens. Grandpa gave us Peter and Paul and we kids treated them as pets. It was only after my mother framed a feather from each with their names inscribed below that we forgave her for serving our pets for Sunday dinner.

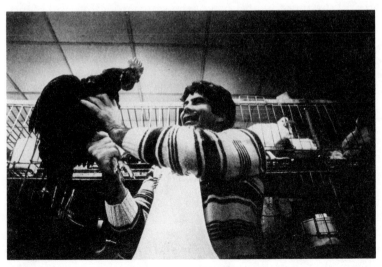

Chris Morris and his chicken.

Meatballs

POLPETTINI

Is there anyone who has not made meatballs? It wouldn't seem necessary to give a recipe, yet my mother, who learned from her mother-in-law, makes particularly tender ones because of the high proportion of eggs. Because they are so tender, she does not fry them first but drops them directly into the simmering sauce. Sometimes, as is often done in southern Italy, my mother would add raisins to the meatballs. This was a problem because not all of the children liked them. So she then added raisins to only half, which was fine as long as the nonraisin lovers could spot them peeking out of the meatball.

1 pound ground beef	Salt and pepper
4 large eggs, beaten	⅓ cup dark raisins
About 1 cup dried	(optional)
breadcrumbs	4 cups meat sauce
¼ cup freshly grated	(pages 79–81)
pecorino or Parmesan	
cheese	

Mix all the ingredients, except the sauce, together and blend well. With wet hands roll into desired-size meatballs. Drop directly into the simmering ragu and cook 30 minutes, or until cooked through. *Serves 6.*

Meat Roll Filled with Spinach

POLPETTONE RIPIENO CON SPINACI

A "polpetto" is a meat ball. Italians add "one" to the end of a word to indicate that something is very large or very important. I guess you could say both about this large meat roll. It is definitely larger than a meatball and the very fact that it is meat made it important to the southern Italians.

1½ cups Italian bread, crusts
removed, broken in pieces
½ cup milk
½ pound Italian sausage,
removed from casing,
crumbled

1½ pounds ground beef
2 eggs, beaten
Salt and freshly ground
black pepper

———————

FILLING

1½ pounds spinach, washed,
stems removed
3 tablespoons extra-virgin
olive oil
⅓ pound prosciutto,
finely chopped
⅓ cup pinoli nuts
(pine nuts)

Salt and pepper
⅔ cup pitted black olives,
preferably Gaeta
1 ounce pecorino cheese
(¼ cup), grated
Olive oil

1. Mix the bread with the milk and mash with your fingers or a fork until well soaked. Squeeze excess milk from the bread.

2. Put the sausage in a bowl. Add the ground meat, bread, eggs, salt, and pepper. Work well together until homogeneous. Put the meat on a moistened sheet of aluminum foil. Cover with a sheet of dampened wax paper and pat or roll into a thin rectangle 12 x 14 inches. Place the meat, on the foil, on a cookie sheet and refrigerate while making the filling.

3. Coarsely chop the spinach. Heat the olive oil and prosciutto in a large sauté pan over medium-low heat 5 minutes. Add the pinoli nuts and sauté just until lightly colored. Add the spinach and salt and pepper to taste, and toss over medium heat until the spinach is cooked. Add the olives and cheese and remove from heat.

4. Preheat the oven to 350°F. Remove the meat from the refrigerator and peel off the waxed paper. Spread the filling over the surface of the meat, leaving a one-inch border all around. Starting with one long side and using the foil to help, roll the meat up, jelly-roll style. Press ends and seam to prevent opening. Using the foil lift, place the meat on the foil in a baking pan with sides. Brush with oil and bake 1 hour, or until a meat thermometer inserted in the center registers 150°F. Let cool at least 20 minutes in the pan before slicing. May be served hot or cold. *Serves 10 to 12.*

Large Meat Roll with Frittata

POLPETTONE CON FRITTATA

We all need recipes that reheat beautifully, taste good at any temperature, and are versatile. This is one of those recipes and I use it often. It can be cooked completely three days before serving and reheated. It is good hot but can also be cooled out of its sauce and sliced thin for picnics or buffets. The recipe can be doubled. The sauce is good on the meat or served over a first course of macaroni. The fact that it is also pretty to look at when sliced is really too much to ask for!

¼ pound pancetta
1 cup fresh Italian bread, crusts removed, broken in pieces
4 tablespoons milk

1 pound ground beef
1 egg, beaten
Salt, pepper, and freshly grated nutmeg

———

FRITTATA

3 large eggs
⅓ cup chopped parsley
⅓ cup grated Parmesan cheese
¼ cup pinoli nuts (pine nuts)

Salt, pepper, and nutmeg
4 tablespoons extra-virgin olive oil

———

SAUCE

¼ cup extra-virgin olive oil
2 garlic cloves, chopped
½ cup chopped onion
½ cup dry red wine
2 cups drained imported canned Italian plum tomatoes (save juices)
2 tablespoons chopped fresh oregano or 2 teaspoons dried

3 tablespoons chopped fresh parsley
3 tablespoons chopped fresh basil (if available; do not substitute dried)
Salt and pepper

1. Put the pancetta and half the bread in the bowl of a food processor and chop with the steel blade until fine. (Do not puree.) Mix the remaining bread with the milk and mash with your fingers or a fork until well soaked. Squeeze excess milk from the bread.

2. Put the ground beef in a bowl. Add the pancetta mixture, drained bread, egg, salt, pepper, and nutmeg. Work well together until homogeneous. Put the meat on a sheet of wax paper. Cover with a second sheet of dampened wax paper and pat or roll into a thin rectangle 12 x 14 inches. Refrigerate in wax paper on a cookie sheet while making the frittata.

3. Beat the eggs. Add the parsley, cheese, pinolis, salt, pepper, and nutmeg. Heat 3 tablespoons olive oil until quite hot in a 10-inch omelet or sauté pan. Add the eggs and swirl with the flat side of a fork. As the eggs set on the bottom, this swirling motion will break up the set eggs and allow the uncooked eggs to run through to the bottom. When the eggs are set on the bottom, turn the frittata onto a plate. Add the remaining tablespoon oil to the pan and slide the frittata, uncooked side down, back into the pan. Cook until set.

4. Remove the meat from the refrigerator. Lay the frittata in the center of the meat and roll, jelly-roll style, starting from the short side. Be sure the frittata is completely enclosed. Press the ends and seam to prevent opening while cooking.

5. Heat ¼ cup olive oil in a pan large enough to hold the meat. Brown the meat on all sides including the two ends. Add the garlic and onion to the pan and cook until translucent. Add the red wine to the pan and cook on high heat one minute. Add the chopped tomatoes, herbs, salt, and pepper. Bring to a boil and reduce the heat. Cover with a sheet of aluminum foil, pressed to the top of the meat and secured tightly around sides. Cover with the pan lid and braise on top of the stove or in a 350°F oven 1 hour. Turn the meat from time to time. If the pan juices do not come at least ⅓ of the way up the sides of the meat, add some of the reserved tomato juices.

6. Remove the cooked polpettone from the cooking juices. Cut into slices and place on a platter. Spoon the pan juices over the meat and serve. Juices should be slightly thickened; if too watery, reduce on high heat. *Serves 8 to 10.*

BY ANY OTHER NAME . . .

When the immigrants first arrived in America, they used their familiar dialect names for their traditional foods and dishes. In Italy these names often varied from town to town and definitely from region to region. Sicilians, for example, call the St. Joseph's Day fritters that Neapolitans call "zeppole," "sfinci." As the immigrant groups mingled and married, dialects mingled and married and the names of dishes were often a blend of dialects. When second- or third-generation Italian-Americans left home for another state, or went to Italy, they found that they had names for foods that no one else knew. "Wandi," for example, seems to be a term that only Rhode Islanders know for the carnival fritters. Eventually, people began to call their heritage foods by American names which might be more generally understood: "ragu" and "sugo" became "gravy" or "sauce," "wandi," "bowknots." The original dialect names have not been totally forgotten, however. Many times when I talk with someone with a Neapolitan background who finds out that my grandparents were from Ischia (off the coast of Naples) he or she will call dishes by their dialect names.

They came here from Italy so that their children would have the opportunity to better themselves.

Large Meat Roll Fried

POLPETTONE FRITTO

As with the other meat rolls, this is equally good hot or cold. I remember eating it mostly cold when I was a little girl. My grandmother put slices of it between crusty pieces of Italian bread on which she had dribbled olive oil and we kids would sit on her back steps, with oil dripping here and there, as we watched the men play bocce (Italian lawn bowling) in the field behind Nonna's house.

⅔ cup stale Italian bread,
   crust removed, crumbled
¼ cup milk
1 pound ground beef
¼ pound Italian sausage,
   casing removed, minced
1 garlic clove, minced
1 egg, beaten
2 ounces freshly grated
   Parmesan cheese
2 tablespoons chopped flat
   leaf parsley
Salt and pepper

3 ounces prosciutto
3 ounces provolone cheese,
   cut in narrow strips
3 hard-boiled eggs, peeled
Whole parsley sprigs
¼ cup olive oil for frying
Juice of 1 lemon

1. Mix the bread with the milk and mash with your fingers or a fork until well-soaked. Squeeze excess milk from the bread.

2. Put the ground beef in a bowl. Add the sausage, garlic, bread, egg, cheese, parsley, salt, and pepper. Work together well. Put the meat on a wet polyurethane cutting board, marble, or piece of aluminum foil. Pat or roll into a rectangle ½ inch thick.

3. Cover the meat with a layer of prosciutto. Arrange the provolone strips on top. Place the hard-boiled eggs in a horizontal row in the center and the parsley sprigs along the sides of the eggs. Carefully roll up, pushing the ends in to secure the filling.

4. Heat the oil in a large frying pan. Brown the polpettone on all sides on medium-high heat. Reduce heat, cover the pan, and cook over medium-low heat 1 hour, turning the meat from time to time. Remove from the pan and let cool. Add the lemon juice to the pan juices, stir in well, and pour over the meat roll. *Serves 6 to 8.*

Steak Pizzaiola

BISTECCA ALLA PIZZAIOLA

"Alla pizzaiola" means that the steak is cooked in a sauce that makes it taste like pizza! In Naples that means that the tomato sauce is flavored with oregano. This was one of my favorite foods growing up. What child can resist something that tastes like pizza?

2 pounds beefsteak (rump or
   round), cut in thin slices
¼ cup extra-virgin olive oil
1 small onion, thinly sliced
2 garlic cloves, chopped
2 cups canned tomatoes,
   drained and chopped

Salt and pepper
½ cup red wine (optional)
1 teaspoon dried oregano or
   1 tablespoon fresh

1. Pound the slices of steak until they are no more than ⅛ inch thick and of even thickness.
2. Put the oil, onion, and garlic in a frying pan and cook over medium-low heat until golden. Remove with a slotted spoon to a side dish and reserve. Increase the heat and brown pieces of steak on each side (1 to 2 minutes). Remove the pieces as they brown and keep warm.
3. Return the onions and garlic to the pan. Add the tomatoes, salt and pepper, and wine. Increase the heat and allow to simmer rapidly until the oil and tomatoes separate (about 15 minutes). Stir in the oregano and return the steaks to the pan. Cook 5 to 10 minutes, or until the steaks are cooked and heated. *Serves 6 to 8.*

• • •

Note: In order to brown meat properly, two techniques are critical. First make sure that the pieces of meat are thoroughly dry. Pat them with paper toweling right before browning. Second, do not crowd the pan. There should be room between the pieces of meat as they brown. If you ignore either of these, the meat will steam and not form a good seared outside layer.

MEMORIES

*"Food was a bonding. It was a thing
that kept the family together."*

*My father's influence on my cooking was greater than my mother's.
My mother's family comes from a different part of Italy and they
would do things like polenta, ravioli, lots of bean dishes. These
things weren't too prevalent in my father's family. They would eat
lots of fish, very light tomato sauces, very lean types of things really.
My grandfather would eat no meat at all.*

*My father used to like to cook on his day off and he was very
demonstrative about it. He really enjoyed what he was doing. He
remembered a lot from his mother. I loved to watch him because he
really got into it. My father's sister, who is eighty-one years old, is
still the greatest cook I've ever known. I used to just watch the both
of them cook for hours on end.*

*The first time my father went to Italy to visit his family there,
they sent us some olive oil and it was like nothing I'd ever had. We
started using it to make the same marinara sauce that my father
remembered my grandmother making. There was a world of difference in that sauce between using the plain olive oil, which was easily
obtained, and this extra-virgin olive oil. This is what the people who
came from my family's region of Italy had; this is what they always
had; this is what they lived with. But when my grandparents were
here, I think they used whatever they could get.*

*My grandfather had been a fisherman in Italy. He was used to
eating a lot of raw fish that they still eat in Bari, where he came
from. There was a type of shrimp he ate raw. They're very sweet and
they're very tiny, and my grandfather would have this little mound
of salt on a plate and he'd dip the shrimp into the salt and eat it.
Once in a while, if he didn't eat them raw, my grandmother would
take the shrimp and make a very light egg batter. She'd dip them in
flour and then the egg batter and she'd hold them in the hot olive oil
with a spoon. They were the size of a quarter maybe. They were
delicious, really delicious.*

My grandfather built a fourteen-foot rowboat when he came here. Believe it or not, in the '38 hurricane, it was the only boat that was still tied and there in the cove in Warwick when the other boats were gone. He would make fenders for wealthy people's boats. He knew how to do all that intricate rope work, really artistic. When he was a fisherman in Italy, he'd be gone for months. He'd go down to Morocco and other places.

I've made bragiolini which were from my mother's mother. We'd stuff a thin eye of the round with ham and cheese, roll them and bake them for about 25 minutes. My grandmother would serve them with peas and red sauce on them. On holidays my grandmother would make the ravioli, there would always be the chicken soup, there would always be a pasta dish beside the ravioli. And then there was a meat course.

The sauces in my family would not be heavy with meat or paste. Just olive oil, the garlic browned in the olive oil and removed, lots of fresh parsley, fresh basil, and squeezed plum tomatoes. My grandmother would put the tomatoes through a fine sieve so that there would be no seeds at all. Very flavorful, very light. My father taught me how to make this sauce. He made kind of a ritual out of it. The color of the garlic had to be right, you couldn't get it too dark because then it would make the tomatoes bitter, you had to remove it at just the right time. They had to be just the right tomatoes, they had to be nice and sweet. You'd put them in and stay with it and simmer it just a short while, it's a quickly made sauce. This, my father taught me how to do.

I grew up speaking Italian. At Easter time, my father would put me out in front of his market with the eggs. I was about nine, and all the old Italian people would come and talk to me and I'd sell them eggs. Every Easter, that was my job. The eggs were a big thing because so many people baked their own Easter pies. That was a big thing at Easter. The ricotta pies, the rice, the barley, the wheat, the pizza rustica with Italian ham in them. They'd have two thick crusts, one on the top, one on the bottom, almost like a bread, with eggs in the middle of it. It was incredible the amount of eggs I sold.

My grandmother was very good at making—this lamb shank dish that she'd do in the oven with potatoes. We called it agnello pudna. She covered it with something like a pizza sauce—tomatoes, olive oil, some garlic, some grated cheese. She'd pour that over the lamb shanks and the potatoes. Then she'd bake it very slowly. My mother used to serve braised escarole with this a lot—just take some escarole and braise it in the olive oil and garlic. Or rabe. We had a lot of rabe. Some of the old dishes are coming back and coming back very strong. Pasta fagiol, for example. Growing up I wouldn't even want my non-Italian friends to see that going on at home. They'd turn their noses up at it. Pasta and beans—that's a lowly peasant dish. But now, that's a gourmet dish.

I think for my father, my grandparents, my aunt, food was a bonding. It was a thing to keep the family together. It was very strong. When I remember my childhood, and I remember my aunts especially, and my father, my mother, my grandparents, this was a reason for getting the family together. When I was a child, my father would get home kind of late—eight o'clock during the week. I couldn't have supper without my father. We all had to wait and have supper with my father. It was important to sit there at that dinner table and talk. Any problems that I had in school and so on would come up at the dinner table. Even though my father worked very many hours, it was that time that we had together. We never went anywhere, my father was tied to his business working an awful lot of hours, but I don't feel like I missed out on anything. Food was always the center of things, the reason for getting together. I think that's why I enjoy cooking so much.

ROZANN DIGIGLIO BUCKNER

Stuffed Beef Rolls

BRACIOLINI (BRAGIOLE) ALLA NAPOLETANA

In Italy these richly flavored meat rolls would be made as below for their own sake and served as a second course with their sauce napping them. Many Italians use the large version of these rolls, braciole, to flavor their meat sauce (pages 79–81) along with pieces of pork and meatballs.

2 ounces dark raisins
  (⅓ cup)
¼ pound prosciutto, finely
  chopped
⅓ cup fresh breadcrumbs
2 ounces pinoli nuts
  (⅓ cup)
⅓ cup minced parsley
3 ounces freshly grated
  Parmesan cheese
Salt and freshly ground
  black pepper

1½ pounds beef top round
  (3 slices, ¼ inch thick)
⅓ cup extra-virgin olive oil
1 small onion (½ cup),
  chopped
1 small carrot, chopped
½ cup dry red or white wine
1 can (35 ounces) Italian
  peeled tomatoes,
  undrained, finely chopped

1. Soak the raisins in warm water to cover for 20 minutes. Drain and dry.

2. In a medium bowl, combine the raisins, prosciutto, the breadcrumbs, pinoli nuts, parsley, Parmesan cheese, salt, and pepper and mix together well.

3. Cut the beef slices to form pieces approximately 4 x 3 inches. Pound with a meat pounder or heavy object until the slices are about ⅛ inch thick. Divide the filling mixture evenly among the meat slices and spread to ¼ inch from the edges. Roll the slices into a sausage shape and tuck the ends in. Secure with toothpicks or tie in both directions with kitchen string.

4. Put the olive oil, onion, and carrot into a heavy cooking pot large enough to hold the braciola in one layer. Cook gently until the onion is translucent. Push to the side and add braciola. Turn up the heat and brown the meat on all sides. Keep the onions and carrots

off to the side so as not to burn. Push the browned meat to the side and pour the wine into the pan. Bring to a boil, scraping up any browned bits from the bottom of the pan. Boil 1 minute to reduce the wine. Reduce the heat, push the meat and vegetables to the center of the pan, and add the tomatoes. Season with salt and pepper and put the cover on slightly askew. Simmer gently 1 to 1½ hours, or until the meat releases easily when tested with a skewer and the sauce is slightly thickened. If the meat is tender but the sauce is watery, remove the meat and reduce the sauce.

5. Transfer the meat to a warm platter and remove the toothpicks or string. Leave whole or slice into ¼-inch pieces. Spoon on the sauce and serve. *Serves 6 to 8.*

Pushcarts covered for the night.

PORK

The winter killing of the family pig was one of the year's most celebrated events in southern Italy. The slaughtered pig provided fresh meat and sausages; pancetta (cured bacon); prosciutto (ham); and numerous other salumi (cured pork). Neck pieces were used to make ragu: fat was rendered for "strutto" (lard), which was used in place of butter for baking and for deep-frying sweet and savory foods. "Lardo" (cured fatback—salt pork) was diced and used to flavor pasta, soup, or vegetables and to make "ciccioli" (cracklings). No part of the pig was wasted and what would not be consumed at home was either sold or traded for items that the family did not grow or produce on its own. The animal was so prized that Calabrians say, "The home has two riches, the pig and the priest. Breed the pig because it anoints the mouth."

Many early immigrants continued to raise and slaughter their own pigs. When ordinances forbade pigs to be raised in the city, many families had a farmer or butcher bring a slaughtered pig to their cellar for butchering and preserving. Gradually, the immigrants began to rely on butcher shops for pork, although many people continued to make their own sausages and salumi, flavoring them according to their own taste. Whole families gathered around the kitchen table and hand-cut the meat. The sausages were eaten fresh or hung in cellars or cool hallways to dry. Some people preserved the dried sausage under oil, as had been the practice in their part of Italy. Before the outbreak of swine fever in Italy that led to the ban of imported pork products, Italians also relied on "paesani" or the "salumeria" (delicatessen) to bring or import their favorite "salumi" from their area of Italy.

Although the live pig has disappeared from the modern Italian-American neighborhood, its products are still an

The Buon Gusto Sausage Factory, 1926.

important part of the diet. All Italian butchers make sausages, sweet with fennel or hot with hot pepper (peperoncino). A large selection of good "salumi" is available from American or Canadian companies, which are usually owned by people of Italian descent. In time many of the bans on importation of these products from Italy may be lifted, as in the case of prosciutto di Parma, and hopefully we will be able to sample many of the southern regional specialties.

The Italian reliance on "lardo" (salt pork) dwindled in America. Originally, cooks diced and mashed the pieces of pork with garlic and parsley and used that as their cooking fat. Most people gave it up because commercial salt pork did not have the same flavor as what they or the family butcher cured. Some of the recipes in this book call for pieces of prosciutto or pancetta to be added to olive oil at the beginning of cooking to give a dish the original southern Italian flavor.

Stuffed Pork Rolls

FAGOTTINI DI MAIALE

Neapolitans call small round tomatoes similar to cherry tomatoes "piennoli." They are considered a winter tomato because they are strung together when ripe, air-dried briefly, and then hung from beams in the kitchen or cool storing room for winter use. The tomato's skin shrivels but the inside remains soft and juicy. The climate of coastal New England was too damp for this kind of drying and most of the early Italian-Americans settled for other methods of preserving. You can simulate the style of these tomatoes by putting the washed cherry tomatoes in a single layer on a baking sheet in a 375°F oven for 5 minutes.

1 pound pork cutlets from the loin (6 pieces)
Olive oil for frying eggplant
1 pound eggplant, cut in ¼-inch slices, salted, and drained 1 hour
2 garlic cloves, minced
¼ cup breadcrumbs
2 ounces grated pecorino cheese (½ cup)
¼ cup chopped parsley
Salt and pepper
2 tablespoons extra-virgin olive oil
1 large onion, thinly sliced
3 tablespoons olive oil
½ cup white wine
18 cherry tomatoes, washed, roasted 5 minutes in a 375°F oven

1. Cut the cutlets in half crosswise and pound thin.

2. Heat ½ inch olive oil in a frying pan. Squeeze the eggplant dry and fry in the hot olive oil until golden on each side. Drain on paper towels.

3. Mix the garlic, breadcrumbs, cheese, parsley, salt, and pepper together. Moisten with 2 tablespoons olive oil. Cover the pork cutlets with the eggplant. Divide the breadcrumb seasoning evenly over each cutlet. Roll up and secure with toothpicks.

4. Fry the sliced onion in 3 tablespoons olive oil until softened but not browned. Push the onion to one side and turn the pork rolls in the pan until lightly browned. Add the wine and reduce by half. Cover the pan and cook over low heat 10 minutes. Cut the tomatoes in half and add to the pan with the salt and pepper. Cover again and

cook 15 minutes, or until the pork releases easily when tested with a skewer. Remove the pork, tomatoes, and onions to a serving platter with a slotted spoon. Reduce the cooking liquid to ⅓ cup and pour over the pork. *Serves 6.*

Grilled Skewered Pork Rolls

UCCELLETTI DI CAMPAGNA

In Italy tiny birds (uccelletti) are often skewered and spit-roasted. They are a rare delicacy, not readily available to everyone. The name of this recipe, "little birds of the country," indicates that this pork dish from Basilicata is cooked in the manner of the little birds. Italians who settled in rural areas of America continued to hunt and spit-roast birds. A woman I know remembers her grandfather shooting birds from a telephone wire and contentedly roasting them in a backyard stone fireplace.

5 garlic cloves, minced
2 tablespoons fresh sage minced or 2 teaspoons dried
1 generous tablespoon freshly grated ginger
½ teaspoon cinnamon
Generous pinch of cloves
8 slices pork scallops, 3 ounces each, cut from the loin
Salt and freshly ground black pepper

8 thin slices prosciutto
16 Italian bread cubes, 1½ inches square (crust may be used)
Extra-virgin olive oil
8 thin slices pancetta

Special equipment:
8 metal skewers or 16 wooden ones, soaked in cold water 1 hour

1. Mix together the garlic, sage, ginger, cinnamon, and cloves. Set aside.

2. Trim any excess fat from the edges of the pork scallops. Pound each piece of pork until it is no thicker than ¼ inch. Season lightly with salt and pepper. Divide the garlic-sage mixture evenly among the scallops and spread to cover entire surface. Lay a slice of

Grilled Skewered Pork Rolls (continued)

prosciutto over each piece of pork, trimming if necessary. Cut each scallop in half crosswise. (If the scallops are very large, cut in 3 pieces each. The width should be approximately 3 inches.) Roll each scallop loosely into a sausage shape, starting at the short end. Push the ends inside slightly to secure the filling.

3. Dip each bread cube in olive oil, coating all sides. Cut the pancetta slices in half and wrap each around a bread cube.

4. Alternate pork rolls and bread on skewers, leaving a tiny space between the pieces. Cook over medium coals or under a kitchen broiler 4 minutes per side. *Serves 8.*

Sausages and Peppers

SALSICCIE E PEPERONI

It is impossible to imagine an Italian street fair without sausages. In Italy, in the late 1800s, fresh sausages were associated with winter celebrations because the family pig met his demise then and the government only permitted the sale of fresh pork in the winter. Fresh pork was available year-round in the United States, and sausages and peppers became part of just about all outdoor festivals.

3 red bell peppers	2 onions, peeled and thinly
3 green bell peppers	sliced
¼ cup extra-virgin olive oil	Salt
2 garlic cloves, smashed	8 Italian sausages, sweet
and peeled	or hot

1. Wash the peppers. Remove the stems, ribs, and seeds. Cut into 1-inch-wide slices.

2. Heat the oil in a frying pan large enough to hold the peppers. Add the garlic and cook until browned. Discard the garlic. Add the onions to the oil and cook until softened but not browned. Add the peppers and salt, cover the pan, and continue to cook over gentle heat until the peppers are soft (about 30 minutes).

3. Prick the sausages all over with a skewer or the tip of a sharp knife. Put in one layer in a heavy frying pan with 2 tablespoons

water. Cook over medium heat, turning often. The water should evaporate and the fat should run so the sausage cooks in its own fat. Cook until the sausage is browned and cooked through (10 to 15 minutes). (The sausage may also be broiled, roasted, or grilled.)

4. Add the peppers and onions to the sausages and heat together 5 minutes. *Serves 4.*

· · ·

Note: At most street fairs sausages and peppers are served inside crusty Italian rolls, simply cut open to hold them.

Roasted Leg of Lamb

AGNELLO AL FORNO

Don't even consider making this Sicilian recipe unless you are passionate about garlic! The cheese on the outside forms a delicious crusty coating.

8 garlic cloves	Olive oil
3 ounces prosciutto	Salt and pepper
6 sprigs fresh rosemary, cut into 1-inch pieces	½ cup freshly grated pecorino cheese
1 whole leg of lamb (about 7 pounds)	

1. Cut the peeled garlic cloves into slivers. Cut the prosciutto into strips ½ inch wide and about 4 inches long. Wrap the prosciutto tightly around the pieces of rosemary to form small rolls.

2. Trim the lamb completely of all fat and fell. With the tip of a paring knife, make small slits over the entire surface of the lamb. Alternately fill the slits with slivers of garlic and prosciutto rolls. Rub the surface well with olive oil. If possible, let the roast rest at least 2 hours.

3. Rub again with the olive oil and roast in a 400°F oven 12 minutes per pound. When the leg is ¾ done, salt and pepper and sprinkle with the cheese. Roast until done (140°F to 145°F). Let rest 20 minutes before serving on warmed plates. *Serves 8 to 10.*

Piquant Roasted Leg of Lamb

AGNELLO PICCANTE

This recipe is based on one of the many recipes that Italo Scanga has shared with me. He explained that in the mountains of Calabria the roast would be goat but here he uses lamb because it is more readily available. The roast provides a good opportunity to open a hearty southern Italian red wine such as a Cirò Rosso.

¼ pound pancetta (substitute prosciutto if unavailable)

¾ cup finely chopped Italian flat-leaf parsley

4 large garlic cloves, smashed and peeled

About ⅓ cup extra-virgin olive oil

1 small leg of lamb or shank half (about 5 pounds)

Salt

1 pound sweet Italian sausage

4 large sprigs fresh rosemary or 1 tablespoon dried

1 cup red wine vinegar

1. Mince the pancetta, parsley, and garlic and mix together. Moisten with a tablespoon olive oil.

2. Trim the lamb of all fell and fat. With the tip of a small sharp paring knife, make a number of ½-inch-deep incisions around the top and bottom of the lamb. Stuff each pocket with some of the pancetta mixture. Continue until all the mixture is used. Rub the entire surface of the lamb with olive oil. The lamb will have more flavor if this is done several hours ahead or the day before roasting.

3. Heat the oven to 400°F. Set the lamb on a rack in a roasting pan. Roast for 12 minutes per pound, brushing occasionally with olive oil and any pan juices. When the lamb is ½ hour from being finished, remove from the oven and keep the oven door closed to maintain the heat. Salt the lamb. Prick the sausages in several places with a skewer and lay them around the lamb. Put rosemary on top of lamb and sausages. Keeping your face averted, pour the vinegar over the surface of the lamb. Return the lamb to the oven and continue to roast. Baste the lamb and sausages and turn the sausages during this last half hour of cooking.

4. When the lamb is finished (internal temperature of 140°F to 145°F for rare) set it aside in a warm place with the sausages to rest for 20 minutes. Meanwhile, remove all but 2 tablespoons of fat from the roasting pan. Place the pan on top of the stove and add ½ cup water. Bring to a boil and scrape any browned juices from the bottom of the pan. Slice the lamb and sausages onto a warm serving platter and strain the sauce over all. *Serves 8 to 10.*

Braised Lamb Shanks

AGNELLO IN UMIDO

I created this recipe from someone else's memory of a favorite dish she enjoyed at her grandmother's house in Bari. She described it so often that I couldn't help but try to duplicate it. My friend feels that it is very close.

6 lamb shanks (2½ to 3
    pounds)
About ½ cup olive oil
1 large carrot, peeled and
    sliced
4 garlic cloves, chopped
1 red onion, sliced
2 tablespoons chopped hot
    pepper or 1 teaspoon
    dried

One 28-ounce can Italian
    tomatoes, drained and
    chopped
Rind of 1 small lemon,
    in strips
1 cup dry white wine
Salt

1. Brown the shanks in a heavy sauté pan using about 4 tablespoons olive oil. Set aside.
2. Put 4 tablespoons olive oil in a large casserole. Add the carrot, garlic, and onion and cook until golden. Add the hot pepper, tomatoes, lemon peel, and white wine. Bring to a boil, reduce the heat, add the shanks, and salt. Cover the pan with foil and with the lid and cook 2½ hours on top of the stove or in a 325°F oven. *Serves 6.*

STREET FAIRS

St. Joseph has been my favorite saint since my earliest remembrance of an Italian street fair in which he was carried in his full, life-sized statuary self along the street with music playing, lanterns and decorations stretched from street to street, and dollar bills tucked all about him. I realized in that wide-eyed moment of wonder that St. Joseph must be special indeed. What I didn't realize was that identical processions were occurring all over the state honoring a number of different saints.

Street fairs had been an integral part of life in Italy for the southern Italian immigrants who came to America. These festivals, characterized by ancient pageantry, had provided a relief from a life that didn't often find much to celebrate. The Bourbon kings of Naples had claimed that the peasant could be kept in line by giving him "farina, feste, and forca" (flour, festivals, and a pitchfork or the gallows, "forca" having both meanings). The "feste" were holidays which usually honored favorite saints or the anniversary of a miracle. There were processions, a high mass, games, food stands, and merrymaking. "Today let's feast, for tomorrow it's famine" was the pragmatic refrain of the hard-working peasant.

Rhode Island town records show that before the twentieth century, numerous communities of immigrants were already requesting permission to hold their festivals. Italians wanted to have the kind of celebrations they had known in their village in Italy, honoring the day with the kind of food and festivities that they had known in their part of the "old country."

Over the years, the festivals began to be less village oriented and to reflect more a combination of general southern Italian and American. The saints retained their individuality, but the food all looked alike—sausages and peppers served in hard Italian rolls, ravioli in meat sauce, dough boys (deep-fried, sweetened pieces of Italian bread dough), along with candied apples and cotton candy. Fireworks and mechanical rides were provided by professional groups that traveled the state.

Recently, I am happy to say, I have seen regional specialties creep back into the fairs. Bakeries especially are making an effort to reproduce the regional breads and sweets that were originally associated with a particular feast day. Hopefully there will be even more of this kind of revival of regional specialties.

St. Anthony's street fair in Boston, Massachusetts.

MEMORIES

"Social life used to be centered around the table . . ."

The food at my husband's market used to come packed differently than in markets today. The potatoes used to come in barrels, and they used to put a whole peck in a bag. His father had a meat market, but he only sold meat. One time he tried to put vegetables in, but it just didn't go. It wasn't traditional.

They used to sell spaghetti loose from boxes. They'd pick it up, weigh it, and wrap it up. All the stuff was like that. It was different.

It took my parents twenty-four days to get over to America on a boat. They said it was a horrible crossing. But when they came here, my mother had a brother in New Jersey where they went first. Then they moved to Rhode Island. My mother used to have a job in a department store making buttonholes in men's suits and jackets. Fifty cents apiece.

I met my husband because I worked with his sister. She was a seamstress also. Bill used to come to pick us up if it rained or poured or something. One night his mother and father came over to our house to see if we would consider a match. I was mortified. My goodness. I didn't know if I liked him or not. I wasn't thinking about marrying.

My mother would always come home with a little something for us. She brought me a little broom once so I could sweep the floor.

We never had the same thing twice in a week for dinner. Monday nights we had soup—either beef soup or chicken soup. We'd put in spinach or pasta or escarole and little tiny meatballs. Tuesday nights we usually had steak. Wednesday night was always fish. The push-cart would come and my mother would go out and get all kinds of delicious fish like calamari or smelts. She used to put the smelts in a frying pan with raisins and pinoli. Thursday night we all had maca-roni with meatballs or braciola. Friday night was fish again and Saturday night was usually a leg of lamb or a big roast with potatoes and macaroni to begin. Sunday was my day off.

My father was a good cook. We used to have an old gas stove and he always had a big pot at the end of the stove. We used to throw all our leftovers in there and it would be a stock pot. He also used to take a piece of steak and make a pesto with lots of parsley, raisins, pinoli, and a little bit of fatback. Then he cooked the steak on a woodstove.

We always put orange peel or pieces of apple or other fruits directly on the woodstove and the smell would go through the house.

My father would always give us, the six kids, wine. He said it was good for us. There was always wine on the table. Sometimes he used to put peaches in the wine for us.

My mother made her own sausage and hung it to dry in the hall where it was cool. She'd send us in with pins to stick in to let some of the air out a little bit so when we cooked it the skin wouldn't break.

My mother-in-law would never stuff green peppers, never. It was always red peppers because they were sweet. She would leave all the seeds in because she said that was what made the red pepper sweet.

Irma Verde (far right) and her family.

Uncle Bill Verde in front of his market.

My mother-in-law made a pastiera with macaroni instead of rice. It was delicious. It was a thin noodle. She boiled it, like the rice, and then she put a few cherries on top and a crisscross pattern of dough.

I used to hand-roll my own pasta. My father made me a roller from a broomstick—it was a nice one, nice and smooth. I used to dry it on a big breadboard.

We used to make cutlets. We never used to put bread on meat cutlets. Just egg. This is new, you know. Now all people do it.

My father watched us like a hawk. We used to wear our hair down to our waists when we were young. He used to bring us beautiful big taffeta bows to wear at the end of our braids. He would wash our heads on Sunday mornings and oh, how he would scrub. When short haircuts came in for girls, I was the first girl in the family to get mine cut that way. He almost killed me. He wouldn't talk to me for weeks—he said only the bad girls had their hair short.

Your social life used to be centered around the table. We used to sit and talk. Now they don't do that. They just eat and run.

IRMA PACIFICO VERDE
(family from Caserta)

Veal Shank with Marsala Wine

STINCO AL MARSALA

What a heavenly combination of flavors! The veal will fall right off the bone and be extremely tender.

2 veal shanks (about 2½ to 3 pounds each)	1 leek, sliced
	2½ cups dry Marsala wine
Flour	Salt
2 tablespoons butter	1 bay leaf
3 tablespoons extra-virgin olive oil	2 sprigs fresh thyme or 1 teaspoon dried
1 carrot, diced	¾ pound mushrooms, wiped clean and sliced
3 scallions, sliced	
1 celery rib, diced	

1. Preheat the oven to 350°F. Tie the veal shanks in 3 places to hold the meat on the bone. Dry the pieces well and dust very lightly with flour.

2. Heat the butter and oil in a large heavy casserole. Working one piece at a time, brown the veal well on all sides, removing pieces when they are browned. Return the veal to the pan. Add the carrots, scallions, celery, and leeks and cook until softened but not browned. Pour the Marsala into the pan and bring to a boil. Remove from the heat. Add the salt, bay leaf, and thyme, cover tightly with foil and the lid, and place in the oven. Cook 2 hours, or until the veal releases easily when tested with a skewer, turning the veal from time to time.

3. Remove the veal from the juices and keep warm. Strain the juices and remove the fat. Return the juices to the pan, add the mushrooms, and simmer until the mushrooms are cooked. Correct the seasonings. Slice the meat from the bone and pour the mushrooms and juices over. Extract the marrow from the bones if desired. *Serves 6 to 8.*

Fennel-Stuffed Veal

VITELLO RIPIENO

In Italy, stuffed pieces of meat such as this often graced the tables of the landowners, "i padroni," not those of the poorer classes which were responsible for the majority of immigrants. When the Italian-Americans' status changed for the better, and they began to add meat to their diet, they often added dishes which represented efforts to emulate the better classes in Italy. Many immigrants had been employed by landowners and had observed their living style and eating habits which they longed to imitate. Fennel-Stuffed Veal is based on a recipe from a friend's grandmother who had been a cook in a wealthy home in Italy before emigrating to America.

3 fennel bulbs, tops removed
6 tablespoons butter
1 small onion, thinly sliced
¾ cup meat or chicken broth
Salt and freshly ground black pepper
One 4-pound boned and butterflied shoulder of veal

¼ pound thinly sliced prosciutto
1 tablespoon vegetable oil
¾ cup finely chopped carrot
½ cup finely chopped onion
¾ cup dry white wine
1 medium tomato, seeded and finely chopped
3 parsley sprigs
1 bay leaf

1. Trim the fennel, remove the cores, and wash the bulbs in cold water. Cut each bulb into eight wedges.

2. Melt 4 tablespoons butter in a large heavy skillet over medium-low heat. Add the sliced onion and cook until translucent. Add the fennel and toss to coat. Add ¼ cup broth and salt and pepper. Cover the pan and braise until the fennel is tender, 20 to 30 minutes. If any liquid remains, uncover the pan and boil until evaporated. Cool.

3. Set the veal on a work surface with the exterior side down. Season with salt and pepper. Cover with the prosciutto. Spread the fennel mixture over. Starting at the long side, roll the veal up, jelly-roll fashion. Tie with string in several places to secure.

4. Preheat the oven to 350°F. Melt the remaining 2 tablespoons butter with oil in a Dutch oven or casserole over medium heat. Add the veal and brown well on all sides. Remove veal from the pan. Add chopped carrot and onion and cook until lightly browned, 5 minutes. Add the wine, scraping up any browned bits. Boil until the liquid is reduced to 3 tablespoons. Add the tomato and return the veal to the pan. Add the remaining broth, parsley, and bay leaf and bring to a boil. Season with salt and pepper, cover the pan with foil and the lid, and transfer to the oven and bake until the veal is tender, about 1½ hours.

5. Remove the veal from the pan. Let stand 10 minutes. Cut into slices and serve with pan juices. *Serves 8 to 10.*

My Aunt Luisa and helpers at Papa's market.

Nonna's Veal and Peppers

SPEZZATINO DI VITELLO ALLA NONNA

One of my most satisfying food remembrances is the smell of veal and peppers in my grandmother's kitchen. Nonna seldom varied the recipe except to add a cupful of peas when they were fresh. Try her simple version and then the variations which follow.

1 medium onion, sliced
4 tablespoons extra-virgin
    olive oil
2 pounds stewing veal,
    trimmed and cut into
    1-inch cubes
¾ cup dry white wine
2 cups canned tomatoes,
    drained and chopped

Salt and pepper
1½ pounds mixed red and
    green sweet peppers
    (peeled, if desired), seeds
    and ribs removed and cut
    into 1-inch strips

1. Put the onions and olive oil into a large sauté pan and cook over medium heat until the onion is translucent. Dry the veal pieces well with paper toweling and add to the pan, pushing the onions to the side. Do not crowd the pan but cook the veal in batches, removing the browned pieces to a side dish. When all the veal is browned, add the wine to the pan, turn up the heat, and reduce the wine to ¼ cup, scraping the bottom of the pan.

2. Return the veal to the pan. Add the tomatoes, salt, and pepper and bring to a boil. Reduce the heat and cook, covered, over medium heat for 30 minutes. Add the peppers, cover the pan again, and cook 30 or 40 minutes, or until the veal is tender. *Serves 6.*

• • •

Variation: Add 1 cup fresh peas blanched 5 minutes, or 1 cup frozen peas, thawed, during the last 10 minutes of cooking.

• • •

Variation: Cook 2 ounces minced pancetta with the onions and oil. Substitute red wine for the white and add a bay leaf to the stew. Add 2 tablespoons minced parsley for the last 10 minutes of cooking.

Stuffed Veal Bundles

INVOLTINI DI VITELLO

Italians have always prized very young animals for cooking and in America veal became a very popular meat. I remember watching my grandfather cutting up the whole animals in his butcher shop. Many people bought whole legs for roasting and before Papa wrapped the meat he would cut the customer very thin scallops from the top.

1 pound thin veal scallops	1 tablespoon fresh sage, chopped
Salt and freshly ground pepper	1 garlic clove, minced
¼ pound mozzarella cheese, chopped	3 tablespoons extra-virgin olive oil
¼ pound prosciutto, chopped	Flour
2 tablespoons parsley, chopped	½ cup dry Marsala
	½ cup meat broth or water
	2 tablespoons butter

1. Cut the veal into pieces 4 x 4 inches. Pound gently to even out the pieces. Season with salt and pepper.

2. Mix together the mozzarella, prosciutto, parsley, sage, and garlic. Season carefully with salt and pepper. Spread some of the filling over each piece of veal. Roll up, pushing edges in, and tie or secure with toothpicks.

3. Heat the oil in a frying pan large enough to hold the veal in one layer. Pat the veal dry and very lightly dust with flour. Brush off any excess. Brown the bundles on all sides. Add the Marsala and meat broth, bring to a boil, reduce the heat, and simmer until the veal is cooked (about 8 minutes). Remove the veal from the pan and remove the string or toothpicks. Reduce the cooking liquid to ½ cup and swirl in the butter. Pour over the veal. *Serves 6.*

Baked Stuffed Tomatoes

POMODORI RIPIENI

Stuffed vegetables, especially tomatoes and peppers, are very common in Italian-American cooking. For a light lunch or supper serve one of these—or two for heartier appetites. Ground pork or beef can be substituted for the veal.

8 large tomatoes
Salt
2 garlic cloves, minced
½ small onion, minced
¼ cup olive oil
1 ounce dried porcini,
   soaked in ½ cup warm
   water for 30 minutes
¼ pound sweet Italian
   sausage, removed from
   its casing
½ pound ground shoulder
   of veal

½ to 1 cup breadcrumbs
2 teaspoons chopped fresh
   sage or dried brushed
   sage leaves
Salt and pepper
2 tablespoons chopped
   parsley
½ cup grated pecorino
   cheese
7 tablespoons extra-virgin
   olive oil

1. Remove ½-inch slice from the tops of the tomatoes and reserve. Gently squeeze the tomatoes to remove the seeds and juices. Scoop out the pulp and chop. Set aside in a bowl. Salt the insides of the tomatoes and turn upside down on the rack to drain.

2. Gently heat the garlic and onion in ¼ cup olive oil until golden. Drain the mushrooms and reserve the juices. Wash the mushrooms well, discard the tough pieces, and finely chop. Strain the mushroom juices through washed cheesecloth or a coffee filter and reserve. Add the mushrooms to the onions. Sauté 3 minutes. Add the sausage meat and veal and cook just until the color turns. Remove the meats and mushrooms with a slotted spoon and add to the chopped tomato. Discard the fat from the pan and add the reserved mushroom juices to the pan. Reduce to a glaze and add to the tomato-meat mixture. Add the breadcrumbs, seasonings, and cheese.

3. Fill the tomatoes. Brush the baking dish with oil, add the tomatoes, and brush or drizzle the oil over. Bake at 350°F 30 minutes. Add the tomato tops to the pan, turn in the oil, and bake 10

minutes more. Remove the tomatoes from the pan with a slotted spoon. Replace the tops. Reduce the cooking juices to a glaze and pour over the tomatoes. Cool slightly before serving. *Serves 4 to 8.*

· · ·

Variation: The filling may also be used for peppers. Slice the tops from 4 small red peppers. Remove the seeds and ribs from the insides of the peppers and discard. Fill the peppers and bake as above for 35 to 40 minutes, or until the peppers are tender.

Fish in Marinara Sauce

PESCE IN SALSA MARINARA

This basic marinara (sailors') sauce has wine in it to add a bit of acidity for the fish. It is a wonderful way to cook any fish, especially a somewhat bland fish such as haddock or cod. The sauce is quick to make and can have numerous variations, depending on your selection of herbs and the amount of garlic or hot pepper you use.

¼ cup extra-virgin olive oil
1 medium onion, chopped
2 large garlic cloves, finely chopped
2½ pounds fresh tomatoes, peeled, seeded, and chopped, or 2½ pounds drained canned tomatoes, chopped
½ cup dry white or red wine
¼ to ½ teaspoon hot pepper flakes (optional)
Salt
3 tablespoons parsley, chopped
2 tablespoons fresh oregano or marjoram chopped
2 pounds fish fillets

Put the olive oil, onion, and garlic in a frying pan large enough to hold the fish. (The fillets can overlap in the pan.) Cook over medium-low heat until the onion and garlic are golden. Add the tomatoes, wine, hot pepper, and salt. Bring to a boil, reduce the heat, and simmer gently 15 minutes. Stir in the herbs and add the fish fillets. Continue to cook over low heat until the fish is cooked. The time will vary according to the size of the fish. Flounder fillets can take approximately 20 minutes; tautog, 30 minutes. *Serves 6.*

Sweet and Sour Sole Fillets

PICCOLI PESCI IN AGRODOLCE

Southern Italians make this dish with many types of fish, especially sardines and a very small variety of tuna known as "alalonga." Italian-Americans used smelts which were available in place of many small fish which were not caught in New England waters. I have never developed a liking for smelts but if they are a favorite with you, do try this method of preparation which the Italians also used to preserve fish, sealing the fish covered with the sauce in glass jars. It is a delicious way to cook sole fillets, which in America are more often than not actually a mild flounder.

⅓ cup extra-virgin olive oil
1 large red onion
   (½ pound), thinly sliced
½ cup red wine vinegar
½ cup water
1 teaspoon sugar
Salt
3 tablespoons coarsely
   chopped parsley

3 tablespoons raisins
1½ pounds fillet of sole
Olive oil for frying
Flour
3 tablespoons pinoli nuts
   (pine nuts)

1. Put ⅓ cup olive oil and the onion in a small pot and cook until the onion is softened but not browned. Add the vinegar, water, sugar, and ½ teaspoon salt and simmer 30 minutes, or until the liquid is reduced ½ cup. Stir in the parsley and raisins and let sit while cooking the fish.

2. Wash the fish fillets, dry well, and cut lengthwise in half to make narrow strips. Heat the olive oil in a pan to ½ inch depth. Lightly flour the fish, shaking off all excess, and fry a few strips at a time, until lightly browned on each side and cooked through (about 1 minute per side). Drain on paper towels.

3. Place the fish on a noncorrosive platter. Sprinkle on a little salt and the pinoli nuts. Pour on the warm sauce. The fish may be served immediately, or cover with plastic wrap and leave 3 hours or overnight for a marinated version. If refrigerated, return to room temperature before serving. *Serves 6.*

Tuna with Fresh Peas

TONNO CON PISELLI FRESCHI

Italians share a straightforward feeling about how fish should be handled: "Il pesce prima nuotare nell' acqua, poi deve nuotare nell' olio e poi nel vino." "The fish first swims in water and then must swim in oil and then in wine," they say. This simple Neapolitan recipe adds a few extras such as tomato and fresh peas, but basically it puts the fish in oil and then wine. Try using other firm fish steaks such as swordfish or shark.

¼ cup extra-virgin olive oil
1½ pounds tuna, cut into
   6 thin steaks
1 small onion, finely
   chopped
1½ pounds fresh tomatoes,
   peeled, seeded, and cut in
   narrow strips

½ cup dry white wine
Salt and pepper
¼ cup fresh parsley
2 pounds fresh peas
   (unshelled weight), shelled

Heat the olive oil in a heavy sauté pan. Pat the fish dry and sauté quickly on both sides on high heat until not quite cooked through. Remove and keep warm. Add the onion to the pan and cook 3 minutes. Add the tomatoes, wine, salt, pepper, and parsley and continue cooking on high heat 10 minutes. Add the peas and cook until tender (about 5 minutes). Return the fish to the pan to finish cooking, about 5 minutes. *Serves 6.*

Tuna Salad

TONNO IN INSALATA

It is natural to think of a small round can when we hear the words "tuna fish," but this Calabrian recipe for "real tuna salad" can make you toss out the can opener. Serve the fish at room temperature with a green salad or "sott'aceti," vegetables under vinegar.

1 large carrot, in large chunks	Salt
1 large onion, in large chunks	1½ pounds fresh tuna, in one piece (2-inch-thick steak)
1 rib celery with top, in large chunks	¼ cup minced parsley
1 bay leaf	2 garlic cloves, minced
Small bunch of parsley stems	2 to 3 anchovies, mashed, or 1 teaspoon anchovy paste
2 tablespoons white wine vinegar	Juice of 1 lemon
5 whole peppercorns	⅓ cup extra-virgin olive oil

1. Put the carrot, onion, celery, bay, parsley stems, vinegar, peppercorns, and 1 teaspoon salt in 1½ quarts water and bring to a boil. Boil 45 minutes, strain, and let cool.

2. Wash the tuna and remove the skin. Tie a piece of kitchen string around the circumference of the fish to hold it together during cooking.

3. Place the tuna in the cooled vegetable broth. The liquid should cover the fish. If not, choose a smaller pan or add a bit of water. Bring to a boil, reduce the heat immediately, and poach about 12 minutes, or until the fish is cooked. At 12 minutes the tuna will still be pink at the center. Let cool in the liquid 20 minutes.

4. Combine the minced parsley, garlic, and anchovies with lemon juice and olive oil. Add salt as needed. Remove the fish from the liquid and cut into ¼-inch-thick slices. If some of the fish separates into smaller pieces, it's all right. Put the fish on a platter. Whisk the dressing and pour over the fish. Serve immediately or let sit for 2 hours at room temperature or overnight in refrigerator. Serve at room temperature. *Serves 4 to 6.*

• • •

Note: Poaching is cooking without boiling. Too often, especially with fish, the cook assumes that the directions to poach mean to boil and allows the liquid to rumble and roll which toughens and breaks apart the fish. The poaching liquid should not go above 205°F. The fish is cooked when the flesh feels firm and tiny beads of milky collagen can be seen between the fibers. If you wait for it to flake it is too late.

CAPERS

I have taught cooking classes for many years in Rhode Island and I am sure that the most-often-asked question was, "What *is* a caper?" The caper is the bud of a small Mediterranean bush. Left to blossom, it opens into a precious, small white flower. Capers are sold either packed in brine or packed in salt. Both will keep in the refrigerator seemingly forever and should be rinsed and dried before using.

Tuna with Two Capers

TONNO CON DUE CAPPERI

Southern Italians fish for a great deal of tuna off their coastline. Combining it with capers which grow wild is a natural. The idea for deep-frying half the capers was Jody Adams's, who is a chef at Michaela's in Cambridge, a longtime friend, and a very talented cook.

½ cup extra-virgin olive oil
½ cup capers (preferably in salt), rinsed and dried
2 pounds tuna steaks (½ inch thick)

Salt and freshly ground black pepper
2 to 3 tablespoons lemon juice

1. Put the olive oil into a small frying pan and heat until very hot. Toss 6 tablespoons capers into the hot oil—they should sizzle when added. Cook until golden and crisped (about 45 seconds). Drain on a paper towel and set aside.

2. Put 6 tablespoons caper cooking oil into a large frying pan. Dry the fish steaks well. Season very lightly with salt and a good grinding of pepper. Put the fish steaks in hot oil, reduce heat, and cook 5 minutes. Turn the fish carefully and season the second side. Cook about 3 minutes, or until done. Remove to a warm platter and keep warm.

3. Add the remaining capers and 2 tablespoons lemon juice to the pan. Heat and taste for seasonings. Pour the juices over the fish, sprinkle on deep-fried capers, and serve immediately. *Serves 6.*

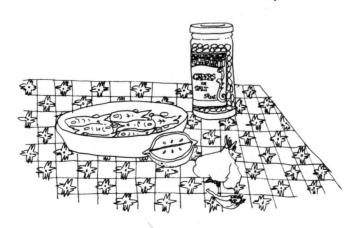

Grilled Tuna Steaks with Piquant Sauce

TONNO GRIGLIATO CON SALSA PICANNTE

This is one of the most delicious ways I know to serve fish. The combination of the piquant sauce with the tuna is extraordinary. Try it with other fish as well. The dish can be served as a main course accompanied by a salad or, instead, the fish may be cut into bite-size pieces and served as an antipasto. In that case, garnish the fish with whole olives and perhaps vegetables preserved under vinegar.

3 pounds fresh tuna steaks, ¾ inch thick
4 tablespoons extra-virgin olive oil

2 tablespoons lemon juice
Pepper
4 to 5 sprigs fresh or dried oregano

———

SALSA PICANTE

½ cup minced flat-leaf parsley
2 tablespoons chopped fresh oregano or 2 teaspoons dried
½ cup extra-virgin olive oil

⅓ cup sliced scallions
1 to 2 tablespoons capers, rinsed
½ cup finely chopped pickled red peppers
¼ cup lemon juice

1. Place the fish in a nonaluminum dish just large enough to hold it in one layer. Season both sides with 4 tablespoons olive oil, 2 tablespoons lemon juice, and a few grindings of black pepper. Place the oregano sprigs on and under the fish and let marinate 30 minutes in the refrigerator.

2. Make the piquant sauce. Put all the ingredients together in a small sauté pan and heat gently for 5 to 7 minutes. The cooking is only to blend the flavors and it is important not to let the heat become so hot as to fry the ingredients. Taste for salt. Set aside at room temperature.

3. Place the fish over hot coals or under a broiler and grill 7 to 8 minutes, turning once and brushing with the marinade. Place the cooked fish on a serving dish and top with the sauce. *Serves 6.*

Tuna Calabrian Style

TONNO CALABRESE

By all means cut down on the amount of hot pepper if this dish proves to be too spicy for you. The same recipe works well for any firm-bodied fish such as swordfish or mako shark.

1 large onion, thinly sliced
¼ cup extra-virgin olive oil
3 garlic cloves, minced
2 cups tomatoes, peeled, seeded, juiced, and chopped
3 anchovies, chopped
1 hot red pepper, seeded and chopped, or ½ teaspoon hot pepper flakes

Salt
2 tablespoons minced parsley
2 pounds fresh tuna, cut in 6 slices
1 tablespoon vinegar

1. Put the onion, olive oil, and garlic in a pan that can go on direct flame and into the oven. Cook until the onion is soft and translucent. Add the tomatoes, anchovies, hot pepper, and salt. Cook 15 minutes. Stir in the chopped parsley.

2. Preheat the oven to 375°F. Put the tuna steaks into the pan with the tomatoes and coat well with the sauce. Drizzle the vinegar on top and bake 20 minutes, or until the fish is cooked. *Serves 6.*

Crisp Fried Salt Cod

BACCALÀ FRITTA

My grandmother always soaked her dried cod in the basement so the odor would not be in the house. When I was very young I was confused as to what kind of "goldfish" had to have its water changed so often in the basement. This is not my grandmother's recipe but one shared with me by Italo Scanga. It's a simple and delicious way to prepare baccalà and when Italo gave it to me he warned me, "And be sure to soak the fish in the basement so the odor won't be in the house!" I have found that not many Americans know about or choose to use dried cod, or if they do, they think it must be boiled to death and smothered in cream sauce.

1 pound dried salt cod, cut
   into 3 x 5-inch pieces
¼ cup extra-virgin olive oil
2 tablespoons vegetable oil
3 garlic cloves, crushed
¼ cup diced prosciutto fat
   or salt pork

All-purpose flour
Freshly ground black pepper
3 tablespoons lemon juice,
   or more to taste
Lemon wedges

1. Soak the salt cod in cold water to cover in a cool place for 24 hours, changing the water at least 6 times to remove the salt. Taste a piece to make sure it is still not too salty and let soak longer if necessary.

2. Drain the fish, rinse well, and pat dry. Put both oils, garlic, and prosciutto fat in a large heavy sauté pan over medium-low heat. Cook until the garlic is golden and the fat is rendered (about 10 minutes). Discard the garlic and the unmelted fat. Increase the heat to medium-high. Mix together the flour and enough pepper to season well on a plate. Coat the fish lightly on all sides with flour, add to the hot fat, and fry, turning once, until golden and cooked through (12 to 15 minutes). Transfer to a heated platter, discard all but ¼ cup drippings, and stir lemon juice into the pan. Pour the pan juices over the fish and garnish with lemon wedges. *Serves 4.*

MEMORIES

"Every day everything was cooked fresh."

Fish was mainstay when I was a kid. One thing we really ate a lot of was squid. Squid, whiting, shellfish of different kinds. Mostly blood-less fish. I remember sometimes in the winter months my father used to take mackerel and marinade it with vinegar and a little bit of garlic, parsley, salt and pepper—no oil, because mackerel is rich, very rich. He would just open them up in half and put them on a hand grill, open the old wood stove, and broil them right over the hot coals. It was delicious.

I hadn't seen octopus from Italy here. They used to come from Spain and Portugal, frozen. When you got them, you thawed them out and they were quite big so as a result they were a little tough. In order to tenderize them a little bit, we had a piece of bluestone, maybe about twelve or fifteen inches square, and my father would lay it down and take the octopus and just beat it on the stone to tenderize it. Then when he cut it in pieces, and fried it or put it in a tomato sauce to serve with pasta, it would be tender.

I started working in meat markets when I was about twelve. In those days they used to sell just meat. No groceries or anything like that. A meat market was just a meat market. For sausage, you bought pork butts. The old-timers in the old days in the winter time used to buy pork butts, take them and cut them by hand into small pieces—it makes a difference when you bite into the piece of meat. Now, we take it and grind it in a coarse cutter. In the old days, they would sit around the kitchen table, kids and all, and cut the pieces very, very small. After it was cut, they would season it and would stuff the sausage by hand with a small funnel. Then they would take it, and dry it and keep it for a few months. The temperature had to be just right. The sausage would be put in the hallway where it was just above freezing. If it was too cold, the water particles in the meat would freeze and spoil once it started to thaw. So, the sausage had to dry gradually to let the moisture come out of the meat. The trick

Joe DiGiglio and his brother-in-law, Henry Ferrara, in their meat-aging room.

was to get the water out slowly, so it was just dripping a little bit and would finally reach a point where the moisture was gone and the sausage would dry up. Then the sausages would be packed in jars and filled with oil, right up to the top, sealed and kept.

In the early fall, we used to go down to the farmer's market and buy a couple of bushels of peppers and some tomatoes, and we would preserve some of this. My father had a little barrel of vinegar, and he would preserve the peppers whole in the vinegar. After a number of days, he would take them out, rinse them off in a little cold water, and cut them in quarters, and put a little olive oil on them. They were delicious.

One of the most popular pastas in the Bari region, where my parents came from, was the "orecchiette," which means "little ears." My mother used to make them by hand, every Sunday without fail. She would cook them with broccoli rabe. She'd steam the rabe and meantime be cooking the pasta. Then she'd put everything together, rabe and pasta, and then put olive oil and crushed black pepper and salt to taste—and that would be all.

Sometimes my mother would cook "orecchiette" with stuffed squid. She would take a small squid and take the pocket of the squid without cutting it, and then make a stuffing with egg, bread crumb, the little tentacles, parsley, and a little garlic, and stuff each little squid. Then she would sew the top of the squid so that the stuffing wouldn't fall out, and cook it in a sauce.

My mother would also make "orecchiette" with whole wheat flour, just for a change. But most of the time, it was made with regular semolina, and I remember for each pound of semolina she would put in one egg and a little bit of flour and some water. She'd mix this dough up and then take a little piece in her hand and roll it out. She'd keep rolling and rolling until she had a dowel about the size of a finger. Then she had a little knife she used to use just for making "orecchiette" because it was very dull and she could cut a little piece off and take it and roll it over her thumb and then just flip it. She would keep spreading them out so that they would dry. She was very fast at it. Very, very fast.

In those days, living in the tenement, your kitchen was your dining room. Every day everything was cooked fresh. We had no freezers. We'd keep things in the hallway because there was no heat in the hallway, but it was just warm enough to keep things so that they wouldn't freeze.

People used to shop daily. Monday mornings, I remember the first thing we'd do when we went in to the market was cut meat bones because on Monday people served soup and they wanted the meat bones to make soup. Tuesday, maybe a little hamburger to make perhaps a little quick sauce. In the middle of the week maybe they would like a little veal or lamb. Their main shopping was done on a Friday or Saturday, so everything would be all gone over the weekend. On Monday, it would start all over again.

JOSEPH DI GIGLIO
Joe's Quality Market
Family from village of Molfetta
near Bari in Apulia

Baccalà with Potatoes and Green Olives

BACCALÀ CON PATATE E OLIVE VERDI

This typical Calabrian stew was often part of the Christmas Eve fish meal. Be careful with salt since the cod and the olives are both salty.

1 pound dried salt cod, cut into 3-inch pieces
½ cup olive oil
2 large onions, coarsely cut
3 pounds all-purpose potatoes, peeled and cut in ¼-inch wedges

Salt, if desired, and pepper
1 tablespoon fresh thyme or 1 teaspoon dried
4 sprigs fresh parsley
1 cup Sicilian green olives, pitted and sliced

1. Soak the salt cod in cold water to cover in a cool place 24 hours, changing the water at least 6 times to remove the salt. Taste a piece to make sure it is still not too salty and leave it soaking longer if necessary.

2. Put the oil and onions in a large soup pot and cook until the onions are softened. Add the potatoes and cook, turning carefully, until lightly colored. Add 3 cups water to the pan and bring to a boil. Reduce the heat, cover the pan, and cook 5 minutes. Uncover the pan, add salt if desired, pepper, thyme, parsley, and olives to the potatoes and stir gently. Lay the pieces of cod on top of the potatoes, cover the pan, and cook over low heat 30 minutes, or until the fish is cooked. Carefully turn the cod halfway through cooking. Serve from the pot. *Serves 4 to 6.*

. . .

Note: Many recipes for this dish call for the cod to first be fried. I like it both ways. Fry the cod in the pan with the onions after the onions have softened. Remove it and return it to the pot as in step 2. It will take less time to cook.

Peppers, Potatoes, and Eggs

PEPERONI, PATATE, E UOVA

Since my grandmother always prepared her major meal at noon, supper dishes were simple. It was often the time she would work her magic with eggs. This satisfying scrambled egg recipe is exactly as I have known it since I was a child and the most I ever do to change it is occasionally fry a small chopped onion in the oil before adding the potatoes.

⅓ cup extra-virgin
    olive oil
2 boiling potatoes,
    peeled and cut in
    1-inch chunks
Salt and pepper
2 large peppers, red,
    green, or yellow
    or a combination
    (peeled, if desired),
    stems and ribs
    removed and cut in
    1½-inch chunks
4 eggs

1. Heat the oil in a sauté pan over medium-low heat. Add the potatoes and toss to coat. Season with salt and pepper, cover the pan, and cook 15 minutes. The potatoes should cook gently so they become tender and lightly golden without forming a hard crust. Add the peppers to the pan, salt lightly, and cook, covered, 15 minutes. Uncover the pan and cook until completely tender (about 20 minutes). The peppers should be completely tender for this dish.

2. Beat the eggs together with salt and pepper. Add the beaten eggs to the vegetables over low heat, and stir with a wooden spoon, as with scrambled eggs, until set. *Serves 2.*

Eggs in Purgatory

UOVA IN PURGATORIO

Being in purgatory is not so bad, that is, so hot, as being "alla diavolo" or like the devil. Hence these eggs are seasoned with only a small amount of hot pepper. You can make them hotter or eliminate the pepper altogether. Choose the Parmesan for a milder flavor, the pecorino for a more robust result. You may use any tomato sauce on hand for cooking the eggs.

3 tablespoons extra-virgin olive oil
½ small onion, minced
3 cups drained canned tomatoes, finely chopped
Salt
¼ teaspoon hot pepper flakes
2 tablespoons snipped basil leaves

2 tablespoons minced fresh parsley
4 large eggs
¼ cup freshly grated pecorino or Parmesan cheese
Four ⅓-inch-thick Italian toasts, lightly brushed with olive oil
(page 7)

1. Put the oil and onion in a 10-inch sauté pan and cook over medium-low heat until the onion is softened but not browned. Add the tomatoes to the pan and bring to a simmer. Add the salt and hot pepper and cook 20 minutes. Stir in the herbs and cook 10 minutes, or until the tomatoes are thick enough to hold their shape on a spoon.

2. Make 4 indentations in the tomatoes with the back of a wooden spoon. Carefully break the eggs into the indentations. Season each egg, cover the pan, and continue to simmer gently until the eggs are cooked (about 6 minutes). Sprinkle with Parmesan cheese.

3. Place 2 slices of toast in each soup dish. Gently spoon half the eggs and sauce over the toast in each plate and serve immediately. *Serves 2.*

EGGS

Nonna never bought her eggs in cartons. She bought them loose from "the chicken man" and I always thought that they were her special secret. Those eggs, collected from baskets that lined the wall in a small, sawdusty shop near her home, were her promise of something light for supper.

Nonna's light suppers were wonderful examples of the versatility of eggs in Italian cooking. Using the staples of her kitchen or leftovers from another meal and her "special eggs," my grandmother created dishes that remain among my most favorite. With a little marinara sauce, some Parmesan cheese, and Italian toast, Nonna made Eggs in Purgatory (page 199). Using a bit of chicken broth, she would cook tiny "pastine" and then poach eggs in the mixture. Her scrambled eggs with peppers and potatoes (page 198) barely made it from the stove to the table before we had finished the dish. And what wonders she created with frittatas! Sometimes they were simple ones with onions and cheese (Farmer's Frittata, opposite page) cooked quickly on top of the stove. Other times she made them thick with fillings and baked them in the oven Baked Spaghetti Frittata, page 205).

I know now that Nonna's chicken-man eggs were not the secret. Traveling so often to Italy and talking with other Italian-Americans, I realize that the wonder is in the Italian imagination and the ability to make so much from so little.

Farmer's Frittata with Onion and Cheese

FRITTATA CONTADINA CON CIPOLLE E FORMAGGIO

This Neapolitan recipe is one of my favorite frittatas. It can be served hot for lunch or supper and is equally good at room temperature cut into wedges for an antipasto. We also love to eat this tucked inside crusty rolls for a very satisfying sandwich. If eight eggs are too many for you to cook at once, cook half the recipe at a time in a smaller sauté pan.

1 cup thinly sliced red onion
4 tablespoons extra-virgin
    olive oil
Salt and pepper
8 eggs

¼ pound scamorza or
    mozzarella cheese, finely
    chopped
1 tablespoon snipped basil

1. Put the onion and 1 tablespoon olive oil in a sauté pan over very gentle heat. Season with salt and pepper and cook until completely softened but not browned (about 15 minutes). Let cool completely.

2. Beat the eggs with salt and pepper. Stir in the cheese, cooled onion, and basil. Heat the remaining 3 tablespoons oil in a 12-inch skillet. When the oil is hot pour the eggs into the pan and immediately begin to swirl with the flat side of a fork, continually breaking the bottom to allow the uncooked egg to run through. When the eggs are soft set on top and the bottom is lightly browned, place a serving-size plate or a flat cookie sheet over the pan and reverse the frittata onto it. Tap the sauté pan firmly to release the eggs. Slide the frittata back into the sauté pan to brown the second side. Slide onto a serving platter. *Serves 4 to 6.*

Celery Frittata with Vinegar

FRITTATA CON SEDANO ED ACETO

This frittata recipe can be used for a light lunch dish or for an antipasto. To serve as an appetizer, let cool to room temperature, cut it into pie-shaped wedges, and serve it either on plates or pass it with napkins.

2½ cups celery, with tops,
   cut in ½-inch pieces
4 eggs
Salt and pepper
2 tablespoons chopped fresh
   lovage (optional)
3 tablespoons extra-virgin
   olive oil
1 large garlic clove crushed
   and peeled
2 tablespoons red wine
   vinegar

1. Blanch the celery in a large pot of boiling salted water 5 minutes, or until tender. Drain, plunge into ice water, drain, and dry.
2. Beat the eggs with salt and pepper. Stir in the celery and lovage. Heat the oil and garlic in a 10-inch omelet or frying pan. When the garlic is well browned, remove with a slotted spoon and add the eggs to the pan. Swirl the eggs with the flat side of a fork, continually breaking the bottom to allow the eggs to run through. When the eggs are softly set and bottom is golden, put a plate over the pan and turn the frittata onto the plate. Slide the frittata back into the pan to cook to brown the underside. Slide onto a serving plate, sprinkle with vinegar, and serve. *Serves 2 to 4.*

Vermicelli Frittata with Anchovies

FRITTATA DI VERMICELLI CON ACCIUGHE

Simplicity itself, this light supper dish may easily become a routine meal for the anchovy lover. Be careful when adding salt since the anchovies already add saltiness. The cheese is optional since many people are purists about not combining fish with cheese. I think it works well in this particular recipe.

¼ pound vermicelli	6 eggs
1 large garlic clove, cut in half	Salt and pepper
¼ cup extra-virgin olive oil	¼ cup grated pecorino cheese (optional)
8 anchovies	

1. Cook the vermicelli in 5 quarts rapidly boiling salted water until slightly firmer than al dente. Drain.

2. Just before draining the pasta, heat the garlic in the olive oil in a frying pan until the garlic is browned. Discard the garlic. Add the drained spaghetti immediately to the hot oil, toss to coat, and cook 5 minutes.

3. Mash 4 anchovies in a bowl. Add the eggs and beat together until combined. Season with salt and pepper. Pour the eggs into the spaghetti and cook until one side is set. Invert onto a plate or a pan lid and slide back into the pan to cook the second side. While the second side is setting, sprinkle with the cheese, if using. Slide out onto a plate and place the remaining 4 anchovies in a spokelike design on top. *Serves 4.*

• • •

Variation: In place of the anchovies, add ¼ cup grated Parmesan cheese and ¼ cup torn basil leaves. Cook in 5 tablespoons butter in place of the olive oil.

Neapolitan Spaghetti Frittata

FRITTATA DI SPAGHETTI NAPOLITANA

Eating leftover spaghetti with tomato sauce from the refrigerator is a secret few people are probably willing to share. I've seen it often enough, however, to know that it is by no means unusual. Neapolitans have an even more savory idea. They turn yesterday's pasta into a frittata. This should be particularly inviting to those people who insist that leftover spaghetti is best for breakfast!

3 cups cooked spaghetti
with tomato sauce
4 eggs, lightly beaten
⅓ cup grated Parmesan or
pecorino cheese

3 tablespoons extra-virgin
olive oil
Salt and pepper

1. Put the spaghetti into a bowl. Add the beaten eggs and cheese, season with salt and pepper, and mix together.
2. Heat the oil in a frying pan. Add the spaghetti to the hot pan and cook over medium-low heat, turning once until set on both sides, about 15 minutes. *Serves 4 to 6.*

Baked Spaghetti Frittata

FRITTATA DI SPAGHETTI AL FORNO

Most spaghetti frittatas, such as the preceding ones, are cooked on top of the stove. This oven method, which I learned from Michi Ambrosi in Naples, works particularly well when the frittata has many fillings.

5 tablespoons olive oil	6 large eggs, beaten
2 garlic cloves, smashed and peeled	2 tablespoons chopped parsley
4 ounces black olives (Gaeta), pitted, sliced	Salt and pepper
1 tablespoon capers, rinsed	2 tablespoons butter for preparing the baking pan
½ pound spaghetti	Dry breadcrumbs
4 ounces canned tuna, drained	

1. Heat 3 tablespoons oil with the garlic until the garlic turns deep brown. Discard the garlic and add the olives and capers to the pan. Heat over low heat 3 minutes and set aside.

2. Cook the spaghetti in 5 quarts rapidly boiling salted water until slightly undercooked—more al dente than usual since it will cook again. Drain and toss with the prepared olives and capers. Cool slightly and add the tuna, eggs, parsley, and salt and pepper.

3. Preheat the oven to 375°F. Butter a 12-inch round baking dish ("ruota") and coat with the breadcrumbs. Fill with the spaghetti, even off the top, drizzle with the remaining oil, and bake 25 to 30 minutes, until the frittata holds its shape and is golden and the spaghetti is cooked. Cool briefly in the pan and then turn out. *Serves 6 to 8.*

Chapter Five

VEGETABLES

In Italy and America, the southern Italians wanted their food to be as fresh as possible. In the case of vegetables, which played such an important role in their diet, that meant growing them themselves. In the "old country," rich and poor alike cultivated gardens at least large enough to feed their own family and usually productive enough to sell or trade crops for other necessary supplies.

It was only natural, therefore, that the immigrants should plant gardens in their new country. Whether it was a tiny patch of front yard, a flower box on a rooftop, or a shared plot of land, the old-timers cultivated it to provide food for their families. Italian-Americans in the northeastern United States found that many of their native fruits and vegetables could be successfully grown. In some cases it required unusual gardening skills such as burying fragile trees for the winter months, but the hardy southern farmer had spent many years fighting the elements in his native land and learned to adapt to the new climate. What he could not grow—artichokes, olives, walnuts, for example—were eventually shipped in from California.

In the early days, however, they had to rely on what they could grow in their garden or buy at the local market. This meant some adjustments to their diets because the growing season of the vegetables they used most was considerably shorter in the United States than it had been in Italy. Tomatoes, zucchini, peppers, and eggplants grew in Italy almost year-round. In America they were summer crops. New Englanders relied on root vegetables—parsnips, turnips, and carrots—for the winter months, but in Italy those were feed for the pigs and the immigrants refused to eat them. Neapolitans would occasionally use carrots in soup or give raw ones to their children, but that was it for root vegetables.

To prepare for the long New England winters, the immigrants put up foods. In late summer and early fall, entire families of Italian-Americans would be involved in the process of preserving the garden's bounty. They used a number of methods—traditional canning process, under salt, under oil, in brine. Although the early Italians were comfortable with home canning, they believed that the commercial methods removed all the taste and nutrition. Not only did they not buy canned goods, they often discarded ones that were left by social workers.

At one time or another, the immigrants did have to rely on vendors to provide some of their produce. It was quite common for vegetable shops and pushcarts to display signs that read THINGS FROM MY OWN FARM, thus assuring the buyer that he was getting the best. Most people bought from their own "paesan" and had no reason to doubt this, but when they went to a different cart or to an American market, they sniffed and pinched suspiciously. Eventually signs that read PLEASE DO NOT TOUCH or DON'T PINCH THE PEACHES appeared on top of produce to protect it from the discriminating Italian shopper.

With all this emphasis on vegetables, one would guess that all entrées were served with a riot of side dishes. Quite the contrary, meat or fish were often served alone or with one simple salad or vegetable. The profusion of vegetables showed up as antipasti, soups, pastas, and quite often as meals in themselves.

Calabrian Artichokes in a Pan

CARCIOFI IN TEGAME CALABRESE

This same recipe is used in Calabria to sauce pasta, in which case the amount of olive oil should be increased to ½ cup and the artichokes tossed with 1 pound cooked penne or similar pasta and sprinkled with pecorino cheese. It is not unusual to find that a vegetable dish is often a sauce for pasta. In Italy, southern Italians relied heavily on these two sources for their evening meal. Combining them was natural.

8 small artichokes
Juice of 1 or more lemons
¼ cup extra-virgin olive oil
2 garlic cloves, coarsely
  chopped
2 small hot peppers,
  chopped, or 1 teaspoon
  hot pepper flakes

¾ cup dry white wine
Salt
¼ cup basil leaves

1. Using a large stainless steel knife, cut off the artichoke stems at the base; rub the cut area with the lemon half to prevent discoloration. Bend back and pull off all the outer green leaves until only the pale yellow-green leaves remain. Cut off and discard the top third of the artichoke. With a small stainless steel knife, pare around the base to remove any tough green patches; rub with lemon. Cut lengthwise into eighths, remove the chokes (fuzzy core), and drop the pieces into a bowl of cold water acidulated with the lemon juice.

2. Heat the oil in a nonaluminum frying pan with the garlic and hot peppers until the garlic is golden. Do not let the garlic brown. Drain and dry the artichoke hearts. Add them to the oil and sauté until golden brown. Add the white wine and reduce to 6 tablespoons. Reduce the heat, add salt, and cook 25 to 30 minutes, or until cooked. Add the basil and additional lemon juice if desired. *Serves 6 to 8.*

Artichoke Hearts with Fennel

CARCIOFI CON FINOCCHIO

This is a rather sophisticated artichoke treatment for southern Italian home cooking. The artichoke hearts do require a little extra work, but the recipe is well worth the effort and the dish can be prepared ahead and reheated. Complete it through step 4 and then heat before serving and add cheese. The trimming is necessary to render the entire artichoke edible. You can make this recipe with two packages of defrosted artichoke hearts. The flavor is not the same but the results are equally delicious.

4 medium artichokes	1 pound small mushrooms,
½ lemon	wiped clean and halved
1 tablespoon fresh lemon	Salt and pepper
juice	¼ cup dry white wine
2 medium fennel bulbs,	¼ cup freshly grated
tops removed	pecorino or Parmesan
¼ cup extra-virgin olive oil	cheese

1. Using a large stainless steel knife, cut off the artichoke stems at the base; rub the cut area with the lemon half to prevent discoloration. Bend back and pull off all the outer green leaves until only the pale yellow-green leaves remain. Cut off and discard the top third of the artichoke. With a small stainless steel knife, pare around the base to remove any tough green patches; rub with the lemon. Cut lengthwise into eighths, remove the chokes (fuzzy core), and drop the pieces into a bowl of cold water acidulated with the lemon juice.

2. Trim the fennel, discarding the tough outer layer. Slice each bulb crosswise into 1-inch-wide strips and discard the tough inner core. Place in a bowl of cold water 20 minutes to wash. Drain and pat dry.

3. In a large skillet, heat the oil. Add the mushrooms and sauté over moderately high heat, tossing frequently, until lightly colored, 3 to 4 minutes. Season with salt and pepper and cook 2 minutes longer, or until the juices run. Drain the artichokes and add them to the mushrooms. Add the fennel and toss to mix.

4. Add the white wine and boil until the liquid is reduced to 2 tablespoons. Lay a sheet of waxed paper on top of the vegetables.

Cover the pan, reduce the heat to low, and cook until the vegetables are tender, 35 to 40 minutes.

5. Remove the lid and the waxed paper. Quickly boil away any excess liquid. Add the cheese and serve hot. *Serves 6.*

. . .

Note: Mushrooms are like little sponges and should simply be wiped clean since washing will cause them to absorb water that will leave them swimming while cooking. If they are extremely dirty, rinse them quickly in cold water with a few tablespoons of flour or corn-starch beaten in. This will reduce any water absorption.

Deviled White Beans with Tomatoes

CANNELLINI AL DIAVOLO

The "deviled" is of course the hot pepper which you can vary according to your own taste. This is a rather hearty side dish and is best used alongside a simple main course such as grilled meat. It is a great buffet dish. Double the recipe for a crowd.

¼ cup extra-virgin olive oil
1 small onion, chopped
4 small garlic cloves, minced
¼ pound prosciutto, diced
1 teaspoon crushed hot pepper flakes
1 pound Swiss chard, washed, stems discarded, coarsely chopped

Salt
2 cups cooked or canned cannellini beans, drained
4 small tomatoes (about 1 pound), peeled, cored, and quartered
¼ cup minced parsley

1. Put the oil, onion, garlic, and prosciutto in a large frying pan. Cook until the onion is translucent (3 to 5 minutes). Add the hot pepper and cook 1 minute.

2. Add the Swiss chard to the pan, salt, and toss over high heat until wilted. Add the beans, tomatoes, and parsley. Cover the pan and cook 5 minutes. Remove the cover and cook 5 to 8 minutes, or until the chard is tender and the flavors have blended. *Serves 6 to 8.*

URBAN LIFE

Although the majority of immigrants had led rural lives in Italy, it was in American cities, not the country, that they settled. In many cases they came to make money in the industrial work force so they could return to the old country, buy a piece of land, and emulate the lives of their former landowner bosses. Instead, most of these temporary moves became permanent and farmers found themselves living urban lives. To be more exact, they attempted to live rural lives in the cities. Gardens and grapevines, tucked behind tenement buildings, shared space with chickens, rabbits, and goats. In some cases, when zoning regulations prohibited livestock, people would attempt to hide a few animals in their cellars. Eventually, some of these reluctant city dwellers bought land in the New England or East Coast countryside and realized their dreams of being landowners. In most instances, however, parents and their city-born children came to prefer an urban life.

A favorite pastime—meeting on "The Hill."

Turnip Greens

BROCCOLI DI RAPE

"Broccoli di rape," or "broccoli rabe," or sometimes simply "rabe" are all names by which southern Italians call turnip tops—the leafy part of the plant with tiny broccoli buds that grows above the ground. In southern Italy, people grew turnips for feed for the animals and ate the tops themselves. In New England, the immigrants discovered that turnips were a winter staple and well-meaning social workers encouraged the Italians to add them to their diet. To the Italians, however, turnips were pig food and they wouldn't eat them. They did continue to grow them for their tops and gradually other people saw the delicious wisdom of this so that today "rabe" is available in many markets.

2 pounds broccoli di rape
¼ cup olive oil
2 to 4 garlic cloves, minced,
  according to taste

Salt and pepper
2 teaspoons lemon juice,
  or more to taste

1. Wash the broccoli di rape and remove any tough outer leaves. With a paring knife, peel the stems to remove the strings in the same way you would remove strings from celery. Cut into 3-inch pieces. Place in a large pot of boiling water and blanch 2 minutes. Drain and refresh under cold water; pat dry.

2. Heat the oil and garlic. Do not let the garlic brown. Add the broccoli di rape, salt, and pepper. Cook until tender, 15 to 20 minutes. Sprinkle with lemon juice and serve. *Serves 6.*

Piquant Broccoli di Rabe (Rape)

BROCCOLI DI RABE PICCANTE

This recipe for broccoli di rape is delicious as well as versatile. Toss it with hot macaroni or use it to fill calzone or top pizza or crostini.

2 pounds broccoli di rape	3 garlic cloves, minced

2 small hot red peppers
    or 1 teaspoon hot
    pepper flakes
	¼ cup extra-virgin olive oil

	½ cup prosciutto meat, diced
⅓ cup prosciutto fat, minced	Salt

1. Wash the broccoli di rape and remove any tough outer leaves. With a paring knife, peel the stems to remove the strings in the same way you would remove strings from celery. Cut into 3-inch pieces. Place in a large pot of boiling water and blanch 2 minutes. Drain and refresh under cold water; pat dry.

2. Cut the hot red peppers in half and working under cold running water, remove the seeds and ribs and cut into thin slices.

3. Cook the prosciutto fat in olive oil slowly until the fat is rendered and the pieces are browned and crisp. Remove the pieces with a slotted spoon and discard. Cook the garlic in the oil and rendered fat until golden. Add the broccoli di rape, prosciutto meat, hot pepper, and salt to the pan and cook over medium-high heat. Toss together well, cover, and cook until the greens are tender (15 to 20 minutes). Add a few tablespoons warm water if the greens begin to stick. Serve warm or at room temperature with additional olive oil and lemon juice if desired. *Serves 6.*

Broccoli with Anchovies

BROCCOLI CON LE ACCIUGHE

This Neapolitan recipe for broccoli may also be used for broccoli rabe. Use 2 pounds rabe and prepare according to the directions for "Broccoli di Rape" (page 213). If there are any leftovers—and there seldom are—I toss them into spaghetti.

2 large heads broccoli,
    about 3 pounds
Salt
½ cup extra-virgin olive oil
5 garlic cloves, minced

10 anchovy fillets, rinsed,
    minced
½ teaspoon hot pepper
    flakes

1. Trim the broccoli. Cut off the flowerets, at about 1 inch, from the stems. Peel the stems and cut into 1-inch pieces. Drop both flowerets and stems into boiling salted water and cook until just tender. Plunge into ice water, drain, and dry well.

2. Put the olive oil and garlic into a sauté pan large enough to hold the broccoli. Cook over low heat until the garlic is golden, about 3 minutes. Add the anchovies and hot pepper to the pan and mash completely with the back of a wooden spoon. Add the broccoli to the pan and toss to heat completely. Taste for salt and serve. *Serves 6 to 8.*

Cabbage with Little Sauce

CAVOLI CON SALSINA

This is another of Italo Scanga's recipes that demonstrate how robust the cooking of Calabria can be. I seem to remember that Italo was a little more generous with the hot pepper and you can be too if you like a little fire in your life! If you can find an Italian butcher, most likely he will be happy to sell you a prosciutto bone, which is the most economical way to get prosciutto fat and meat. The bone will keep for several days in the refrigerator or you can cut off pieces and bag them for the freezer.

4 tablespoons extra-virgin
    olive oil
1 medium onion, coarsely
    chopped

1 large head savoy cabbage,
    cut in small wedges
1 cup water
Salt and pepper

―――――――

SALSINA

½ cup diced prosciutto fat
2 tablespoons extra-virgin
    olive oil
¾ cup prosciutto meat, cut
    in ½-inch pieces
2 tablespoons minced fresh
    oregano or 2 teaspoons
    dried
¼ cup chopped parsley

½ jalapeño or other hot
    pepper, seeded and thinly
    sliced, or ½ teaspoon
    crushed dried hot pepper
½ cup dry white wine
1 cup drained canned
    tomatoes, pureed
Salt

1. Heat the olive oil and onion in a large sauté pan and cook over medium heat until the onion is translucent. Add the cabbage and toss to coat. Add the water, salt, and pepper and bring to a boil. Reduce the heat and cook until the cabbage is tender (20 to 30 minutes). Add more water if the cabbage begins to stick.

2. For the sauce, sauté the prosciutto fat in oil over low heat until the fat is rendered (about 15 minutes). Remove and discard unrendered pieces. Add the remaining ingredients to the pan and sauté until the oil separates (about 30 minutes).

3. When the cabbage is cooked, drain off excess liquid or reduce it over high heat. Pour hot sauce over the cabbage, toss together, and serve. *Serves 6.*

Spicy Cabbage and Beans

CAVOLO E FAGIOLI PICCANTI

Cabbage and beans was very often dinner for the poor farmers of Basilicata. It is a delicious accompaniment to grilled Italian sausages.

3 tablespoons extra-virgin olive oil

4 ounces prosciutto, cut in thin strips ½ inch x 1 inch

3 large garlic cloves, minced

1 small onion, chopped

½ teaspoon hot pepper flakes

1½ pounds savoy cabbage, shredded

2 tablespoons tomato paste

1 cup water

2 cups cooked cannellini beans (white beans)

⅓ cup chopped parsley

Salt if needed

1. Place the olive oil, prosciutto, garlic, and onion in a large sauté pan and cook over medium heat until the onion is translucent. Add the pepper flakes and stir together 30 seconds. Add the cabbage to the pan and mix together well. Blend the tomato paste into the water and add to the cabbage. Cover the pan and cook over medium heat 20 minutes.

2. Add the beans and ¼ cup parsley to the pan, cover again and cook 5 minutes, or until the cabbage is tender and the beans are heated through. If any liquid remains in the pan, turn the heat to high to reduce. Taste for salt and stir in the remaining parsley. *Serves 6.*

Eggplant Parmesan

PARMIGIANA DE MELANZANE

There is probably no dish as sublime as eggplant Parmesan and yet there is probably no dish more often mishandled. I have never seen a recipe in Italian that calls for a breadcrumb coating and yet almost all Italian-American restaurants prepare it that way. Furthermore, the eggplant is often cut so thick that it remains raw in the center, which isn't immediately noticeable because the diner has to first wade through a heavy layer of cheese and sauce to find the vegetable. Nonna's method for cooking eggplant Parmesan results in a delicate —yes, ethereal—affair that balances all the flavors. Her initial secret is to cut the eggplant as thin as possible. A light hand with both the sauce and the cheese results in a layered dish that literally melts in your mouth. Eggplant Parmesan is often served as a main course.

1 medium eggplant, 1¼ pounds	1½ cups tomato sauce (page 82 or pages 79–81) (see note)
Salt and pepper	
4 large eggs	2 tablespoons Parmesan cheese
Olive oil for frying	

1. Peel the eggplant and cut it into paper-thin slices. Place in a colander, salting each layer, and place a plate and weight on top. Let sit at least 1 hour to draw out the water. Dry with paper towels and squeeze gently but firmly with your hands to remove all excess liquid.

2. Beat the eggs, salt, and pepper together in a pie pan. Pour a little over ¼ inch oil into a flat-bottomed 10- or 12-inch frying pan. Heat the oil to 375°F. Working with a few slices at a time, dip the eggplant into the egg, hold up to drain off excess egg, and slide into the hot oil. Cook a few seconds on each side, removing as soon as slightly golden. Drain on paper towels or brown paper bags.

3. Layer the cooked eggplant and tomato sauce into an oven-proof shallow pan or dish. Sprinkle the cheese over the top layer and bake in a 400°F oven 10 minutes. Serve hot or at room temperature. *Serves 6 to 8.*

· · ·

Note: Southern Italians in Italy always made eggplant Parmesan with a marinara sauce because ragu was only made in the winter when eggplants were not in season. In the United States, the Italians began to make ragu almost year-round and use it with vegetables in a way they hadn't in the "old country."

BACKYARD

When I picture my grandparents' house, which is no longer standing, I think first of the backyard. The small garden was crammed full of vegetables and grape-vines which climbed up and over a pergola providing shelter from summer rains. And that was the way it was all along the street behind those three-story city houses. The old-timers were often out under those vine-covered arbors doing household chores, putting up foods, or visiting "paesani." It brought back something of their life in Italy.

Stuffed Escarole

SCAROLA RIPIENA

If you grow your own escarole, this Neapolitan recipe is a delightful reason to plant a large crop and harvest it while the heads are still small and tender. If you rely on the supermarket, it will probably be necessary to trim away a great many of the outer leaves. Save them to use in salad, escarole soup, or calzone. You could also make this with endive.

6 small heads escarole, about ¼ pound each
⅓ pound black Gaeta olives, pitted
1 generous tablespoon capers, rinsed
3 anchovy fillets, rinsed
2 garlic cloves, minced

½ cup pinoli nuts (pine nuts)
½ cup raisins, soaked in tepid water for 30 minutes and drained
⅓ cup extra-virgin olive oil
Salt and pepper
¼ cup vegetable broth or water

1. Preheat the oven to 400°F.
2. Trim the escarole, leaving the root end intact, and blanch in boiling salted water 5 minutes, or until just tender enough to spread the leaves. Plunge into ice water to stop cooking. Drain in a colander, squeeze gently to remove excess water, and dry.
3. Mince the olives, capers, anchovies, and garlic together. Put into a bowl and stir in the pinoli nuts and raisins. Add 2 tablespoons olive oil or enough to moisten the filling and season carefully with salt and pepper.
4. Spread out the leaves of escarole. Fill the center with about ¼ cup filling. Close and reshape the head of escarole. Put the remaining oil into a baking dish large enough to hold the vegetable in one layer. As each is put in the dish, turn it to coat completely with the oil. Pour ¼ cup vegetable broth or water into the pan, cover, and bake 25 minutes, or until tender. If any water remains, remove the escarole; boil to a glaze, then pour over the vegetables. *Serves 6.*

Baked Fennel with Parmesan Cheese

GRATIN DI FINOCCHI AL PARMIGIANO

It is not unusual in southern Italy to find fresh, crisp bulbs of fennel tucked into a fruit bowl at the end of a meal. It's a surprisingly sweet finale that I wish we encountered here. More commonly, this winter vegetable is found either raw in salads or cooked for soups or "contorni."

6 small fennel bulbs, about 3 pounds	Salt and pepper
4 tablespoons unsalted butter	⅓ cup hot chicken broth
	¼ cup freshly grated Parmesan cheese

1. Remove the fennel tops. Trim away the outer tough layer and the base of the bulb. Quarter the bulbs and put them in a large bowl of cold water to soak 20 minutes. Drain and place the fennel in a large pot of boiling salted water to blanch 5 minutes. Drain and rinse in cold water. Squeeze pieces in a towel to dry well.

2. Preheat the oven to 350°F. Using 1 tablespoon butter, butter the bottom and sides of a low-sided baking dish large enough to hold the fennel in no more than 2 layers. Put in a layer of fennel, cut the butter into small cubes, and dot over fennel; season with salt and pepper. Add a second layer of fennel and push into the spaces of the first layer. Pour on the broth, cover the pan with aluminum foil, and bake 45 minutes. Remove the foil, increase the temperature to 400°F and cook until the liquid has evaporated. Sprinkle with the cheese and bake at 400°F until golden, about 10 minutes. *Serves 6.*

• • •

Note: Fennel comes in two shapes, one bulbous and round, the other elongated and slightly flattened. If possible, choose the elgonated ones for cooking and the bulbous ones for eating raw.

Roasted Green Beans

FAGIOLINI ARROSTITI

These wrinkled green beans are a family favorite. Roasting vegetables was very much a part of the cooking style of the early Italian-Americans. In Italy, stoves were little more than a charcoal or wood brazier, often located outdoors. Housewives used that space mostly for simmering—for making soup or sauce or stew. All families except the very poorest had a large brick or stone oven either in the kitchen or outside. This is where bread was baked and foods were roasted. The immigrants transferred this method of cooking to their "modern" American indoor woodstoves and continued to roast vegetables. Eating them will tell you why. Choose whichever herb is available or particularly liked.

1½ pounds green beans,
  trimmed and washed
3 garlic cloves, smashed
  and peeled
3 sprigs fresh rosemary,
  oregano, or thyme

Salt and freshly ground
  black pepper
⅓ cup extra-virgin olive oil

1. Preheat the oven to 450°F.
2. Put the beans, garlic, and herb in a large metal roasting pan so that the beans are in one layer. Sprinkle with salt and pepper. Pour the olive oil over all and toss to coat well. Place in the preheated oven and roast 12 to 15 minutes, tossing occasionally, until the beans are tender and browned. *Serves 6 to 8.*

• • •

Variation: Toss 2 teaspoons red wine vinegar or Balsamic vinegar into the cooked beans for a tangy version.

• • •

Variation: Mix together 3 mashed anchovies, grated zest of 1 lemon, and 2 teaspoons lemon juice and toss into the hot beans. A good accompaniment to fish dishes.

Green Beans and Onions

FAGIOLINI E CIPOLLE

Green beans cooked this way will not keep their bright color but Italian sensibilities are not troubled by this. Try to choose the smallest beans possible and, at any rate, choose beans that are as regular in size as possible. This is not easy since grocers have no concern for the fact that a big fat bean will not cook in the same amount of time as a small skinny one. It usually takes me some time to pick through beans and I feel quite conspicuous as other shoppers reach by me to grab handfuls willy-nilly.

¼ cup extra-virgin olive oil
3 garlic cloves, smashed
  and peeled
1½ cups sliced red onion
1½ pounds green beans,
  washed and trimmed

2 tablespoons chopped fresh
  mint or parsley
Salt and freshly ground
  black pepper
¼ cup dry white wine

1. Put the oil and garlic in a sauté pan large enough to hold the beans. Cook over low heat until the garlic is well browned. Discard the garlic. Add the onions to the pan and cook until softened (about 10 minutes).

2. Add the beans to the onions in the pan and toss together well. Season with mint or parsley, salt, and pepper. Add the white wine and turn the heat to high to reduce the wine 1 minute. Cover the pan, reduce the heat to medium-low, and cook until the beans are tender. If at any time the beans begin to stick, add 1 to 2 tablespoons hot water. *Serves 6.*

• • •

Note: If fresh mint is just not available, you can use about 1 teaspoon dried mint, reconstituted with a bit of boiling water, and mixed with 1 tablespoon chopped parsley.

Braised Mushrooms with Pancetta

FUNGHI STUFATI CON PANCETTA

It is amazing how such a small amount of dried mushrooms can flavor a dish. This "contorno" goes particularly well with grilled or roasted meats.

1 ounce dried porcini
  mushrooms
¼ pound pancetta, cut in
  ⅛-inch dice
2 tablespoons extra-virgin
  olive oil
¼ cup pinoli nuts
  (pine nuts)

1 large garlic clove, minced
1 small onion, minced
1 pound mushrooms, wiped
  clean and sliced thin
Salt and pepper
¼ cup Marsala
¼ cup chopped parsley

1. In a small bowl, cover the dried porcini with warm water and let soak at least 30 minutes. Drain, strain soaking liquid through washed cheesecloth or a coffee filter, and reserve. Rinse the mushrooms well to remove all sand, discard any tough pieces, dry, and coarsely chop. Set aside.

2. In a large sauté pan, cook the pancetta in the olive oil until slightly crisped. Remove with a slotted spoon. Add the pinoli to the pan and cook over low heat until just golden. Remove with a slotted spoon and reserve with the pancetta.

3. Add the garlic and onion to the pan and cook over low heat until softened. Add the reserved porcini, the fresh mushrooms, salt, and pepper and turn the heat to high. When the mushrooms release their juices, add ½ cup reserved soaking juices and the Marsala and reduce the liquid until it just glazes the mushrooms. Stir in the parsley, pancetta, and pinoli and correct the seasonings. Serve hot. *Serves 6.*

• • •

Note: As noted before, many vegetable dishes are delicious over pasta. Braised mushrooms are wonderful mixed either with an egg noodle such as tonnarelli (page 132) or a short macaroni such as penne. Increase the oil to ⅓ cup and toss the finished dish with 1 pound cooked pasta. They are also delicious added to scrambled eggs.

Neapolitan Onions

CIPOLLE NAPOLITANE

My grandmother roasted onions whenever she roasted lamb, pork, or chicken. The combination of aromas was as enticing as the blending of flavors. The onions are roasted until their natural sugars are released and form an almost caramel glaze. Serve them warm or at room temperature. They can be made a few days ahead and reheated or brought back to room temperature before serving. You may use all red or all yellow onions if you prefer. Neapolitans also make these with red wine or Marsala in place of the vinegar. Try either for variety.

3 large yellow onions
3 large red onions
Salt and pepper

About ½ cup extra-virgin olive oil
¼ cup red wine vinegar

1. Preheat the oven to 400°F.

2. Remove the papery outside from the onions but leave most of the peel on. Do not trim the roots of the onions, which must be left on for the onions to hold their shape. Quarter the onions through the roots, being careful that each quarter has part of the root to hold it together.

3. Put the onions in one layer in a large metal baking pan. Season with salt and pepper. Pour the oil over and turn the onions to make sure all the sides are coated. Use more oil if necessary. Cover the pan tightly with aluminum foil and place in the preheated oven 30 minutes. Remove foil and continue to bake, turning and basting, until the onions are tender (20 to 30 minutes).

4. Remove the onions with a slotted spoon to a serving dish. Put the baking pan on top of the stove over high heat and stir the vinegar into the pan juices. Deglaze the pan over high heat and pour the juices over the onions. *Serves 6.*

Sweet and Sour Onions

CIPOLLINE IN AGRODOLCE

Southern Italians often make these up in large batches and put them up in glass jars to have on hand as needed. You may not want to process them, but they will keep a week refrigerated. Be sure to bring them to room temperature before serving. Sweet and sour onions are a classic southern Italian accompaniment for game. I like them with any roasted meat and make them often for buffets since their staying power is remarkable.

2 pounds small white onions	1¼ cups water
3 tablespoons extra-virgin olive oil	½ cup red wine vinegar
	1 tablespoon sugar
2 ounces prosciutto with fat, shredded	⅓ cup raisins
	Salt and pepper
1 tablespoon tomato paste	1 bay leaf

1. With the tip of a paring knife, make 2 cross cuts in the root ends of the onions. Plunge into boiling water and cook 1 minute after the water returns to the boil. Remove to cold water, drain, dry, and peel carefully, keeping the onions whole.

2. Heat the olive oil and prosciutto gently in a straight-sided frying pan 2 minutes. Do not let the prosciutto crisp or brown. Add the onions and cook until just golden.

3. Mix the tomato paste with the water to dissolve. Add to the onions with all the remaining ingredients, bring to a boil, reduce the heat, and simmer gently, turning occasionally, 1½ hours, or until the onions are tender and the liquid has reduced to coating consistency (almost a glaze). If the cooking liquid has not reduced but the onions are tender and brown, remove the onions with a slotted spoon and boil until the liquids are reduced to their proper consistency. Discard the bay leaf. Serve warm or at room temperature. *Serves 6.*

Herbed Onions in White Wine

CIPOLLE AL VINO BIANCO

This finished dish keeps well for a day in the refrigerator. Reheat to serve.

2 pounds small white
  boiling onions
¼ cup extra-virgin olive oil
½ cup dry white wine
¼ cup meat or chicken
  broth

Salt and pepper
2 tablespoons chopped fresh
  thyme
1 tablespoon chopped
  parsley

1. With the tip of a paring knife, make 2 cross cuts in the root ends of the onions. Plunge into boiling salted water and cook 1 minute after the water comes to a boil. Plunge in cold water, drain, dry, and carefully peel.

2. Put the oil in a covered pan large enough to hold the onions in no more than 2 layers. Add the onions and turn to coat. Add the remaining ingredients except the parsley, bring to a boil, reduce the heat, and simmer, covered, 40 minutes. (This may also be done in a 300°F oven.) Remove the cover and cook 20 minutes more, or until the onions are tender and the liquid is reduced to a glaze. Stir in the parsley and serve. *Serves 8.*

Sweet and Sour Peppers with Almonds

MANDORLATA DI PEPERONI

This delicious and unusual pepper dish from Basilicata may be served hot or at room temperature. It is wonderful with grilled meat, especially Italian sausages. Peeling the peppers, with a vegetable peeler and a light hand, is not something my grandmother ever did. Marcella Hazan made me aware of how the little extra work makes peppers succulent. This peeling method is not the same as roasting and peeling, which gives the peppers an entirely different taste. It is not *necessary* to peel the peppers. The dish is delicious either way.

3 medium sweet red bell peppers	⅓ cup dark raisins, soaked 20 minutes in warm water, drained
2 medium sweet green bell peppers	2 tablespoons sugar
3 tablespoons extra-virgin olive oil	3 tablespoons red wine vinegar
⅓ cup slivered almonds	Salt

1. Wash the peppers; peel if desired. Cut in half lengthwise; remove the seeds and ribs. Cut each pepper into ½-inch strips.

2. Heat the oil in a sauté pan large enough to hold the peppers. Add almonds and cook 2 minutes without browning. Add the raisins and heat 1 minute. Add the peppers, sugar, vinegar, and salt and toss together well. Cover the pan and cook over medium heat 15 minutes. Uncover and continue to cook until the peppers are tender (5 to 10 minutes) and a glaze forms. If at any time during the cooking the peppers begin to stick, add 1 to 2 tablespoons warm water. *Serves 6 to 8.*

Roasted Potatoes with Onion

PATATE CON CIPOLLA AL FORNO

I have my own proof of how American and Italian eating habits have melded. My sons greedily gobble these crispy potatoes, but insist on putting ketchup on them! Nonna would do what all horrified grand-mothers do from beyond. The large amount of olive oil is an indul-gence. I've tried reducing it but we just don't like them as well.

5 medium new white
    potatoes, about 2½
    pounds
1 medium onion, cut in
    16 wedges
5 sprigs thyme, oregano,
    rosemary, or marjoram

2 bay leaves
¾ cup extra-virgin olive oil
Salt and freshly ground
    black pepper

1. Preheat the oven to 450°F.
2. Scrub the potatoes but leave the skin on. Cut each potato in half crosswise, then cut each half into 8 wedges. Rinse in cold water and pat dry.
3. Put the potatoes, onion, herb, and the bay leaves into a large roasting pan. Pour the olive oil over and toss to coat. Roast in a hot oven 35 to 40 minutes, or until browned on the outside and tender within. Turn occasionally with a flat spatula. Season the cooked potatoes with salt and pepper. *Serves 6.*

• • •

Note: Use a roasting pan large enough to hold the potatoes in one layer so they have a chance to form a crisp outer coating.

Baked Potato Cake

GATTÓ DI PATATE

Although I have never encountered this dish in an Italian-American restaurant, I discovered that it was one that many people of Neapolitan backgrounds have maintained as part of their home cooking. In traditional Neapolitan cooking, it is most often seen as a first course. I prefer to serve it as a side dish especially on a buffet table. The recipe can be doubled or even tripled and may be assembled the day before and baked when ready to serve.

2 pounds all-purpose potatoes, peeled and quartered	Salt and pepper
	¼ cup chopped parsley
¼ pound unsalted butter	¼ pound fresh mozzarella cheese, chopped
2 ounces Parmesan cheese, freshly grated	¼ pound smoked provola cheese (smoked mozzarella), chopped
2 ounces pecorino cheese, freshly grated	3 tablespoons olive oil
¼ pound prosciutto, chopped	Dried breadcrumbs made from Italian bread
2 large eggs, lightly beaten	

1. Put the potatoes in a pot with cold water and bring to a boil. Salt and cook until tender (about 20 minutes). Drain and put through a potato ricer or mash with a potato masher.

2. Cut 5 tablespoons butter into small pieces and add to the hot potatoes along with the Parmesan, pecorino, prosciutto, eggs, salt, pepper, and parsley. Blend together well.

3. Mix the mozzarella and provola with the olive oil and season with salt and pepper.

4. With one of the remaining 3 tablespoons butter, grease the bottom and sides of an 8-inch square or round baking dish. Coat the bottom and sides completely with breadcrumbs. Spread ½ the potato mixture in the bottom and up the sides of the prepared dish. Cover the potatoes with the seasoned cheeses. Cover with the remaining potatoes. Sprinkle with breadcrumbs and dot with the last 2 tablespoons butter.

5. Place the "gattó" in a 375°F oven 40 to 50 minutes, or until hot and slightly browned on top. Cool 15 minutes and unmold or serve directly from the dish. *Serves 8.*

Potatoes with Peppers

PATATE COI PEPERONI

A terra-cotta baking dish is perfect for cooking and serving this colorful country dish. I like to leave the fresh herb in sprigs for a more rustic look.

3 medium all-purpose
    potatoes (about 1 pound),
    peeled and cut into
    ½-inch-thick slices
2 medium onions, cut into
    eighths
4 medium red peppers, stem,
    seeds, and ribs removed,
    cut in ¾-inch-wide slices

¼ pound thinly sliced
    prosciutto, shredded
3 rosemary sprigs or
    2 teaspoons chopped
    dried
Salt and pepper
¼ cup extra-virgin olive oil

1. Preheat the oven to 400°F.
2. Rinse the potatoes well in cold water. Pat dry. Put the potatoes, onions, and red peppers in a large roasting pan. Add the prosciutto, rosemary, salt, and pepper. Drizzle on the olive oil and toss to coat. Bake, turning 2 to 3 times, 30 to 40 minutes, or until the potatoes are tender. *Serves 6.*

. . .

Note: Be sure to use a pan that is big enough to hold the vegetables in one slightly overlapping layer or they will steam and become soggy. To turn the cooking vegetables without breaking them, use a thin metal spatula pressed firmly against the pan. Slide under the vegetables and turn.

Mixed Vegetable Stew

CIANFOTTA (CIAMBOTTA)

This colorful vegetable dish, which is equally good hot or at room temperature, is known by many dialect names throughout southern Italy. The variations are almost as numerous as the names themselves since the vegetables will change according to season and region. Eggplant, zucchini, and celery may all find their way into this country vegetable stew. A wonderful Calabrian touch is the addition of green olives.

⅓ cup extra-virgin olive oil
3 garlic cloves, crushed
   and peeled
3 medium onions, peeled
   and cut into large wedges
3 bell peppers (red, green,
   and yellow if possible)
Salt
3 all-purpose potatoes
   (about 1 pound), peeled
   and cut into ¼-inch
   wedges

1 pound tomatoes, peeled,
   seeded, and juiced,
   coarsely chopped
6 large green olives, pitted
   and sliced into strips

1. Put the oil, garlic, and onions into a wide sauté pan. Cook over gentle heat until the onions are translucent and the garlic is golden.
2. Wash the peppers. Peel with a peeler if desired. Cut in half and remove the ribs and seeds. Cut into 1-inch-square pieces and add to the onions. Salt lightly and cook, covered, 2 minutes. Rinse the potatoes under running water until water runs clear and add to the pan. Salt lightly, cover the pan, and cook 20 minutes. Add the tomatoes, a bit more salt, cover, and cook 30 minutes more, or until the potatoes and peppers are cooked. Fold in the olives 5 minutes before the cooking is finished. If the pan becomes dry during cooking add 1 to 2 tablespoons warm water. *Serves 6.*

Calabrian Side Dish for Fish

CONTORNO CALABRESE PER PESCE

There is absolutely no reason why this delicious potato dish has to be saved for a fish meal even though it is perfect for such a menu. The typically southern use of pickled vegetables adds a wonderful zip to the potatoes. Served warm or at room temperature, it's a great change from regular potato salad.

5 all-purpose or boiling potatoes (1¾ pounds), washed
Salt and freshly ground white pepper
4 hard-boiled eggs, cut in large chunks

⅔ cup chopped small white pickled onions (see note)
2 scant tablespoons capers, rinsed
6 tablespoons or more extra-virgin olive oil

1. Put the potatoes in a pot and cover with cold water, bring to a boil, salt, cover the pan, and cook until tender. Drain and let sit until cool enough to handle. Peel and carefully cut into 1-inch squares. (The potatoes should be warm; if too hot, they will not cut evenly but break apart.)

2. Toss the warm potatoes gently with the eggs, onions, and capers. Fold in the olive oil and salt, using 1 or 2 more tablespoons oil if the potatoes absorb more. Serve warm or at room temperature. *Serves 6.*

. . .

Note: I have found pickled white onions, one inch in diameter, in many markets. If you cannot find them, you will have to resort to a few jars of tiny cocktail onions. You could pickle your own according to the directions for preserved peppers (page 36) but you will have to wait at least a month to use them.

Sautéed Spinach and Romaine

SAUTE DI SPINACI E LATTUGA

When I was growing up, I remember thinking how strange it was that my grandmother cooked her salads. Escarole or romaine or dandelion greens might be found in a soup or a calzone, or appear at the table sautéed or stuffed and baked. Now, of course, it makes perfect sense. Italians make frugal use of whatever the garden or countryside provides. Using lettuces for salads only is a limitation Italian cooks knowingly shun.

2 pounds spinach
1 medium head romaine
    lettuce
4 tablespoons extra-virgin
    olive oil
⅓ cup golden raisins
    (dark raisins may be
    substituted)

¼ cup pinoli nuts
    (pine nuts)
Salt, pepper, and nutmeg
¼ cup freshly grated
    pecorino cheese

1. Remove the tough stems from the spinach and wash well. Put the leaves in a large pot with only the water clinging to them. Cover and cook just until beginning to wilt (about 5 minutes). Drain well, dry, and chop coarsely.

2. Remove the tough spines from the romaine lettuce and wash the leaves well. Dry and chop coarsely.

3. Heat the oil in a large skillet. Add the raisins and pinoli nuts and cook over gentle heat until the pignolis are lightly colored. Add the lettuce and cook over high heat, tossing well, 30 seconds, or just until the lettuce begins to wilt. Add the spinach, salt, pepper, and nutmeg and cook just until the spinach is heated. Sprinkle on the cheese. Toss briefly over the heat and serve. *Serves 6.*

Tomatoes with Herbs

POMODORI CON ERBE

Southern Italy is rife with recipes for tomatoes—baked, stuffed, fried, grilled, and so forth. This particular recipe was inspired by my dear friend, Dagmar Sullivan, who, although French, has an Italian heart in the kitchen. It is one of the most flavorful ways to cook tomatoes since the many hours of cooking concentrates the flavor incredibly. They may be served as a "contorno" or as an antipasto with toasted, oiled Italian bread. If there are any leftovers—highly unlikely—toss them into hot spaghetti.

6 large ripe salad tomatoes	2 garlic cloves, minced
¾ cup extra-virgin olive oil	½ cup chopped parsley
Salt and pepper	½ cup chopped basil
Pinch of sugar	2 tablespoons chopped mint

1. Wash the tomatoes. Remove the stems and cut in half. Heat ¼ cup olive oil in a sauté pan large enough to hold the tomatoes in one layer. Put the tomatoes in the pan, cut side up, and cook over medium-low heat 15 minutes. Salt and pepper the cut side after 15 minutes. Add a pinch of sugar and turn the tomatoes. Reduce the heat to low and cook gently 2½ to 3 hours.

2. Heat the remaining ½ cup olive oil and the minced garlic in a small sauté pan over gentle heat. Soften the garlic but do not allow it to color. Add the herbs, salt, and pepper and cook gently 3 to 5 minutes.

3. Gently remove the cooked tomatoes from the pan, being careful not to break them. Place, cut side up, on a serving platter and pour the garlic-herb mixture over the top. Serve hot or at room temperature. *Serves 6.*

• • •

Note: The tomatoes may also be cooked in a slow oven (225°F).

Oven-Baked Piquant Tomatoes

POMODORI PICCANTI AL FORNO

What could be more inviting than a white platter brimming with red tomatoes! That is how I first encountered this zesty vegetable in Naples. I ate them with grilled lamb and was very content. They also make a fine antipasto—just be sure to serve them on a white platter.

4 medium fully ripe salad
   tomatoes, 1¾ pounds
Salt
1½ cups breadcrumbs,
   from day-old bread
⅓ cup chopped parsley
1 tablespoon capers

3 anchovy fillets, chopped
2 tablespoons minced
   soppressata or other
   hard salami
5 tablespoons extra-virgin
   olive oil
Freshly ground black pepper

1. Preheat the oven to 350°F.

2. Remove the stems from the tomatoes and cut in half. Squeeze gently to remove the seeds and juice. Sprinkle the insides lightly with salt and place upside down to drain.

3. Mix the breadcrumbs, parsley, capers, anchovies, salami, and 3 tablespoons olive oil together in a small bowl. Taste for seasonings and add pepper and salt as needed. Divide the filling among the tomato halves.

4. Lightly oil a baking dish large enough to hold the tomatoes in one layer. Place the tomatoes upright in the pan and drizzle on the remaining oil. Bake 25 minutes, or until the tomatoes are lightly browned on top. Serve at room temperature. *Serves 8.*

MEMORIES

"When you're married you please your husband . . ."

I learned cooking from my mother, but when I married I had to change my way of cooking because this is what my husband liked. When you're married you please your husband. Right? So I learned to cook more my mother-in-law's way than my mother's.

My mother couldn't read. Neither could my mother-in-law. They had to learn by themselves or by what other people told them. That's how we learned from them. By watching and asking questions.

My mother was a very simple, plain cook. My mother-in-law was different. For instance, on Christmas Eve in my house we had aglio olio with raisins and walnuts for Christmas Eve dinner; my mother-in-law had clams in red sauce. I had never had the red clam sauce and my husband had never had the other that I had. They were from different paes'.

Margaret Sullo Alfano and Francesco Alfano, Mary's parents.

A Christmas Eve dinner that I learned from my mother-in-law was spaghetti in red clam sauce, stuffed quahogs, squid salad, snail salad, fried smelts, baked stuffed shrimp, codfish or "baccalà" salad, and fourteen or fifteen different kinds of cookies. The cookies were my own addition to the meal.

The neighborhood was typically Italian. Everyone knew everyone else. There were about six or seven large families on the street, all related somehow. A very close-knit section of town. The church was close by. There was a Mr. De Pazio who had a pushcart in our neighborhood, which was outside the city. He sold beautifully made sweets, more or less like marzipan, and his own gelato. He used to come around all year long. There was a meat market where they made their own sausage. There was a variety store. They're all pretty well gone now and it's changed its look.

My father had a big garden. He grew potatoes, tomatoes, string beans, peas, corn, radishes, cucumbers, squash. He tried peanuts one time and they grew. That was one of our chores—we had to go and take the potato bugs off the potatoes before we could go play. We had to pick blueberries and tomatoes. We sold our produce around the neighborhood because back then we needed the money. There were six of us in the family and we all had to do our share.

My mother put up her own tomatoes and that was a chore we had to help with. She had a big galvanized tub down in the basement and she used to put a nice clean cloth over it. Then she had a strainer which was like a flat tray with raised sides and holes in it. We would squeeze the tomatoes on that so all the skins and seeds would remain on top and all the good stuff would come out on the bottom. Then she would pour it into this big cloth and all the water would drain out; then we would scoop that and put that in bottles. We used to squeeze baskets and baskets of tomatoes in this way. We weren't allowed to touch anything while doing this—if you had an itch you had to use your elbow. It was a tradition for girls, if they were having their periods at the time, they weren't supposed to do this. Sometimes if you didn't feel like squeezing tomatoes, you would pray that you got your period.

To preserve her tomatoes, my mother kept them in soda bottles. We'd keep all these green bottles around and we'd wash them out with bottle brushes. Sometimes we put in whole tomatoes and we had a stick that we'd push the tomatoes down in the bottles with.

My father used to make wine. He had a wine-pressing machine and he'd buy crates of grapes. When he'd open the first batch he and my uncles would get together under the grapevine and have a great time. It was an altogether different life-style than we have now. As busy as they were, they always had time for things like this.

My father was a produce peddler when we were young. He had a truck that he would drive around and sell his vegetables from. On

Wine pressing machines

Sundays, he'd clean it out and we'd go for a ride in it. It had canvas sides that we rolled up on nice days. He had a very serious accident once in the truck and he never drove again.

On New Year's Eve my grandmother used to come over. I don't know what the significance of this is—perhaps it is to ask the new year to come in peacefully—but she used to bring over a small, empty Christmas tree. She took it and stood outside and stamped it three times saying "Bossa grazi?"—"May I come in?" She was symbolizing the new year. We'd say yes and open the door. And aunts would come and they'd bring jugs of wine and they'd start singing Christmas carols in Italian. That was our New Year's Eve growing up.

On the day before Easter, we weren't allowed to eat anything until noontime. My mother made the sweet bread with the traditional eggs in there with crosses of dough over them. She also made "pastiera," rice pie, and also one with spaghetti. The spaghetti would get very crunchy on top and it was delicious. She would put all the food on the table and in those days the priest used to come around on Saturday afternoon with the holy water and bless everything that the families made. We'd wait for the bells to ring at 12 o'clock on Saturday which meant our fast was over so we could eat.

My mother used to make these cookies at Christmas that took a lot of steps. She started to make the dough right after Thanksgiving. They were called "mostaccioli." It was a very spicy cookie. She used flour, cloves, cinnamon, lemon, and orange rind. She mixed it very well, then covered it and put it in a closet for about a month to age it. Then she would make her own peach preserves. When it was time to make the cookies, she rolled the dough into a log shape and filled it with the preserves. She put chopped nuts in there too. Then she would cut the cookies in different shapes such as diamonds. She would bake them in a lot of flour to make sure that the preserves wouldn't stick. So, after they cooked we had to put them on the table and brush off the flour with clean paintbrushes. It was a big job—the house got to be a mess. Finally, she made this chocolate frosting for the cookies that she thinned out with coffee. It had to be the right consistency or else it wouldn't stick to the cookies. Then she put little colored confetti on them. After all this she put them up in a closet because we weren't supposed to touch them until Christmas—but little did she know we used to sneak them at night.

My mother-in-law never baked. She did not have time with nine kids. But she was a great cook. If she could keep nine children fed that was enough. My mother-in-law taught me how to make "polpettone," which is a large meatball shaped like a football. She made it like she was going to make a meatball. She took a couple of hard-boiled eggs, peeled them, and put them in the center of the hamburg. She really patted them in there so that they wouldn't break through. Then she browned it first in a frying pan and then dropped it in tomato sauce to cook. When it was done, she put it on a platter and sliced it so you could see the egg. Then she sautéed peas and onions and put them around the "polpettone" and drizzled tomato sauce over it all. It was a pretty dish and very tasty. She would make it for Sundays or special meals as a second course, served after the pasta.

MARY ALFANO CODOLA
(family name Alfano, near Naples;
mother-in-law's family from Atrani,
near Amalfi)

Piquant Zucchini

ZUCCHINI PICCANTI

Is zucchini a popular Italian vegetable because it grows everywhere or does it grow everywhere because Italians love it? It is an extremely versatile vegetable, and is cooked in many ways and found as antipasti, in soups and pasta, and as "contorni." In Italy, it may be dark green, pale green, or green with pale stripes. I have found striped zucchini in my market and use it just as I would the more common dark green. This piquant recipe should accompany dishes that are not highly spiced.

5 tablespoons extra-virgin olive oil	Salt
1 medium onion, minced	¼ teaspoon crushed hot pepper
2 small garlic cloves, minced	3 tablespoons red wine vinegar
3 pounds small zucchini, cut into thin matchsticks or coarsely shredded	2 tablespoons minced parsley

Heat the oil, onion, and garlic in a large heavy skillet over medium-low heat until the onion is softened but not browned. Add the zucchini, salt, and hot pepper. Increase the heat to high and sauté, tossing often, until the zucchini is tender, about 3 minutes. Stir in the vinegar and parsley and let boil until reduced to a glaze. *Serves 8.*

• • •

Note: Choose zucchini that are firm with tight, glossy skins. They must be washed well to remove all dirt. I scrub them lightly with a vegetable brush. Trim both ends.

Zucchini Parmesan

PARMIGIANA DI ZUCCHINE

A few years ago, *P.M. Magazine* came to my house to tape a story about me and my work. They wanted a clip of the boys, who were ten and twelve years old. They asked them on tape if there was any food that they didn't like. In unison, without hesitation, they answered, "Zucchini. Definitely zucchini." A challenge was mounted! It was not until they had finished the entire pan of "Parmigiana di Zucchine" that I declared myself the victor. If you have 2½ cups of marinara sauce on hand, use that and begin with step 2.

¼ cup extra-virgin olive oil
1 small onion, minced
3 pounds fresh plum
   tomatoes, peeled, seeded,
   and finely chopped or
   3 pounds drained canned
   tomatoes, chopped
Salt
¼ teaspoon sugar (optional)

2 pounds zucchini
Olive oil for frying zucchini
Flour
½ pound fresh mozzarella,
   thinly sliced
¾ cup fresh basil leaves
1 ounce freshly grated
   Parmesan (about ¼ cup)

1. Put ¼ cup olive oil and the onion into a noncorrosive pot. Cook over low heat until the onion is golden. Add the tomatoes and salt and cook 30 minutes, or until the water is evaporated. Stir in the sugar if necessary.

2. Meanwhile, trim and wash the zucchini. Cut into long thin slices (about ⅜ inch thick). Place in a colander, salting each layer, and let drain 1 hour. Gently squeeze and pat dry. Heat the olive oil to a depth of ½ inch. Very lightly flour zucchini, pat off the excess, and fry in hot oil until golden on each side (about 3 minutes). Drain on paper towels.

3. Preheat the oven to 375°F. Oil a shallow baking dish approximately 8 x 12 inches. Put in a layer of tomato sauce, a layer of zucchini, pieces of mozzarella, torn basil leaves, and Parmesan cheese. Continue to layer and end with a layer of mozzarella drizzled with tomato sauce and sprinkled with Parmesan. Bake 20 minutes, or until the cheese melts and the sauce bubbles. Cool at least 10 minutes before serving. *Serves 6 to 8.*

Sweet and Sour Zucchini

ZUCCHINE AGRODOLCE

In this Sicilian recipe, the sweet comes from the raisins. There is no sugar added. It is less intense than other "agrodolce" preparations.

1 garlic clove, smashed and peeled
3 tablespoons extra-virgin olive oil
6 small zucchini (about 2 pounds), washed and trimmed and cut into ¼-inch slices
3 tablespoons vinegar
3 tablespoons water
3 tablespoons pinoli nuts (pine nuts)
3 tablespoons raisins (dark or white)
2 anchovies, mashed
Salt as needed

Heat the garlic in the olive oil in a frying pan until the garlic is browned, then discard. Add the zucchini to the pan and toss over high heat until the pieces are lightly browned. Add the vinegar, water, pine nuts, raisins, and anchovies. Let boil, then reduce the heat, cover the pan, and cook 10 minutes. Remove the cover and cook until the liquid is reduced to a glaze. Taste for salt. *Serves 6.*

Fried Zucchini in Batter

FRITTELLE DI ZUCCHINE

Use this same batter for any vegetable cut in small pieces. Particularly hard vegetables such as carrots or cauliflower should be blanched briefly first. Italians often serve a "fritture mista" (mixed batter-fried vegetables) for an antipasto or as a side dish with fried fish. For a lighter batter, separate the egg, beat the white until stiff, and fold into the batter.

1½ pounds zucchini	About ⅓ cup water
1 egg	Olive oil or vegetable oil
½ cup flour	for deep-frying
Salt	

1. Trim the zucchini ends, wash, and cut into ⅛-inch-thick rounds.

2. Beat the egg well in a small bowl. Gradually sift the flour and salt into the egg, making a smooth mixture. Slowly add enough water to make a smooth batter the consistency of heavy pancake batter. Let rest at least 20 minutes.

3. Put ¾ inch oil in a deep skillet and heat to a temperature of 350°F. Dip the zucchini into the batter and slide into the hot oil a few pieces at a time so as not to crowd the pan. Cook, turning until golden on both sides, about 1 minute. Remove with a slotted spoon to paper towels to drain. Sprinkle with salt, fine or coarse, just before serving. *Serves 6 to 8.*

Zucchini Cooked Like Mushrooms

ZUCCHINE AI FUNGHETTI

I'm not exactly sure why mushrooms are the yardstick for how other vegetables are cooked but I do know that this simple method of cooking zucchini is a treat. Be sure that the frying pan is large enough so that the zucchini is not crowded. Keep it moving about so that it browns all over quickly. Otherwise the vegetable will steam and become mushy.

4 pounds zucchini, washed and ends trimmed
⅓ cup olive oil

3 garlic cloves, chopped
Salt
¼ cup chopped parsley

Cut the zucchini into ½-inch dice. Heat the oil and garlic in a frying pan. Do not brown. Add the zucchini and cook over medium heat, tossing, until the zucchini is tender and lightly browned. Add the salt and parsley. *Serves 6 to 8.*

Romaine Salad with Parmesan Cheese

INSALATA DI LATTUGA E PARMIGIANO

My grandmother always insisted that we eat a little salad after a big meal, even when we were sure that we couldn't handle another bite. She said that it would help us digest. Of course, she was always right and within minutes we were hunting for the *dolci*—the sweet! Adjust the amount of mint to your liking. It will depend on the size of the leaves and the strength of their flavor. Omit the cheese if the salad is to accompany or follow a fish entrée.

2 small heads romaine lettuce
1 small red onion, very thinly sliced, soaked 1 hour in cold water (change the water 3 times)
About 12 to 15 mint leaves
6 tablespoons best-quality extra-virgin olive oil
2 tablespoons red wine vinegar or lemon juice
Salt and pepper
3 tablespoons freshly grated Parmesan cheese

1. Discard the bruised outer leaves and tough spines from the lettuce. Wash the remaining leaves, dry, and break into bite-size pieces. Drain the onion and pat dry.

2. Place the lettuce in a salad bowl. Toss the onions and mint leaves with the lettuce. Pour on the olive oil, vinegar, salt, and pepper. Toss. Mix in the cheese and serve immediately. *Serves 8.*

• • •

Note: Soaking red onion in cold water removes a great deal of its astringency, thus making it sweeter and more digestible.

• • •

Note: To remove the tough spines from the romaine, simply hold the leaf in both hands, one end in each, and bend until it snaps. The spine beneath the snap should be discarded.

DRESSING SALADS

Italians do not make salad dressings but simply dress the salad with oil and vinegar or, less commonly, lemon juice before serving. I have heard many adamant statements as to the order in which salt, oil, and vinegar should go on the salad. My way is to hold a large tablespoon over the greens. Put the suggested amount of oil in the spoon and pour it over the salad. Next put the vinegar or lemon juice in the spoon and pour that on the salad. Sprinkle the salad with salt and pepper if desired and toss well. Taste the salad and adjust the seasonings. Some Italians put the salt in the spoon with the vinegar to dissolve it but I don't find that necessary. A good way to add a mild garlic flavor to the salad is to sprinkle the bowl lightly with salt and rub the salt around the bowl with cut garlic cloves.

A woman weighing greens.

Mixed Salad

INSALATA MISTA

A mixed salad may combine all or any of the following ingredients. It should be dressed just before serving. You may want more or less oil and/or vinegar. It should be to your taste.

1 garlic clove	1 carrot
1 small romaine or Bibb lettuce	6 tablespoons extra-virgin olive oil
2 heads radicchio	3 tablespoons red wine vinegar or lemon juice
1 fennel bulb	Salt and freshly ground black pepper
1 sweet red pepper	
2 small ripe salad tomatoes	

1. Cut the garlic clove in half and rub the inside of the salad bowl with the cut side of the clove, then discard. Wash and trim the lettuces. Discard any bruised leaves. Break into bite-size pieces and put into the salad bowl.

2. Remove the feathery top from the fennel bulb. Discard any bruised layers. Wash the bulb well and cut into julienne strips. Put into the salad bowl.

3. Wash the pepper, tomatoes, and carrot. Remove the stems from the peppers, cut in half, and remove the seeds and ribs. Cut into ½-inch strips. Remove the stems from the tomatoes and cut into 8 wedges. Peel and trim away the ends from the carrot. Cut into thin slices. Add the vegetables to the salad bowl. Cover and refrigerate until ready to serve.

4. Pour the olive oil and vinegar on the salad and season with salt and pepper. Toss and serve immediately. *Serves 6 to 8.*

Escarole Salad

INSALATA DI SCAROLA

Escarole is a slightly bitter green in the chicory family. I like to combine it with other, milder greens to balance its flavor.

2 teaspoons anchovy paste
  or 4 anchovies, mashed
2 tablespoons lemon juice
1 head escarole
1 head romaine lettuce
1 large red onion, cut in very
  thin slices, soaked 1 hour
  in cold water (change the
  water 3 times)

3 tablespoons snipped basil
6 tablespoons extra-virgin
  olive oil
Salt

1. Put the anchovy paste in the bottom of a salad bowl. Add the lemon juice to it and beat them together until well combined.

2. Wash the lettuces. Remove the tough spines, break into pieces, and add to the salad bowl. Drain the onions and pat dry. Add the onions and basil to the lettuce and chill until ready to serve.

3. When ready to serve, pour the oil over the lettuce and toss well. Taste for salt and serve immediately. *Serves 6 to 8.*

· · ·

Variation: Rub the salad bowl first with garlic (see Dressing Salads, page 247).

· · ·

Variation: Sprinkle the salad with 3 tablespoons freshly grated pecorino cheese.

Bean Salad with Tomatoes

INSALATA DI FAGIOLI CON POMODORI

Large open bags holding an assortment of dried beans have stood by the door of the shop where I buy my vegetables at least since I was a little girl. As a child I found it impossible not to run my hands through them and listen to them tick against one another. I just loved the way they looked and felt and to this day I love to buy and cook dried beans. Although canned beans are a satisfactory substitute for soups and some vegetable dishes, I think that bean salads are really best when made with fresh or freshly cooked dried beans. I use this salad often for room temperature country buffets. It is a good accompaniment especially to the "Tonno in Insalata" (page 188) or platters of grilled sausages.

1 cup dried white beans (Great Northern, cannellini)	1 small red onion, diced and soaked 1 hour in cold water (change the water 3 times)
1 celery stalk, with tops	
1 medium onion, cut in half	1 garlic clove, minced
1 bay leaf	2 tablespoons red wine vinegar
6 medium salad tomatoes	
⅓ cup extra-virgin olive oil	¼ cup chopped fresh mint
Salt and pepper	Mint leaves for garnish

1. Soak the washed and picked-over beans in cold water to cover overnight or at least 4 hours. Drain and rinse. Or use the quick soak method: place the washed and picked-over beans in a large saucepan. Add enough cold water to cover them by 2 inches and bring to a boil. Boil 2 minutes. Remove from heat and let soak in their cooking water, covered, 1 hour. Drain and rinse.

2. Put the soaked beans in a large pot and add fresh cold water to cover by 2 inches. Bring to a boil, reduce the heat, and add the celery, onion, and bay leaf. Simmer 45 minutes to 1 hour, or until the beans are tender. Drain and discard the celery, onion, and bay leaf.

3. While the beans are cooking, peel, seed, and chop the tomatoes into ½-inch dice. Season with a few tablespoons olive oil and some salt and pepper. Set aside.

4. Drain and dry the red onion and add to the warm beans. Add the remaining olive oil, garlic, vinegar, chopped mint, salt, and pepper. Toss often as the beans cool. When the beans are completely cooled, spoon into the center of a platter. Surround with tomatoes and decorate with mint leaves. Serve at room temperature. *Serves 8.*

· · ·

Note: Beans should not be salted during either the soaking or cooking stages or they will toughen and not absorb water properly to soften.

Jimmy Pandozzi could always be found in the morning at his son's fruit stand, 1936.

Calabrian Potato Salad

INSALATA DI PATATE CALABRESE

Although Calabrians serve this salad mainly as an antipasto, I like it best as a side dish. Use it in place of your regular potato salad. The mint makes it refreshingly different.

3 pounds boiling potatoes, peeled	Salt and pepper
2 medium-large red onions, very thinly sliced and soaked 1 hour in cold water (change the water 3 times)	¼ cup chopped parsley
	½ cup chopped fresh mint
	About 9 tablespoons extra-virgin olive oil
	About 3 tablespoons red wine vinegar

1. Slice the potatoes into rounds ¼ inch thick. To remove excess starch, rinse in cold water until the water runs clear. Put potatoes into a pot of cold water, bring to a boil, salt, and simmer gently until just tender (about 7 minutes). The potatoes should remain just slightly firm at the center.

2. Drain the onions and pat dry. Place ⅓ of them on a serving platter. Cover with ⅓ of the hot potatoes and season them with salt and pepper. Sprinkle with ⅓ the amount of parsley, mint, oil, and vinegar. The oil and vinegar should just coat the entire surface but not drown the vegetables. Use a bit more if necessary to coat the layer. Continue layering until all the ingredients are used. Set aside to cool and serve at room temperature. Do not refrigerate. *Serves 6 to 8.*

• • •

Note: It is important to dress the potatoes while still hot. I do not drain the potatoes, but working very quickly, I remove one-third of them at a time from the hot water with a strainer and place them directly on the platter. The other ingredients are right at hand and I assemble the salad rapidly.

Green Bean Salad

INSALATA DI FAGIOLINI

If you have access to tiny, garden green beans scoop them up for this salad. If they are very young and tender there is no need to even trim the ends. Just remove the stem.

1½ pounds green beans,
   trimmed
¼ cup extra-virgin olive oil
3 tablespoons minced
   fresh mint
3 tablespoons minced
   fresh parsley

Salt and freshly ground
   black pepper
2 tablespoons lemon juice
4 teaspoons grated or
   shredded lemon peel

Cook the beans in a large amount of boiling salted water until just tender, about 5 minutes. Drain and plunge into ice water. Drain well and pat dry. Place in a bowl and add the oil, mint, parsley, salt, and pepper. Just before serving, mix in the lemon juice and lemon peel. Toss and serve at room temperature. *Serves 6.*

Any area not planted might well be used for bocce ball.

Fennel, Mushroom, and Cheese Salad

INSALATA DI FINNOCHIO, FUNGHI, E FORMAGGIO

This is an extremely well-traveled salad. It has moved back and forth between the antipasto chapter and here innumerable times. It is equally welcome both places. Its crisp, clean flavor is a pleasing prelude to what's to come and a refreshing finish to what has been.

4 fennel bulbs
½ pound mushrooms
¼ pound Parmesan or best-
    quality pecorino cheese
3 tablespoons lemon juice

6 tablespoons extra-virgin
    olive oil
Salt and freshly ground
    black pepper

1. Remove the fennel tops. Trim the bulbs, removing the tough outer layer and the hard core. Wash well in cold water. Dry and cut into julienne pieces.

2. Wipe the mushrooms clean and cut into thin slices. Break the cheese into slivers.

3. Scatter the fennel on plates or a serving platter. Top with the mushrooms and cheese slivers. Sprinkle on the lemon juice, olive oil, and salt and pepper. Toss before serving. *Serves 6.*

• • •

Note: Hard grating cheeses are meant to be broken, not cut for eating. There is a special small, wedge-shaped knife specifically for this. If you do not have one, use the tip of a blunt knife, and simply press it into the cheese, which will break. Continue until the cheese is in a number of irregular-size pieces.

• • •

Note: The pecorino cheese must not be too sharp or astringent for this salad. I have found excellent pecorino sardo in Italian neighborhoods.

Neapolitan Cauliflower Salad

INSALATA DI RINFORZO NAPOLETANA

"Insalata di rinforzo" is a traditional Neapolitan Christmas salad that is "reinforced" or strengthened during the holidays by the addition of more of the ingredients or, in some cases, by other pieces of leftover boiled vegetables. In that way some is always on hand for the holidays. It is customary today to think of the Christmas holidays as December 25 and New Year's Eve or Day. But traditionally in Italy and for the early Italian-Americans, the feast of the Natale spanned the twelve days from Christ's birthday to the feast of the Epiphany, January 6, when the Three Wise Men arrived in Bethlehem. It was a more celebratory time, filled with special foods, required visits to relatives, and tradition. My grandfather always gave us gifts on Epiphany, which is the day the friendly Italian witch Befana brings gifts to Italian children. So much of this has disappeared today, but I do give my boys gifts from Befana on January 6. On the other hand, I make this festively colored salad any time of year and serve it with fish or chicken or as an antipasto.

1 large head cauliflower
⅓ cup extra-virgin olive oil
3 tablespoons red wine vinegar
Salt and pepper
3 tablespoons minced fresh oregano or marjoram or 1 tablespoon dried

8 anchovy fillets in oil or salt, rinsed
½ cup oil-cured or brine-cured black olives
¼ cup capers, rinsed
1½ cups pickled red peppers

1. Cut the cauliflower into flowerets. Wash and drop into boiling salted water. Cook 3 to 5 minutes, or until just tender. Drain and plunge into ice water. Drain and pat dry.

2. Put the cauliflower in a bowl and pour on the olive oil and vinegar and season with salt, pepper, and herb. Cut the anchovies into narrow strips. Cut the peppers into ¼-inch strips. Toss the anchovies, olives, capers, and peppers with the cauliflower. The salad should be allowed to mellow at least 3 hours but is best after a few days. *Serves 8.*

MINT

One of the lovely surprises of the cooking of southern Italy is the use of fresh mint. It shows up in some of the most surprising places (see Calabrian Potato Salad, page 252). In Italy, the Italians use wild mint which has a similar but different flavor. It does not grow in this country so some Italian-Americans substituted domestic mint (menta spicata). Others simply eliminated the herb from their cooking. In both cases, the traditional tastes were changed. However, I find domestic mint, sometimes with the addition of a little lemon peel or juice, a satisfactory substitute. Since it is so easy to grow, it is always possible to have your own fresh supply.

Grapefruit Salad

INSALATA DI POMPELMO

The grapefruit is a relatively new fruit to the Italian table so I can hardly claim that this recipe is anything but an invention. It came about because I was craving the refreshing taste of orange salad (page 258) but had only grapefruits on hand. I feel very comfortable adapting traditional recipes to what is good in America. Our Italian-American ancestors did this, often with outstanding success. Veal Parmesan, for example, does not exist in Italy. The immigrants arrived with recipes for eggplant Parmesan, and when they became meat eaters they simply adapted the recipes to the new food. Today, it is one of the most popular dishes in Italian-American restaurants. Who knows where grapefruit salad might go?

10 radishes
3 small pink grapefruit
1/3 cup mint leaves
2 tablespoons lemon juice
6 tablespoons extra-virgin
   olive oil

Salt and freshly ground
   black pepper
18 Gaeta olives

1. Wash the radishes and trim the ends. Slice as thinly as possible.
2. With a sharp paring knife, remove the skin and all the white pith from the grapefruits. Cut between the membranes to remove the segments. Remove the seeds. Toss the radishes and grapefruit in a bowl. Tear in the mint leaves. Pour on the lemon juice and olive oil and season with salt and pepper. Add the olives and serve immediately. *Serves 8.*

Orange Salad

INSALATA DI ARANCE

The color of this Sicilian salad is as inviting as its refreshing flavor. In Sicily it is made with blood oranges (red flesh oranges) and has a particularly dramatic look. Blood oranges are occasionally available in the United States. I especially like to serve this salad after a fish meal.

4 navel oranges
½ red onion, thinly sliced, soaked 1 hour in cold water (change the water 3 times)
12 small mint leaves
18 black Gaeta or other brine-cured black olives

3 tablespoons extra-virgin olive oil
1 tablespoon red wine vinegar or lemon juice
Salt and freshly ground black pepper

1. With a very sharp knife, carefully peel the oranges, being sure to remove all the pith (white part). Slice into ¼-inch rounds. Drain the onion and pat dry.

2. Layer the oranges, onions, mint leaves, and olives in a shallow bowl. Pour on the olive oil and vinegar or lemon juice and salt and pepper. Toss. Serve immediately or let sit 2 to 3 hours. *Serves 6.*

Bread Salad

INSALATA DI FRISEDDE (FRISELLE)

"Frisedde" or "friselle" are flat ring-shaped rolls made with whole wheat flour. After the first baking, they are cut in half and baked again so that they become quite crusty. They can be found in Italian-American bakeries and some large specialty food stores. "Insalata Frisedde," a cousin of the Tuscan panzanella (bread salad), was a very typical light meal for the southern Italians in Italy and America. I serve this often for lunch in the summer when tomatoes and basil are an arm's length from my kitchen door.

Twelve 4-inch or six 6-inch "frisedde"
½ cup extra-virgin olive oil
6 ripe salad tomatoes, chopped
1 medium red onion, minced and soaked in cold water 1 hour

3 garlic cloves, minced
1 tablespoon capers
24 fresh basil leaves, torn in strips
2 tablespoons red wine vinegar
Salt and freshly ground black pepper

Run the "frisedde" under cold water to soften. Squeeze dry. Place in a single layer on a large serving platter. Pour a little of the olive oil on each slice. Cover with the tomatoes. Sprinkle with the onion, garlic, capers, and basil. Pour the remaining olive oil over the top and sprinkle with the vinegar, salt, and pepper. Let sit at least 1 hour before serving. *Serves 6.*

Chapter Six

BREAD AND
PIZZA

There is an Italian saying, "Without bread everyone is an orphan." Whatever its size or shape, crusty Italian bread has always played an important part in the Italian diet. Neither my grandparents' nor my parents' home was ever without it. Loaves appeared fresh for dinner. We sliced and toasted it in the morning, spread on butter, and dipped it into hot cups of milky coffee. Pieces of bread were the base of soups and stale loaves were grated for breadcrumbs for meatballs, stuffings, and coatings. If we were without bread we didn't quite know how to begin to prepare a meal!

It was common in southern Italy for families to have a brick or stone oven, usually outside, that was used for baking bread and pizza. Small towns often did not have bakers and, if they did, bread was still cheaper to bake than to buy. Women often baked large round loaves that might last the family a week.

It wasn't long after the first immigrants arrived in America that Italian bakeries were opened to serve their countrymen. Although some rural families, without the benefit of a neighborhood baker, built backyard ovens for baking, most people relied on the baker for brick oven crusty loaves. What people did continue to make at home were some of the traditional recipes of their paese, such as the Easter cheese bread "crescia" and the special pork crackling bread "tortano," which were unavailable unless the baker happened to emigrate with them.

This chapter is merely a sampling of some of those special breads and pizzas, which could fill volumes. These are recipes that are not difficult for the home cook to reproduce even with only a smattering of bread-baking knowledge. Bread dough is very forgiving. It seems to want "to be" regardless of what insults it might be forced to endure. When my son Brad had his eleventh birthday, he had ten friends all making pizza in our kitchen for their supper. Each little person mixed, and pushed, and struggled and tossed the dough with his or her own flair. It was amazing to discover that no matter what technique they used, they all produced a very decent pizza. I was charmed and secretly grateful that I had not revealed the backup dough I had made earlier to buffer any disappointments.

Perhaps one of the reasons they all met with such success is that they loved the kneading part. They were happy to spend the ten required minutes pushing the dough (usually toward each other) until it had developed the right amount of elasticity. You can't cheat at this stage or your dough will have none of the characteristic chewiness. However, the dough may be successfully made and kneaded in a food processor or an electric mixer with a dough hook attachment.

Pizza Dough

PASTA PER PIZZA

It is difficult to determine exactly how much dough each person will need for what size pizza. When I taught hands-on pizza classes, I discovered that everyone has his or her own idea about how thick or thin the crust should be. Some had ideas, but were unable to stretch the dough to the size they wanted. (If you don't work quickly and the dough becomes overhandled, it will develop an excess of gluten which will make the dough behave like a rubber band. You stretch; it retreats.) I prefer a thin crust, about ⅛ inch before baking, but I sometimes make it paper-thin as in the Parsley Pizza (page 270) or thicker for heartier fillings. Pizza making has become serious business, but for my family it is a favorite—not a solemn—food. More often than not, my son Andrew makes it for the family and has been doing so since he could reach the counter standing on a stool.

1 package dry yeast	1 teaspoon salt
1 cup warm water (110°F)	
3¼ to 3½ cups all-purpose flour	

1. Dissolve the yeast in ¼ cup of the warm water.
2. By hand: put 3 cups flour on a counter. Mix in the salt. Make a well in the center and add the yeast and remaining water. Gradually work together and gather into a ball. Knead 10 minutes, adding more flour to make a soft dough that does not stick to the counter.

By machine: put 2 cups flour into the bowl of food processor fitted with steel or plastic blade. Pulse in the salt. Add the yeast and the remaining water through the feed tube and process 10 seconds. Add 1 cup more flour and knead 40 seconds, adding more flour as necessary to make a soft dough that does not stick when poked with a finger.

3. Put the prepared dough in an oiled bowl, turn to coat, cover with a towel, and leave to rise in a warm spot 1½ to 2 hours, or until doubled in bulk. Punch down and let rest 10 minutes before rolling and shaping. *Makes enough for approximately two 12-inch pizzas or one 12 x 17-inch pizza.*

• • •

Pizza Dough (continued)

Note: For a crunchier crust with a slightly nutty flavor, substitute half semolina flour for the all-purpose flour. The dough will require more water and will take longer to rise.

· · ·

Note: The dough may be placed on a pizza peel which has been dusted with cornmeal to help the pizza release easily. The pizza is then transferred to tiles or a pizza stone which has been preheated in the oven. Otherwise the pizza can be cooked in pizza pans. I have had great success with both black steel and heavy aluminum pans.

STRETCHING PIZZA DOUGH

Anyone who has seen the stereotypical pizza man at work knows that dough can be stretched with a great deal of flair. With practice anyone can learn to turn and toss it in the air, but it isn't necessary, just fun. Until that technique has been mastered, follow these more simple guidelines.

Once you have punched the risen dough down, let it rest about 10 minutes to relax the gluten. Otherwise it will snap back at you as you roll it out. Once you start, it is best to work quickly, with a minimum of handling, since the more you work it the more gluten you develop.

Begin by rolling the dough with a rolling pin on a lightly floured counter. Use firm, swift strokes that visibly enlarge the dough. When the dough is about three inches shorter than the sides of your pan it is ready for the final stretch. Now you can use your fists to toss it in the air and thin it out if you know how. Otherwise, put it in the center of an oiled pizza pan or on a pizza peel dusted with flour or cornmeal and push it to the edges with the flats of your hands. Do not oil the rim of the pan so the dough will not slide back. If the dough becomes too elastic and resists you, let it rest in the refrigerator at least thirty minutes before continuing—or settle for a smaller, thicker pizza!

Angry Pizza

PIZZA ARRABBIATA

The pizza is not angry, of course, but hot and spicy. You can adjust the amount of "anger" to your liking by cutting down—or increasing—the hot pepper. This pizza has a rich topping and I like to bake it in a 12 x 17-inch rectangular pan and cut it into small squares. I use an Italian rectangular pizza pan but a jelly-roll pan works fine.

SAUCE

2 garlic cloves, crushed
2 tablespoons extra-virgin
  olive oil
1½ cups fresh or canned and
  drained tomatoes, peeled,
  seeded, and chopped
1 tablespoon tomato paste
¼ teaspoon hot pepper
  flakes or ½ hot pepper,
  seeded and chopped
2 teaspoons snipped basil
1 tablespoon fresh marjoram
  or 1 teaspoon dried
Salt and pepper

PIZZA

1 recipe pizza dough
  (1½ pounds) (page 263)
1 cup finely chopped
  mozzarella
Salt and pepper
⅔ cup grated or finely
  chopped caciocavallo
  cheese
⅓ cup freshly grated
  Parmesan cheese
6 thin slices prosciutto
1 large salad tomato, thinly
  sliced
Extra-virgin olive oil

1. Make the sauce: sauté the garlic in 2 tablespoons olive oil until brown, then discard. Add the tomatoes, tomato paste, and seasonings to the oil. Cook over medium-low heat until very thick (about 20 minutes).

2. Preheat the oven to 500°F and set the rack in the lower third of the oven. Lightly oil a 12 x 17-inch pan.

3. Roll, stretch, and spread the dough to fit in the pizza pan (page 264). Spread the prepared sauce evenly over the dough, leaving a 1-inch border. Sprinkle the mozzarella, caciocavallo, and Parmesan cheeses over the sauce. Lay the prosciutto slices on top of the cheese and place the tomatoes on top of the prosciutto. Season with a little olive oil. Bake 12 to 15 minutes, or until the cheeses are melted and the bottom is crisp. *Makes one 12 x 17-inch pizza.*

White Pizza

PIZZA BIANCA

Pizza means tomato sauce to so many people that it is easy to overlook some of the delicious recipes that combine other toppings. Make the crust a bit thicker for this pizza since the topping is dense.

1½ cups ricotta cheese, drained in a sieve 30 minutes
⅓ cup freshly grated Parmesan cheese
⅓ cup freshly grated pecorino cheese
⅓ cup freshly grated mozzarella cheese

½ cup shredded prosciutto
8 ounces mushrooms, wiped clean and thinly sliced (about 2 cups)
2 tablespoons extra-virgin olive oil
Salt and pepper
1 recipe pizza dough

1. Preheat the oven to 475°F. Put the rack in the lower third of the oven.

2. Mix the ricotta, Parmesan, pecorino, mozzarella, and prosciutto together just until blended. Season with salt and pepper and set aside.

3. Sauté the mushrooms in the olive oil with the salt and pepper until the juices run and evaporate and the mushrooms are lightly browned.

4. Roll, stretch, and spread the dough in a lightly oiled pizza pan(s) or on a prepared pizza peel (page 264). Brush with oil. Spread the cheese mixture over the crust and sprinkle on the mushrooms. Bake 12 minutes. *Makes one 18-inch pizza or two 9- to 10-inch pizzas.*

•   •   •

Note: American ricotta cheese often has a tendency to be very wet. I always let it drain before using it in any recipe where its moisture may produce a problem.

Margherita Pizza with Canned Tomatoes

PIZZA MARGHERITA CON PELATI

Pizza Margherita is a classic Neapolitan recipe which was created in honor of Queen Margherita. Its ingredients are red, white, and green to symbolize the Italian flag. It is one of the simplest of pizzas to make and hardly needs a recipe. I include one because few people know that it can be made successfully with canned plum tomatoes.

1 recipe pizza dough
2½ cups well-drained canned Italian plum tomatoes
1½ cups chopped mozzarella
1 tablespoon olive oil
Salt and pepper
½ cup freshly grated Parmesan cheese
¼ cup shredded fresh basil
1 teaspoon chopped fresh oregano (optional)

1. Preheat the oven to 475°F. Place the rack in the lower third of the oven.

2. Roll and stretch and spread the dough in lightly oiled pizza pans or on a pizza peel (see page 264). Chop the tomatoes and place evenly over the dough. Mix the mozzarella with the olive oil, salt, and pepper and sprinkle over the tomatoes. Scatter the Parmesan, basil, and oregano (if using) on top and season with salt, pepper, and a little olive oil. Bake 12 minutes, or until the cheeses are melted and the bottom is crisp. *Makes two 12-inch pizzas.*

• • •

Note: Unless your oven is large enough to hold two pans at a time with breathing space between, bake only one pizza at a time for best results. I put the first pizza in the oven and prepare the second while the first is baking. However, at Brad's famous pizza party, we found that unbaked pizzas will keep with the toppings on for 15 to 20 minutes. Pour the oil on top just before baking.

Flat Bread

PIZZA DI PANE

It is very common in Italian neighborhoods to see morning shoppers eating small, rectangular strips of pizza that are topped with olive oil and a smidgen of tomato. In the old days the immigrants ate this flat bread topped only with oil and salt as had been and still is the custom in the areas around Rome and Naples. School children flock to the bakeries for a midmorning snack of what the Romans call "pizza bianca" and Neapolitans "pizza di pane." I serve this flat bread, similar to the northern Italian "foccacia," with meals or as part of an antipasto.

1 teaspoon dry yeast	Salt
1 cup warm water (110°F)	About ⅓ cup extra-virgin
3¼ to 3½ cups all-purpose	olive oil
flour	

1. Dissolve the yeast in ¼ cup of the warm water.

2. By hand: put 3 cups of flour on a counter. Mix in 1 teaspoon salt. Make a well in the center and add the yeast, and the remaining water. Gradually work together and gather into a ball. Knead 10 minutes, adding more flour to make a soft dough that does not stick to the counter.

By machine: put 2 cups flour into the bowl of food processor fitted with steel or plastic blade. Pulse in 1 teaspoon salt. Add the yeast and the remaining water through the feed tube and process 10 seconds. Add 1 cup more flour and knead 40 seconds, adding more flour as necessary to make a soft dough that does not stick when poked with a finger.

3. Put the prepared dough in an oiled bowl, turn to coat, cover with a towel and leave to rise in a warm spot 4 hours or in a refrigerator overnight. Punch down and let rest 10 minutes before rolling and shaping.

4. Preheat the oven to 450°F. Roll the dough into a rectangle 14 x 7 inches. Put it on an oiled baking pan or onto a wooden pizza peel that is dusted with flour. Using two knuckles, dimple the entire surface of the dough. Brush well with olive oil. Put the baking pan

into the oven or transfer the dough from the peel to oven preheated bricks. Bake 8 minutes, brush again with oil and continue to bake 8 to 10 minutes or until pizza is golden brown. Remove from the oven and immediately brush again with oil and sprinkle with salt. *Makes one 14 x 7-inch pizza.*

. . .

Variation: Before baking, brush the dough with the olive oil and top with 6 plum tomatoes, fresh or canned, peeled, juiced, and cut into narrow strips. Drizzle olive oil on top halfway through baking and sprinkle with salt.

. . .

Variation: Before baking, brush the dough with olive oil and sprinkle on 1 tablespoon chopped rosemary, or other herb, or minced garlic. Drizzle olive oil on top halfway through baking and sprinkle with salt.

Mr. Sciallo in his bakery on "The Hill" in Providence, Rhode Island.

Parsley Pizza

PIZZA DI PETRUSINO

Parsley is everywhere in Italian cooking but perhaps nowhere as abundantly or as deliciously as in this pizza, which I often cut into small pieces and pass to guests before dinner.

1 recipe pizza dough	Pinch of hot pepper flakes
10 large garlic cloves,	(optional)
finely minced	1¼ cups extra-virgin
3 cups minced flat-leaf	olive oil
parsley	Salt

1. Preheat the oven to 425°F. Place the rack in the bottom third of the oven.

2. Roll, stretch, and push the dough to fit into two 18-inch lightly oiled pizza pans (page 264). The dough should be very thin on the bottom with a slightly rolled edge around. Brush the crust with a bit of the olive oil.

3. Mix together the garlic, parsley, and hot pepper flakes if using. Sprinkle the mixture over the dough and pour the olive oil over the pizzas. Sprinkle generously with salt. Bake the pizzas one at a time 12 to 15 minutes, or until the bottom is crisp and the sides are golden. Watch carefully to prevent burning. Slide the pizza onto a cutting board and cut into pieces. *Makes two 18-inch pizzas.*

Vegetable Calzone

CALZONE DI VERDURE

These delicious individual pizza turnovers make wonderful picnic fare since they are equally good warm or at room temperature. The recipe below is for escarole, but you can use beet greens, turnip greens, spinach, or a combination of greens. When I am making them for picnics or snacks, I divide the dough into 16 pieces instead of 8 and bake them about 15 to 20 minutes.

2 pounds escarole, trimmed and cored
1 pound fresh mozzarella or scamorza cheese, grated
¼ cup extra-virgin olive oil
1 cup brine-cured black olives (such as Gaeta), pitted and coarsely chopped
¼ to ½ teaspoon hot pepper flakes, depending on taste
Salt
1½ pounds pizza dough

1. Preheat the oven to 400°F. Separate the escarole leaves and boil in salted water until tender (about 10 minutes). Drain and rinse with cold water. Squeeze well with your hands or in a kitchen towel until completely dry and chop fine. Mix together with the cheese, olive oil, olives, hot pepper, and salt. Set aside.

2. Divide the dough into 8 equal pieces. Roll each piece into an oval shape approximately 4 x 6 inches. Place about ½ cup filling along the center of each piece of dough, leaving a thin border around the edges. Dampen the border with a pastry brush or your fingers dipped in water. Fold the dough over the filling and press the damp edges together to seal. Brush calzone with olive oil.

3. Put the calzone on a baking sheet lightly brushed with oil and bake 25 to 30 minutes, or until golden brown. Serve hot or at room temperature. *Makes 8 calzone.*

Little Pizzas Neapolitan Style

PIZZETTE ALLA NAPOLETANO

What a delightful treat these little pizzas make! As children, we would gobble them up as fast as my grandmother could fry them. You can use a ready-made marinara sauce and begin with step 26.

4 garlic cloves, chopped
½ hot red pepper, seeded
   and chopped, or
   ¼ teaspoon dried
3 tablespoons olive oil
2½ cups fresh Italian plum
   tomatoes, peeled, seeded,
   and juiced, or 2½ cups
   drained canned, chopped

Salt
Sugar, if necessary
1 recipe pizza dough
Olive oil or vegetable oil
   for frying
¼ cup snipped basil

1. Cook the garlic and hot pepper in 3 tablespoons olive oil over medium-low heat in a wide frying pan until the garlic is golden. Add the tomatoes, salt, and a pinch of sugar if necessary. Cook until the liquid has evaporated (about 20 minutes).

2. Roll the pizza dough on a lightly floured counter into a long roll 1 inch in diameter, and cut pieces 1 inch long. Roll each piece into a thin circle 5 inches in diameter. Put the oil in a heavy pan to a depth of ½ inch. Heat to 375°F and cook the pizzas a few at a time, turning once until they are puffy and light brown, about 1 minute per side. Drain on paper towels.

3. Put the pizzas on a large serving platter. Add the basil to the sauce and top each pizza with about 1 tablespoon sauce. *Makes 24.*

• • •

Note: If you already have fresh tomato sauce on hand, you will need about 1½ cups for this recipe.

• • •

Note: If you wish to add cheese, sprinkle the sauced pizza with grated mozzarella seasoned with olive oil, salt, and pepper, and put in a 400°F oven until the cheese melts.

PARSLEY

In Neapolitan dialect, parsley is called "petrusino" and when someone is always interfering in everything, Neapolitans say that he is like "un petrusino ogne menesta" (like parsley, he's in every dish), because parsley is in every recipe. When I buy artichokes, my greengrocer automatically tucks in a small bunch of parsley in case I get home and find that I have none. He is so sure that they would be tasteless without this addition! I always use the flat-leaf variety, sometimes called Italian parsley. The leaves have a good strong flavor and the stems are more tender than those of curly parsley. Hence you can chop up a bit of the stem with the leaf. If a dish has cooked a long time with parsley in it, it is necessary to put some in again at the end if you want the fresh parsley taste.

MEMORIES

"What are we doing here? . . .
They don't even know how to make bread."

My family came from Sicily and there the kind of sauce my mother made was a plain sauce, very plain. It is different from the Neapolitan's. They use a lot of tomato sauce. In Sicily, we used less. You can actually see the spaghetti's color through the sauce. Mostly it is a marinara sauce, sometimes the ragu, but Sicilians like mostly a marinara.

We have in Sicily a fish that comes from Holland. This was after the Second World War. It is a special dried "stoccafisso," the same family as a "baccalà." The people from Denmark or Holland, they use this during Christmas time. This kind of fish needs very cold waters to live, that is why we get it from Holland and Denmark. There they make a stew similar to the French zuppa de pesce. In Sicily, they put this fish in water for about three days because it is so dry, but it comes back nice and fresh. It smells awful until you put it in a frying pan and cook it. You use chunks of this fish, plus pieces of tomatoes, potatoes, scallions, Sicilian black olives, olive oil, and a few other things, depending on what the housewife feels like to make this dish. Also you can boil the fish and then put it in the refrigerator

Tony and his mother before leaving Italy for America.

and make it as a salad with a little garlic, olive oil, and oregano. Also you can roast this type of fish with little baby tomatoes and garlic and make an appetizer.

I used to watch my mother make her own bread. I used to try and help her too. She had a place where she'd put the flour and add the water. Then she used to tell me to punch the dough down. Then she'd put it underneath a blanket so that it would rise. With a knife, she would slice a design on top and put it in the oven. She used to break off a small piece of dough to make a little roll just for me. I'd slice it while it was hot and put in a little piece of "cicoli" (pork crackling) and it would melt just like butter.

I remember she used to make me a dish with the little black eye beans. She used to do those specially with the diced potatoes. She used to get the tomato sauce and put in on potatoes and mix it together with tubettini.

I came to America in 1947. I was fifteen years old. My mother and I took an American boat from Palermo, the S.S. Pierce, which was carrying back GI soldiers from Europe. On the boat, they served us bread with butter. It was soft bread. I had never had this kind of bread before in my life. I knew the Sicilian loaf bread that was round and dense and you sliced with a knife. I was so disappointed. I said to my mother, "Ma, what are we doing here? We're going to the wrong country. They don't even know how to make bread!"

When my mother and I came to America we adopted American ways. My mother found that all the ingredients she wanted to make a good sauce, she could find in America—she didn't have to go to Sicily. She shopped at the Italian markets. She did fantastic.

I used to enjoy her food better here, I think. For example, my mother used to make meatballs. She would grind her own top sirloin with her own grinder. Then she'd put eggs inside, grated Romano cheese, grated breadcrumbs, and pieces of garlic. She used to sauté them in a frying pan and then put them into her gravy. They were delicious.

It took my mother about seven years to buy her own home. In the back of this home there was a lot, about forty by eighty feet. As soon as she moved there, she made a garden. She planted corn, zucchini, peppers, scallions, garlic. She grew different types of to- matoes. The Italian ones, plum tomatoes. Then there were beefsteak tomatoes, for salads. She also grew eggplant.

My mother used to make a fantastic dish out of the zucchini she grew. She sliced it and sautéed it in a frying pan with olive oil. When it was nice and brown, she cooked angel hair spaghetti, capellini. She poured the zucchini over the angel hair and it wouldn't stick because it's cooked al dente and it's 100 percent semolina.

My mother was a very talented person. She was quite a creative cook. Out of nothing she used to make a meal and it never took her a long time to do. If she had company, in about an hour and a half, she had a meal for six or seven people.

When we moved here we used to be invited for dinners a lot with other people who came from the same town in Sicily. In the town

where I came from, practically everybody cooks the same. One might give a little more color to the dish than the other, but they are basically the same. For example, everybody in my hometown knew eggplant croquette. You boil the eggplant and you cut it into pieces. Then you put in Romano cheese, dry breadcrumbs, parsley, and pieces of garlic and you roll it up

Tony's family gathered in Providence.

like little weenies. Then you fry them and use them as an appetizer. You had to make sure to leave the skin on the eggplant to give them firmness. Everybody from my hometown knew how to make them, but others here didn't know about them.

Food is a first priority for people who come from my region of Messina [in Sicily]. They sit for hours and hours at the table. They start at one o'clock and very slowly you have the first course, then the second, then the salad. The salad, "insalata," comes after the dinner, before the dessert. It's a digestive.

ANTONIO FAMA
*(from San Pier Niceto, Sicily;
wife Anna Calderone Fama)*

Filled Ricotta Pitta

PITTA RIPIENA CON RICOTTA

Calabrians refer to a filled pizza as a "pitta." They make "pitte" with any number of combinations of fillings. This is excellent picnic food because it tastes best at room temperature and will keep for three to four days.

3 tablespoons olive oil	2 hard-boiled eggs, sliced
1½ pounds pizza dough	¼ cup chopped parsley
¼ pound thinly sliced prosciutto	⅓ cup oil-packed sun-dried tomatoes, drained and cut in thin strips
1 pound ricotta cheese, drained in a sieve 30 minutes	¼ cup freshly grated pecorino cheese
Salt and pepper	

1. Preheat the oven to 400°F. Place the oven rack at the lowest setting.

2. Brush 1 tablespoon olive oil on the bottom of a round pan 12 inches in diameter and about 3 inches deep (a springform pan works well). Divide the pizza dough in 2 pieces with 1 piece slightly larger than the other. Roll the larger piece of dough on a lightly floured counter until large enough to fit in the pan and come up over the sides. Put the dough in the pan, bring it up the sides, and let it hang slightly over the top.

3. Lay the prosciutto slices evenly over the crust. Spread the ricotta cheese over the prosciutto. Season the cheese with salt and pepper and lay hard-boiled egg slices over the cheese. Sprinkle with the parsley, salt and pepper, sun-dried tomatoes, and grated pecorino. Roll the second piece of dough into a circle large enough to cover the pan. Moisten the edges with water and place on top of the filling. Pinch the edges of the top and bottom dough together well to seal. Make three 3-inch slits in the top of the dough, brush with the remaining olive oil, and bake on the lowest oven rack 35 to 40 minutes, or until browned and the bread is cooked. *Serves 8 to 10.*

• • •

Filled Ricotta Pitta (continued)

Variation: Remove the casing from ¾ pound hot or sweet Italian sausage and sauté it in 1 tablespoon olive oil just until no longer pink. Drain on paper towels and sprinkle it over the bottom crust. Cover with 1 pound ricotta beaten with 2 eggs. Tear ⅓ cup basil leaves over the ricotta and cover the leaves with 3 peeled plum tomatoes cut into ⅛-inch-thick rounds. Sprinkle with ¼ cup freshly grated Parmesan or pecorino cheese and finish as above.

Spinach Pie

PITTA DI SPINACI

One of my earliest food surprises was the discovery of olives cooked in foods. It was my grandmother's spinach pie which opened my eyes to the fact that they need not be relegated only to the condiment tray. It seems to me that Nonna always had a bit of spinach pie on the counter in her kitchen. I would nibble little pieces, bit by bit, until I had eaten a good-size portion. To this day I am unable to resist a piece when I find it on the counter of my Italian grocer.

DOUGH

2 packages dry yeast	4½ cups flour
1½ cups warm water (110°F)	2 teaspoons salt

FILLING

2½ pounds spinach, stemmed	3 garlic cloves, minced
Salt	6 ounces brine-cured black olives, pitted and chopped
¼ cup extra-virgin olive oil plus additional for brushing	½ cup raisins
¼ cup minced onion	¼ teaspoon hot red pepper or freshly ground black pepper

1. Make the crust: dissolve the yeast completely in ½ cup warm water.

2. Put 4 cups flour on a counter. Mix in the salt. Make a well in the center and add the yeast and the remaining water. Gradually incorporate the flour and work together to form a dough. Knead 10 minutes, adding more flour to make a soft dough that does not stick to the counter. This may also be made in the food processor or in a mixer with a dough hook.

3. Place the prepared dough in an oiled bowl, turn to coat, and let rise, covered with a towel, 1½ to 2 hours, or until doubled in bulk. This makes 2 pounds dough.

4. Make the filling: rinse the spinach and place in a large pot with only the water clinging to it. Salt and cover and cook over low heat until just wilted, about 3 minutes. Squeeze dry and chop coarsely.

5. Heat ¼ cup olive oil, the onions, and the garlic in a sauté pan over low heat until soft. Mix in the olives and raisins and cook 2 minutes, stirring constantly. Add the spinach and pepper and cook 5 minutes, or until the spinach is dry.

6. Preheat the oven to 400°F. Brush the bottom of a 9 x 13-inch rectangular metal or enameled cast-iron baking pan with olive oil. Break the dough into 2 pieces, one 1½ times larger than the other. Let rest 15 minutes to relax. Roll and stretch the larger piece on a lightly floured surface to an 11 x 5-inch rectangle. Fit the dough into a prepared pan, covering the bottom and sides. Brush the dough with olive oil. Spread the filling over the dough. Roll and stretch the remaining piece of dough on a lightly floured surface into a 9 x 13-inch rectangle. Brush the edges with water and place, wet side down, atop the filling. Pinch the top and bottom crusts together. Cut three 3-inch slits in the top. Bake until well browned, about 35 minutes. Cool slightly and serve warm or at room temperature. *Makes one 9 x 13-inch "pitta."*

·   ·   ·

Variation: My grandmother never put cheese in her spinach pie but I know that many people are used to it made that way. If you would like to add cheese, mix ¾ pound chopped mozzarella with 2 tablespoons olive oil, salt, and pepper and sprinkle it over the spinach.

Cheese Bread from Marche

CRESCIA DELLE MARCHE

Vicki Giustini Moran, the sister-in-law of a friend, shared this recipe which her grandmother Nerina made primarily for Christmas and Easter, although the bread was originally an Easter treat. The golden color and grand size of this tasty bread makes it a dramatic addition to any table. The name comes from the verb "crescere," "to grow or rise up," and that is exactly what this bread does. Vicki said that her grandmother always gave it that long rise and baked it in a deep pot to accommodate its height. Use a deep casserole or a soup pot.

5 to 6 cups all-purpose flour
10 ounces pecorino romano
    cheese, grated
1½ teaspoons salt
1½ teaspoons pepper
¼ cup milk, warmed
¼ pound butter, melted

8 eggs
4 ounces yeast
¾ cup warm water
¼ pound mild provolone
    cheese, cubed
2 tablespoons soft butter

1. Mix 5 cups flour with the pecorino cheese, salt, and pepper. Stir in the milk and butter. Beat in the eggs one at a time until well combined.

2. Dissolve the yeast in the warm water. Add to the flour mixture. Turn onto a counter or attach a dough hook to an electric mixer and knead, adding the provolone cheese and using the additional flour as necessary to produce a soft dough. Turn into a greased bowl and let rise, covered, until tripled in bulk (about 5 hours).

3. Punch the dough down and place in a deep—at least 8-inch deep, 10-inch round—pan. Cover and let rise 2 hours. Bake 1 hour in a preheated 350°F oven. While still warm, rub with butter. *Makes 1 loaf.*

Pizza Campofranco

PIZZA CAMPOFRANCO

Pizza Campofranco is a traditional Neapolitan two-crusted pie that is similar to what other regions call "pizza rustica." They have in common a rich crust and the fact that they are usually baked during the Easter season. I ate many pizza rusticas growing up but I never had one with a brioche crust like this one that Michi Ambrosi, a Neapolitan cooking teacher, showed me one spring in Naples.

BREAD

3 cups flour
1½ teaspoons salt
¾ cup softened butter,
    in cubes
1 package yeast

¼ cup warm milk (110°F)
4 eggs
2 ounces grated Parmesan
    cheese

_____

FILLING

1 cup peeled, seeded, and
    chopped tomatoes
3 tablespoons extra-virgin
    olive oil
Salt
4 ounces thinly sliced
    prosciutto, cut in narrow
    strips

4 ounces shredded
    mozzarella
¼ cup snipped basil or
    parsley

1. Mix the flour and salt together. Beat in the butter (this may be done in a food processor or a bowl with flat paddle). Dissolve the yeast in the warm milk and stir into the flour. Beat in the eggs one at a time. Beat in the cheese. The batter will be loose.

2. Quickly sauté the tomatoes in 2 tablespoons olive oil in a sauté pan. This is only to dry the tomatoes, not to cook them. Season with salt.

3. Generously butter a deep 12-inch round pan (a springform pan is fine). Pour half the dough into the prepared pan without letting it touch the sides. Spread the tomatoes on top of the dough, leaving ½-inch border. Scatter the prosciutto over the tomatoes and

cover with mozzarella and basil, keeping all within the ½-inch border. Put the remaining dough over the filling and pinch the top and bottom crusts together. Cover with a towel, place in a warm spot, and let rise 1 hour.

4. Preheat the oven to 350°F. Brush the top of the pizza with the remaining tablespoon olive oil. Bake the pizza in the preheated oven 35 to 40 minutes, or until golden brown. Serve warm. *Serves 8 to 10.*

Cicoli Bread

TORTANO CU' CICOLI

"Cicoli" is the Neapolitan word for "ciccioli," which are pork cracklings. They add a very distinctive flavor to this bread. At Easter time, a "tortano" is baked with whole eggs in their shells, set on top and held in place with strips of dough. The bread is then called "casatiello." A "tortano" may also be baked with a rich filling of ham, cheese, salami, and hard-boiled eggs, in which case it is known as "tortano imbottiti" (filled tortano).

CRACKLINGS

1½ pounds lean pork fatback

———

DOUGH

1 package dry yeast	1 teaspoon salt
1¼ cups warm water (110°F)	1 teaspoon coarsely ground black pepper
4 cups all-purpose flour	

1. Trim off the rind and chop the fatback into small pieces. Put in a pan with water to cover over medium-low heat until the fat is completely rendered. Remove "cicoli" (pork cracklings) with a slotted spoon. Boil the water away and measure 4 tablespoons fat.

2. Dissolve the yeast in ½ cup warm water. Sift 1 cup flour into

a bowl, add the yeast, and mix well with a wooden spoon. Cover and let proof 1 hour.

3. Mix the remaining flour, salt, and pepper together on the counter, in a food processor, mixer, or in a large bowl. Make a well in the center. Punch down the dough from step 2—the sponge—and add to the well. Add the remaining water, "cicoli," and 2 tablespoons rendered fat. Knead 20 minutes by hand or in an electric mixer with a dough hook until the dough is smooth and elastic. Place in an oiled bowl, cover with a towel, and let rise in a warm spot 1½ hours.

4. Brush a 12-inch ring-shaped pan with 1 tablespoon rendered fat. Roll dough into a rectangle 12 inches long and 6 inches wide. Roll up, jelly-roll style, and form a circle. Put into the prepared pan, dampen ends, and pinch together. Let rise 45 minutes. Brush with the remaining fat and bake at 375°F 1 hour, or until the bread is browned and sounds hollow when tapped on the bottom. *Makes 1 loaf.*

．　．　．

Note: This bread begins by forming what is known as a sponge. Yeast and a small amount of the flour are allowed to proof alone before being mixed with the remaining flour. The resulting bread has a special texture and flavor. Be sure not to add salt to the sponge.

MARKETS

Italian neighborhoods were easily recognizable in the early days of settlement. Markets huddled together cheek by jowl along streets that were lined with produce stands and pushcarts. Blocks of shops were often anchored on the corner by a variety store that sold Italian-language newspapers, candy, cigarettes, and cigars. "Salume" (dried cured meats) and provolone cheese hung by ropes in the windows and from the ceilings of "salumerie" (delicatessens). And there were always people, gathered in groups, standing outdoors.

Stores were very specialized in those days. The butcher sold only fresh meat; "the chicken man," poultry and eggs; the "latticini" shop, freshly made cheese and other dairy products. Fish, fruits, and vegetables were offered from pushcarts or stands. Bakeries were either bread bakeries or dessert bakeries but never both. My grandfather was a successful butcher and an innovative man. He thought he could increase business by also selling a little produce and some basic groceries along with his meat. It was just too alien a concept for the early Italians and he eventually had to give up his entrepreneurial ways.

No matter how small the neighborhood, there was never just one of any type of store. There were numerous butcher shops, "latticini," and "salumerie," almost enough to represent all the areas from which the immigrants had come. The Italians had arrived with the food preferences of their own villages and they wanted to maintain them. So the early shopkeepers opened their stores to serve their "paesani," the people from their area of Italy— to import their favorite salume or cheese, to make sausages as they knew them, to bake the breads of their native villages. Since native dialects and food customs varied, the immigrant chose a store where his language and his cooking needs would be understood—and, most important, where he could trust his "paesan" and count on him for credit in hard times. I can remember, as a little girl, wondering why my grandmother sent me past what seemed to be two or three perfectly good shops to buy what she needed from her own "paesan."

Over the years the flavor of Italian market streets has changed. Second-generation Italians did not have the same sense of village loyalty that influenced their parents. The dialects began to meld into one language and cooking differences became less so. Americans began to shop in the stores and the vendors added products to meet their wishes. Except for the occasional fish man, pushcarts have all but disappeared.

Furthermore, stores today are less specialized, and although there are still some that sell only one type of product, many are like mini-supermarkets. I can still buy chicken from "the chicken man" and bread from the bread bakery but I pick up my macaroni along with my meat and cheese and pass a Chinese restaurant on the way.

There have been many changes in the markets of the Italian neighborhood, but the greatest change is the most positive. The stores are now carrying products that were unavailable to the early immigrants. Freshly made mozzarella, imported Italian prosciutto, an endless selection of virgin olive oils are all available in the stores and are being bought not

Peter Melaragno's cigar store with Italian library and opera scores, 1916.

only by Italian-Americans but by people who claim no relationship other than a passion for their food.

Wine Biscuits

BISCOTTI DI VINO

Wine biscuits have existed in one form or another since at least Roman times. In *Di Agricultura,* Cato gives a recipe for Sweet Wine Cakes. These were crumbly cookies baked on bay leaves. The only leavening used was the fermenting wine must. Today, baking powder is used as a leavening. Italian-Americans baked these at home if they did their own baking. If not, they found them, as I always have, loose in boxes or bags at the Italian bakery. Today they are also sold in beautiful packages at specialty food stores.

4½ cups all-purpose flour
¾ cup sugar
2 teaspoons salt
1 tablespoon baking powder

1 cup sunflower or vegetable oil
1 cup full-bodied red wine

1. Preheat the oven to 350°F. Set the rack in the upper third of the oven.

2. Sift 4 cups flour and the remaining dry ingredients together onto a counter or into the bowl of an electric mixer with a paddle attachment. If working on the counter, make a well in the center. Add the oil and wine and gradually incorporate the flour until a soft dough is formed. Knead, using as much of the remaining flour as necessary to make a dough that is soft but does not stick to the counter. If the dough is too dry, the "biscotti" will break as they are being shaped.

3. Divide the dough into 40 pieces, roll each piece into a 5-inch-long rope, and form the ropes into rings, pinching the ends together firmly. Place on an ungreased heavy cookie sheet 2 inches apart. Bake in the upper third of the oven 20 minutes. Reduce the heat to 300°F and bake 15 to 20 minutes more, or until they are golden. Let the biscotti cool on cake racks and store them in airtight containers. *Makes 40 "biscotti."*

Pepper Biscuits

BISCOTTI DI PEPE

Pepper biscuits, made from seasoned bread dough, are common to Italian-American neighborhoods. I have not seen them as such in Italy. They were probably created here to resemble the "taralli," which is the same shape but is boiled before baking. "Taralli" may be sweet or savory as these biscuits.

1 package dry yeast
About ½ cup warm water
  (110°F)
4 cups all-purpose flour
½ teaspoon salt
1½ teaspoons cracked
  black pepper

½ cup olive oil
1½ teaspoons fennel seeds
  (optional)
Olive oil

1. Dissolve the yeast in ¼ cup water. Sift the flour, salt, and pepper onto the counter. Make a well in the center and add the yeast, the remaining water, and the oil. Blend together and gradually begin to incorporate the flour. Add more water if necessary to work in all the flour. This may also be done in a food processor or an electric mixer with a dough hook. Add fennel seeds if desired. The dough will be stiff. Knead 10 minutes, put in an oiled bowl, turn to coat, cover with a towel, and let rise until doubled in bulk.

2. Preheat the oven to 375°F. Break off small pieces of dough and roll into small ropes about 6 inches long. Form a ring and pinch the ends together. Place on a heavy baking sheet and let rise 20 minutes. Brush with oil and bake 12 to 15 minutes, or until firm and lightly browned. *Makes about 36 biscuits.*

Chapter Seven

SWEETS

here is a special joy to Italian sweets that goes beyond the obvious delights of the palate. It is the joy of association—the link with festive occasions. Although today traditional sweets are often baked at any time of the year, hardly a classic dessert exists without an alliance to a legend, a feast, or a saint's day. No doubt many of the ancient recipes owe their long and continued existence to their association with Italian traditions which die hard even when the initial belief has faded. For example, each St. Joseph's Day in Rhode Island, bakeries sell thousands of "zeppole," the deep-fried pastry which has been associated with that saint for centuries in the south of Italy. People line up at the doors of the Italian shops from early morning to buy a box to bring to family or friends. And yet, a few years ago when the city newspaper did an article on the pastry and questioned bakers and consumers alike about the origins of this tradition, few people had any idea why they repeated this process year after year other than that their families had always done it!

The myths and legends surrounding Italian sweets are almost as numerous as the sweets themselves. The stories, and names of the sweet, might vary from region to region or even from town to town. In many cases the derivation of the association is only hinted at by the name or by the fact that they were always made on a certain day of the year. "Fave dei morti" (dead man's beans), for example, are small, bean-shaped cookies usually baked on All Soul's Day, November 2. In ancient times it was considered a prudent practice to place beans on the tombs of the dead to ward off evil spirits. The cookies became a symbol of the gesture.

Often the descriptive candor of the cook reveals more about the appearance of the sweet than about its history. A myriad of graphic names provides those mental pictures worth so many words. Whisper-light meringues are known as "sospiri" (sighs); a pile of deep-fried, honeyed pieces of dough are known as "struffoli" (a heap of shreds).

When they were in Italy, the immigrants associated sweets only with festive occasions. At all other times, they ended their meals with a piece of fresh fruit and perhaps some cheese before it. The higher standard of living in America enabled them to consume more sweets just as it had enabled them to eat more meat. For the most part the sweets were eaten midmorning or afternoon, sometimes for breakfast, but in the early days they did not replace fruit for dessert. That occurred after the Americanization of the next generation. Most old-timers still prefer a piece of fruit at the end of a meal.

Irma Verde's family gathered around the table.

Aunt Irma's Deep-Fried Bowknots

WANDI ALLA ZIA IRMA

My grandmother said that these delicious carnival pastries, which are sometimes knotted and sometimes not, were named "wandi" because, as they wiggled in the hot oil, they resembled the empty fingers of gloves (guanti) which in a Neapolitan accent sounded like "wandi." Rhode Island seems to be the only place that calls them that. In Naples they are called "chiacchiere" (to chatter) because of the way they move while cooking. In Italy, they were originally made during carnival week when the streets were lined with vendors who fried outdoors rather than inside their small shops. Today they are available year-round in many Italian-American shops but homemade ones such as my Aunt Irma's are always better.

3 cups all-purpose flour	4 large eggs, beaten
1 tablespoon sugar	Vegetable oil for deep-frying
Pinch of salt	Powdered sugar

1. Sift the flour, sugar, and salt together and put into the bowl of an electric mixer or onto the counter. Make a well in the center and add the eggs. Mix together until a dough forms. Knead in the machine or on the counter, adding more flour if necessary, until a soft dough that does not stick is formed. Divide into 3 balls and set aside under an upturned bowl to rest 30 minutes.

2. Working with one ball at a time, roll the dough into a very thin sheet no more than $\frac{1}{16}$ inch thick. The dough may also be rolled in a pasta machine. Using a fluted ravioli wheel, cut the dough, on the bias (at an angle), into strips 1 inch wide by 8 inches long. Gently pull and stretch the strips as you tie each one into a loose knot.

3. Heat 2 inches oil to 370°F in a deep pan. Drop 2 to 3 strips of dough into the hot oil at a time. Turn immediately and remove with a slotted spoon onto paper towels to drain as soon as they are lightly golden. The "wandi" cook very quickly and should go in and out of the oil rapidly. Layer "wandi" and paper towels until all are cooked. Sprinkle both sides of cooled "wandi" generously with powdered sugar. Serve piled on a serving plate. "Wandi" will keep, loosely covered, for many days. *Makes about 54 pieces.*

Aunt Irma's Deep-Fried Bowknots (continued)

. . .

Note: My aunt Irma was a seamstress before she was married and knew from experience that the pieces of dough would stretch more easily if they were cut on the bias.

Sweet Ricotta Balls

DOLCETTE DI RICOTTA

Variations of this sweet exist all over Italy. They are at their best served warm, but I certainly don't shun them at room temperature. They can be reheated in a 400°F oven for about 5 minutes but they will not repuff.

1 pound ricotta cheese, drained in a sieve 30 minutes	1 tablespoon flour Grated rind of 1 lemon (no pith)
2 eggs	Vegetable oil for deep-frying
3 tablespoons sugar	Powdered sugar

1. Push the ricotta through a sieve into a bowl and beat until smooth and creamy. Beat in the eggs and sugar. Stir in the flour and lemon rind. Let rest 20 minutes.

2. Put the oil 2 inches deep in a deep heavy pan and heat to 370°F. Drop the batter into hot fat by scant ¼ cup measure. Cook, turning until golden on all sides and slightly puffed. Remove with a slotted spoon and drain on paper towels. Sprinkle with powdered sugar and serve. *Makes about 12.*

Sweet Half-Moon Ravioli

RAVIOLI DOLCI A MEZZA-LUNA

Deep-fried sweets have always been part of southern Italian celebrations, especially street fairs. These are a specialty of Calabria and are most often made in the shape of square ravioli. I prefer the looks of them when they are made in fluted half-moon shapes.

PASTA FROLLA

2 cups all-purpose flour
2 tablespoons sugar
¼ teaspoon salt

4 tablespoons butter
2 eggs, beaten
White or Marsala wine

———

FILLING

1 cup ricotta cheese
½ cup powdered sugar
4 ounces candied citron or
   other candied fruit, diced
2 ounces unsweetened or
   bittersweet chocolate,
   chopped

½ cup toasted peeled
   hazelnuts, chopped
1 teaspoon cinnamon
Vegetable oil for frying

———

Vanilla-flavored powdered
   sugar

1. Make the dough: sift the flour, sugar, and salt onto the counter. Work the butter in with your fingertips until the mixture is the consistency of coarse grain. Make a well in the center and add the eggs. Incorporate the flour and add a few tablespoons wine or Marsala as needed to make the dough hold together. Knead briefly until the mixture is a smooth dough. Set aside, covered with a towel, 30 minutes.

2. Make the filling: push the ricotta through a sieve. Beat the ricotta and the powdered sugar until completely smooth. Fold in the chopped fruit, chocolate, nuts, and cinnamon.

3. Working with half of the dough at a time, roll out on a floured counter to about ⅛ inch thickness. Cut fluted circles 3½ to 4 inches

Sweet Half-Moon Ravioli (continued)

in diameter. Put a well-rounded teaspoon of filling in the center of each circle. Fold in half and press well around the filling to seal the edges. Use a bit of water if necessary to close securely.

4. Heat the oil in a heavy pan with high sides to a depth of 1 inch. When the oil is hot (350°F) slip in 2 or 3 ravioli. Do not crowd the pan. Fry until golden on both sides (about 1 minute). Drain on paper toweling. Sprinkle with vanilla-flavored powdered sugar. *Makes about 28.*

• • •

Note: Vanilla-flavored powdered sugar is available in Italian markets. You can make your own by steeping a vanilla bean in powdered sugar in a tightly closed container for several weeks.

CANDIED FRUITS

I suspect that supermarket candied fruits are not fruits at all but some chemical concoction. There is no way that those tough little Kelly-green squares ever grew on a tree! Do try to find good-quality candied fruits, which are usually sold loose, not in jars. Some specialty food stores will mail-order them. Check the markets in Italian neighborhoods because many of them at least carry citron around holiday time. Buy a large piece because it keeps indefinitely in the refrigerator.

Honey Cluster Dessert

STRUFFOLI

"Struffoli," honey-coated pastry balls shaped into circles or pyramids, are a traditional part of a Neapolitan Christmas dinner. Quite often it is the centerpiece, waiting for the end of the meal when diners cut a slice or, more commonly, break off the little balls. Italian-Americans usually make "struffoli" at home and only during the Christmas season, so I was very surprised to find them in Naples in bakeries and restaurants year-round. The candied fruit gives the dessert a festive appearance, but "struffoli" are just as often made without it.

2 to 2¼ cups sifted all-purpose flour	½ teaspoon vanilla or anise extract
3 tablespoons grated orange rind	Vegetable oil for deep-frying
1 tablespoon grated lemon rind	1 lemon, cut in half
¼ teaspoon salt	¾ cup honey
3 eggs at room temperature, beaten	1 tablespoon sugar
	1 cup best-quality mixed candied fruits (optional)

1. Combine the flour, 1 tablespoon orange rind, all the lemon rind, and salt on a counter or in the bowl of an electric mixer. Make a well in the center and add the eggs and vanilla and gradually combine with the flour until a dough is formed. Knead until smooth, adding more flour if necessary to prevent from sticking. Cover loosely and let rest at least 20 minutes.

2. Break off large walnut-size pieces of dough. Using your palms, roll each piece on the counter to a 14- to 15-inch pencil-thin strip. Cut each long dough strip into ¼-inch pieces.

3. Put the oil 2 inches deep in a heavy pan and heat to 370°F. Fry pieces of dough, a few at a time, until golden on all sides (45 seconds to 1 minute). Remove with a slotted spoon to paper towels to drain.

4. Rub a serving plate with the cut side of a lemon. Boil the honey and sugar in a large pan over medium heat until the sugar has

Honey Cluster Dessert (continued)

melted and the mixture is golden brown (about 5 minutes). Add the remaining orange rind, "struffoli," and the candied fruit if using. Mix together and pour onto the prepared plate. Use the cut lemon to push the "struffoli" into a pyramid or ring shape. If the "struffoli" are too warm to form a shape, wait a few minutes and try again. Cool completely. *Serves 8.*

• • •

Note: The amount of crunchiness of the "struffoli" depends on how long the honey and sugar are cooked. The closer the mixture gets to a caramel, the crunchier the finished dessert.

• • •

Note: My Aunt Irma, who wouldn't let a Christmas go by without "struffoli," taught me to shape the "struffoli" with a cut lemon because it does not stick to the honey coating.

Lemon-Glazed Egg Biscuits

FROLLI DI UOVA

Originally associated with Lent and Easter, egg biscuits are now available year-round in many Italian-American bakeries. During holiday times the tops of these cookies are often decorated with colorful candied sprinkles. If you wish to do this, be sure to apply them as soon as the glaze is brushed on so that they will stay put.

1 stick softened butter (4 ounces)	Grated rind of 2 lemons
1 cup sugar	1 tablespoon lemon juice
1 large egg	2 cups all-purpose flour
½ pound ricotta cheese	½ teaspoon baking powder
1 teaspoon vanilla	½ teaspoon baking soda
	½ teaspoon salt

LEMON GLAZE

1 cup powdered sugar
4 teaspoons lemon juice

1. Place the oven rack in the upper third of the oven. Preheat the oven to 350°F.

2. Cream the butter in the bowl of an electric mixer, adding the sugar gradually to make a light and fluffy mixture. Add the egg and beat well. Beat in the ricotta cheese, vanilla, lemon rind, and lemon juice.

3. Sift the flour, baking powder, baking soda, and salt together. Blend into the batter either by hand or on the slow speed of the mixer. Be sure the mixture is thoroughly blended but do not overbeat.

4. Drop by rounded tablespoons on an ungreased cookie sheet 2 inches apart. Bake 14 minutes, or until cooked through. Remove to a wire rack and cool 5 minutes. Sift and blend powdered sugar with the lemon juice to make the glaze. Brush on the cooled biscuits. *Makes 40 cookies.*

Aunt Irma's Easter Egg Biscuits

BISCOTTI DI PASQUA ALLA ZIA IRMA

Aunt Irma prefers this version of egg biscuits because, without the ricotta, they keep longer. But then, there are seldom any left over to keep. Pastries knotted like these have very old, religious origins. They were meant to simulate arms crossed over the chest in prayer.

6 cups all-purpose flour
1½ cups sugar
3 tablespoons baking
   powder
1 teaspoon salt

6 eggs, lightly beaten
1 cup vegetable oil
½ cup milk
½ ounce lemon extract

———

ICING

1 pound powdered sugar
4 tablespoons milk
½ ounce lemon extract

1. Preheat the oven to 325°F.
2. Sift the dry ingredients together into a bowl. Make a well in the center and add the liquid ingredients. Gradually incorporate the dry ingredients into the liquids (may be done with the slow speed of an electric mixer) until a dough is formed. Let rest, covered, 20 minutes.
3. Break off small pieces of dough and roll into pencil-thin strips 6 inches long. Knot the ropes. Place on a buttered and lightly floured cookie sheet. Bake 12 to 15 minutes, or until lightly colored.
4. Sift the powdered sugar into a bowl. Beat in the milk and flavoring to make a smooth, runny icing. Dip the warm cookies into the icing and place on a cake rack to cool. *Makes 60 biscuits.*

Instant Biscotti

BISCOTTI RAPIDI

Rosemary Manell, Julia Child's longtime associate, designed this method of baking what I call "instant biscotti" because the cookie dough is simply pressed into the pan, cut, and left in the pan for its second baking. The results are a flat, hard cookie which, like the traditional almond "biscotti," is hard and keeps for a long time in cookie tins.

¾ pound walnuts
¼ pound hazelnuts, toasted at 350°F 6 to 8 minutes
3 cups all-purpose flour
½ cup sugar
1 cup light brown sugar
2 teaspoons cinnamon

½ teaspoon salt
1 teaspoon baking powder
3 large eggs, beaten
⅓ cup unflavored vegetable oil (safflower, sunflower, or corn)

1. Preheat the oven to 350°F.
2. Coarsely chop the nuts and mix together. Sift the flour, sugars, cinnamon, salt, and baking powder together twice. Blend in the nuts.
3. Remove 2 tablespoons beaten egg for brushing the top of the "biscotti." Add the remaining eggs and oil to the flour mixture and work together until homogeneous. Add a few tablespoons water if necessary to blend but the mixture should be a bit dry and crumbly.
4. Pat the dough into a lightly oiled 10½ x 15½-inch jelly-roll pan. Working with a wet hand makes this easier. Brush the top with the reserved egg.
5. Bake in the oven 30 minutes, or until the edges begin to color slightly. Leave the cookies in the pan and make diagonal cuts 1½ inches apart so that cookies are a diamond shape. Return to the oven in the same pan and bake 30 more minutes. Cool in the pan. *Makes approximately 48 pieces.*

Almond Cookies

BISCOTTI DI MANDORLE

These nutty "biscotti" are often called "quaresimali" because they were originally made only during Lent ("quaresima"). Loosely translated, "biscotti" means "cookie," but the derivation of the word is from "bis" (twice) and "cottare" (to cook), or "twice cooked" because traditional biscotti are first baked in a long loaf or roll and then cut into individual pieces before being rebaked until browned. This method of baking produces a hard, nutty cookie, perfect for dipping in sweet wine or cappuccino. The cookies will continue to harden as they sit and may be kept in cookie tins for months.

¾ pound whole unpeeled almonds
¾ cup sugar
2 cups all-purpose flour
2 teaspoons cinnamon
½ teaspoon salt

2 teaspoons baking powder
¾ cup light brown sugar
3 tablespoons unflavored vegetable oil (safflower, sunflower, or corn)
4 large eggs

1. Preheat the oven to 350°F.
2. Put ¾ cup almonds and ¼ cup sugar in a food processor and grind until very fine. Set aside. Toast the remaining almonds 10 to 12 minutes, or until lightly browned. When cool enough to handle, chop very coarsely, leaving the pieces in about thirds.
3. Sift the flour, remaining sugar, cinnamon, salt, and baking powder together twice. Combine with the coarsely chopped nuts in a large bowl or in an electric mixer with a paddle attachment. Stir in the brown sugar and reserved nut sugar.
4. Stir the oil into the mixture. Beat 3 eggs together and add to the dough. If necessary, beat the fourth egg and add enough of it to make a homogeneous but not sticky dough. Reserve the remaining egg for brushing on top.
5. Turn the dough out onto a lightly floured counter and knead briefly until the dough holds together. Divide the dough into 2 pieces, then roll each piece back and forth under your palms to form a 12-inch-long log. Transfer to an oiled baking sheet and pat the log into a shape about 1 inch high and 2½ inches wide. Brush the top

with the reserved beaten egg. Bake 40 minutes. Remove from the oven and reduce the heat to 300°F. Immediately hold a large knife at an angle to the log, cut it into slices ¾ inch wide, and separate the pieces slightly from each other. If the center pieces are very long, cut them in half. The "biscotti" should be about 3 inches long. Return to the oven and bake 20 minutes, or until dry. Remove and cool in the pan. *Makes approximately 40 cookies.*

ITALIAN-AMERICAN CELEBRATIONS

Aunt Irma is eighty-four years old and still does her own baking, especially for the holidays when she makes the same traditional southern Italian sweets that her mother and mother-in-law made. She also bakes American desserts and tries new recipes from food magazines and cookbooks, and that is more or less what has happened to Italian-American holiday meals—"biscotti di Pasqua" and "wandi" share table space with lemon meringue pie and "three-layer-chocolate-mousse wonder." An elegant, typically American wedding dinner or First Communion meal may well begin with ziti (macaroni which means "bridegrooms") and ragu because it is unthinkable not to. Maintaining these traditions, no matter how small or seemingly insignificant, gives Italian-Americans a sense of connection with their Italian-born ancestors. It is this sense that allows thoroughly modern Americans, who speak no Italian whatsoever, to find relatives in a tiny remote town on a first visit to Italy and feel at home.

Sesame Seed Cookies

BISCOTTI REGINA

Pyramids of Italian cookies are always a part of holidays, weddings, and celebrations of the like. In fact, it is often the custom for relatives and friends to bring a large tray of cookies to a wedding. I can remember as a young girl staring in wonder at the large pyramids of cookies and wondering whether to politely take one from the top or risk pulling one from underneath.

3 cups flour	2 eggs, lightly beaten
¾ cup sugar	¼ cup milk
2 teaspoons baking powder	2 teaspoons vanilla
⅛ teaspoon salt	¾ cup sesame seeds
4 tablespoons unsalted butter, softened	Water
4 tablespoons vegetable shortening	

1. Preheat the oven to 375°F. Lightly grease a cookie sheet.

2. Sift the flour, sugar, baking powder, and salt together into a bowl. Blend in the butter and shortening until the mixture resembles coarse meal. Make a well in the center and add the eggs, milk, and vanilla. Gradually incorporate the dry ingredients to make a soft dough.

3. Divide the dough into 4 pieces. Form each piece into a long roll ½ inch in diameter. Cut into 2-inch pieces. Brush with water and roll in the sesame seeds. Place 1 inch apart on the cookie sheet. Bake 20 to 25 minutes, or until golden brown. Cool on a rack. Store in an airtight container. *Makes 3 dozen.*

Frozen Zabaglione

SEMIFREDDO DI ZABAGLIONE

A "semifreddo" or "half frozen" is a refrigerated or frozen dessert that is never quite frozen but has a somewhat soft texture. This simple one combines a bit of "new country" with the old by using an American technique for the crust with a typical Italian filling.

CRUST

5 tablespoons butter, melted
¾ cup crushed amaretti cookies
¾ cup crushed toasted almonds
1 tablespoon cocoa

ZABAGLIONE

6 egg yolks
6 tablespoons sugar
⅓ cup dry Marsala wine
1¼ cups heavy cream, whipped to soft peaks

1. Brush 1 tablespoon melted butter on the bottom of a 13 x 8-inch glass or ceramic dish with at least ¾-inch-high sides. Mix the crust ingredients together in a bowl until they are well combined. Press all but 2 tablespoons of the mixture into the bottom of the prepared pan.

2. For the zabaglione, whisk the egg yolks and sugar together in a 1½-quart heavy pot until well mixed. Place on a Flame-Tamer over medium-low heat and gradually whisk in the Marsala, beating continuously until thick and foamy. Remove from the heat and set the pot in a bowl of ice water to cool quickly. When the zabaglione is thoroughly cooled, fold in the whipped cream. Pour into the prepared crust, even the top with a spatula, and sprinkle with the reserved crumbs. Freeze a minimum of 3 hours. Cut in squares and serve with chocolate sauce flavored with coffee (page 304). *Serves 8.*

• • •

Note: Zabaglione is usually made over direct heat. This can be tricky because if the mixture gets too hot the eggs will scramble. Many people use a double boiler but I find it a terrible nuisance. The very easiest method is with a Flame-Tamer, which can be purchased for about five dollars in a kitchen or hardware store. A Flame-Tamer is a round metal flame diffuser with a short handle that sits on top of

Frozen Zabaglione (continued)

a gas or electric stove. It allows the bottom of the cooking pot to be evenly heated at a controlled temperature. I use a Flame-Tamer whenever a double boiler might be called for.

Chocolate Sauce

I use imported Italian bittersweet chocolate for all my recipes that call for bittersweet chocolate. It has a very distinct taste that I haven't found in other chocolates. Perugina bittersweet bars, known as "Luisa," are available in the United States. You can substitute a good grade semisweet chocolate if you cannot find Italian bittersweet.

This is a quick, easy chocolate sauce that is delicious over semifreddos, ice cream, or poached fruit. Choose a flavoring to blend with the dessert.

½ cup heavy cream
¼ cup sugar
4 ounces bittersweet
  chocolate

½ cup strong espresso
  coffee or 2
  tablespoons liqueur

Blend the ingredients together in a small pot and cook over low heat until the chocolate and sugar have melted. *Makes about 1½ cups.*

Molded Frozen Nougat Cream

SEMIFREDDO DI TORRONE

Torrone, a traditional Christmas nougat candy, is still made by Italian-American bakeries, but only during that season. When I was growing up, nougat from Italy was available almost year-round. The most popular one, and the one that my grandmother always kept on hand, came wrapped in silver in a tiny box decorated with an Italian lady in regional dress. I think we loved them as much for their wrapping as their taste. Today there are many good brands of imported nougat, both hard and soft, in Italian markets. You will need the hard torrone for this dessert.

4 ounces hard Italian nougat
    candy (torrone)
4 ounces bittersweet
    chocolate
3 eggs, separated
½ cup sugar
1¼ cups heavy cream

1 tablespoon vanilla
2 tablespoons rum

½ cup shaved chocolate
    pieces for decoration
    (optional)

1. In a food processor or with a heavy rolling pin crush the torrone into rice-sized pieces. Chop the chocolate into similar-size pieces and combine it with the torrone.

2. Beat the egg yolks and gradually add the sugar, beating well until the mixture is lightly ribboned.

3. Beat the heavy cream to soft peaks. Beat the egg whites until they are stiff but not dry. Fold the cream, egg whites, vanilla, and rum into the egg yolks.

4. Line a 10 x 5-inch loaf pan with plastic wrap, letting the ends extend out far enough to cover the pan after it has been filled. Sprinkle ⅓ torrone mixture into the bottom of the pan. Cover with ⅓ cream mixture, pressing the cream with a spatula to adhere to the torrone. Continue to layer, ending with the cream. Fold the plastic wrap over the top. Freeze 3 hours. Unmold and let rest in the refrigerator 20 to 30 minutes, or until soft enough to slice, before serving. Sprinkle with the shaved chocolate pieces if desired. *Serves 8.*

Drowned Coffee Ice Cream

COVIGLIA AL CAFFÉ AFFOGATA

"Coviglia" is a Neapolitan term for what would be called a "semi-freddo" elsewhere. It is a softly frozen dessert. This one is "drowned" with hot coffee.

2 cups milk	2 tablespoons instant coffee
4-inch piece vanilla bean	1 cup heavy cream, whipped
5 egg yolks	to soft peaks
1 cup sugar	3 ounces Italian bittersweet
1 cup espresso coffee or	chocolate, shaved
strong coffee	

1. Scald the milk with the vanilla bean and keep warm.

2. In a heavy 2-quart pot, beat the egg yolks, gradually adding the sugar, until they are lightly ribboned. Gradually stir in the warm milk with the vanilla bean, ½ cup coffee, and the instant coffee. Place over low heat or on a Flame-Tamer (page 303) and cook until the mixture coats a spoon and forms a custard. *Do not let boil.* Cool and refrigerate until well chilled.

3. Remove the vanilla bean. Fold in the heavy cream and freeze in an ice cream maker. Let rest to ripen 1 hour.

4. To serve, spoon "coviglia" into 8 individual dishes. Top with the shaved chocolate and pour on about 1 tablespoon hot espresso. Serve immediately. *Serves 8.*

Mascarpone Pudding

BUDINO DI MASCARPONE

Whenever there were more than two or three "paesans" gathered at our house the conversation invariably turned to food. A Neapolitan-American friend of my family's married a woman whose ancestors came from Lombardia, in the north of Italy. The southern Italian-Americans pretended great pity for her because she didn't know how to eat. "No calzone. No lasagna. Mama mia!" Her defense was always to talk about the cream and cheese used in her family's cooking.

1 cup mascarpone cheese
½ cup powdered sugar
⅓ cup dry Marsala wine
1 teaspoon vanilla
3 ounces bittersweet
  chocolate, grated

1 cup heavy cream
2 egg whites
About 10 amaretti cookies,
  crushed

1. In a large bowl, beat the mascarpone cheese with a wooden spoon until smooth. Sift in the powdered sugar and blend together well. Stir in the Marsala and vanilla and fold in the chocolate.

2. Beat the heavy cream to soft peaks and fold it into the mascarpone mixture. Beat the egg whites until stiff but not dry. Stir ¼ of the volume of the beaten egg whites thoroughly into the cheese mixture and then carefully fold in the remaining whites.

3. Spoon the mixture into a deep, 8-inch round glass bowl or 8 individual glass coupes. Sprinkle the amaretti on top and chill 3 hours before serving. *Serves 8.*

MEMORIES

"They never wrote anything down.
They cooked by feeling . . ."

It was the Italian custom that when a woman was married, she went to live with the husband's family. She became part of his family. That was the custom. When my wife and I were married, my sister lived downstairs from us and my mother wasn't too far away. They taught my wife to cook.

When my father was living we had to have Sunday dinner and supper. It was a must. We had to be there and had to sit throughout the meal. Today, we have Sunday dinner, the phone rings, and the girls disappear. We would never do that.

There are dishes that are forgotten now. When I get together with my family, my sisters, and I think of it, I realize that you just don't see them anymore or hear of them anymore.

"Pastiera." My mother used to make a rice pie and then one especially for me because I didn't like rice. It was made with noodles. It was the best I've ever had.

Mr. Rossi with his father, mother, brother, and sister.

They never wrote anything down. They cooked by feeling a little bit of this and a little of that.

There was a well-known family who had a lot of property and people could go there and make a garden. A lot of the people from my parents' area who lived in apartments without land would go there to garden.

When my parents finally built a house, my mother had a garden. In fact, when she was eighty-something and the doctor told her, "Don't do anything," she'd be out there in the garden, weeding.

They knew how to preserve. Once a crop was ready to pick, they had to think about preserving it somehow. You couldn't eat it all. They'd cut apples and tomatoes into pieces and leave them out in the sun to dry. Then you'd have them all winter.

Sunday mornings it was our [the children's] job to make pasta. Couldn't go out to play baseball. We had to make cavati. We had to hollow them out. Now I imagine they have a machine.

AMERICO ROSSI
(family from Orchi near Naples)

Mr. Rossi's father, Giacomo Rossi, and grandfather Tomasso Rossi in Orchi, Italy.

Sponge Cake

MADDALENA

"Maddalena" is what Italians call a genoise-type sponge cake, i.e., one made with whole eggs. They call a sponge cake that is made with separated eggs a "Pan di Spagna" (bread from Spain) because it was indeed the Spanish who brought the cake to southern Italy in the fifteenth century. I prefer to make a "Maddalena" because it is more straightforward. It freezes beautifully and I even save trimmed pieces because they are perfect for triflelike desserts. Many traditional southern Italian cake desserts use a combination of sponge cake and ricotta cheese (see "Cassata Siciliana," page 312, and "Zuppa Inglese Napoletana," page 313).

4 large eggs
⅔ cup sugar
¼ teaspoon salt
1 teaspoon vanilla

2 teaspoons grated lemon or
    orange rind
1 cup sifted cake flour

1. Preheat the oven to 325°F.
2. Generously butter the bottom and the sides of a cake pan. Flour the bottom lightly. If you are making a sheet cake, butter the bottom of a 12 x 15-inch jelly-roll pan, line with wax or parchment paper, and butter and flour the paper.
3. Beat the eggs in the bowl of a heavy-duty electric mixer. Gradually add the sugar and continue beating until the batter begins to swell. Add the salt, vanilla, and grated rind and beat until the batter is pale, doubled in volume, and forms a heavy ribbon.
4. Sift the flour onto the batter and fold in quickly but completely. Hold the bowl close to the bottom of the prepared pan and pour in the batter. Bake in the bottom third of a preheated oven until done (a round cake takes 40 minutes, a sheet cake 25 minutes). Test with a cake tester, which should be dry and feel warm to the heel of your hand. Immediately turn the cake out onto a cake rack to cool. *Makes one 9-inch round cake or one 12 x 15-inch sheet cake.*

• • •

Note: The only leavening agent in this cake is the volume that is beaten into the eggs. The eggs need warmth in order to swell and a good heavy-duty electric mixer produces that warmth by the friction it generates. If you do not have a heavy-duty mixer, work in a heat-proof bowl set over a Flame-Tamer (page 303) on low heat. Because there is no other leavening, the swelled batter should be transferred to the baking pan carefully so it does not deflate and should be baked immediately.

Chocolate Cake from Capri

TORTA CAPRESE

It is close to impossible to visit any place even close to Capri and not encounter a version of this wonderful chocolate cake. Yet, in spite of the fact that we have a large population from that area of Italy, I have never seen it here. I am sure that it would have been an extravagant use of ingredients for "la cucina povera" but it is about time it emigrated.

½ pound butter
½ pound bittersweet or
    semisweet chocolate
5 eggs, separated
1 cup sugar
¼ cup potato or cornstarch

1 tablespoon baking powder
¼ teaspoon salt
2½ cups finely chopped
    walnuts
1 teaspoon vanilla
Powdered sugar

1. Melt all but 1 tablespoon butter with the chocolate. Transfer to a large bowl and cool. Beat the egg yolks until light and lemon-colored. Gradually add the sugar and beat well until lightly ribboned. Combine well with the cooled chocolate. Sift the starch, baking powder, and salt together and add to the eggs, stirring until blended. Stir in the nuts and vanilla.

2. Preheat the oven to 350°F. Use the remaining tablespoon butter to butter a 9-inch springform pan. Lightly flour the bottom and sides of the pan. Whip the egg whites until peaks form and fold into the chocolate mixture. Put in the cake pan and bake 45 minutes. Cool completely in the pan. Remove the cake from the pan and sprinkle with powdered sugar. *Serves 6 to 8.*

Sicilian Ricotta Cake

CASSATA SICILIANA

Many versions of the Sicilian "cassata," including a frozen one, exist both in Italy and the United States. Pastry chefs often cover the cake with a chocolate frosting and elaborate decorations. I am most fond of this simple version. Ricotta cheese is frequently part of southern Italian desserts since it was readily available even to the poorest of households. In fact, it was usually homemade, in Italy of sheep's milk, and here eventually from the more abundant cow's milk.

1½ pounds ricotta cheese	3 ounces walnuts, chopped
½ pound mascarpone cheese	(about ¾ cup)
¾ cup powdered sugar	2 tablespoons orange liqueur
½ cup chopped candied	⅓ cup water
citron or other candied	2 tablespoons sugar
fruit (3 ounces)	½ cup orange liqueur
5 ounces bittersweet or	
semisweet chocolate,	
finely chopped	

———

1 "Maddalena" cake with	Sweetened cocoa for
orange rind baked in	decoration
12 x 15-inch jelly-roll pan	
(page 310)	

1. Push the ricotta through a sieve into a bowl. Add the mascarpone and cream together until well combined. Sift in the powdered sugar and blend well. Fold in the citron, chocolate, nuts, and orange liqueur.

2. Combine the water, sugar, and orange liqueur in a small heavy pot. Heat until the sugar melts and the mixture is clear. Pour into a pie pan or a similar flat dish.

3. Using a 6 x 10-inch loaf pan as a guide, cut pieces from the cake to fit the bottom, sides, and top of the pan. Line the pan with plastic wrap. Dip the top piece of cake quickly on both sides in the prepared syrup and place in the pan. Repeat with the side pieces. Spoon the filling into the pan and tap the pan soundly on the counter to settle the filling. Dip the last piece of cake into the syrup and cover

the filling. (If necessary, use patchwork pieces to cover the top of the cake.) Wrap the pan in plastic wrap and refrigerate 3 hours or overnight.

4. When ready to serve, unmold, using plastic wrap to coax the cake from the pan. Dust with sweetened cocoa. *Serves 8 to 10.*

Neapolitan Cherry Ricotta Cake

ZUPPA INGLESE NAPOLETANA

When I was growing up I was fascinated by the little boot-shaped glass jars that held steeped cherries from Bari. Little did I know what wonders they could make.

8 ounces bittersweet or semisweet chocolate	1 "Maddalena" cake with lemon rind baked in a 9-inch round cake or springform pan (page 310)
2 pounds fresh ricotta cheese	
1 cup powdered sugar	
5 tablespoons dark rum	
¼ cup sugar	1 cup imported cherries in rum, drained (see note)
¼ cup water	
½ cup rum	

1. Break the chocolate into pieces and pulsate in a food processor until broken into small bits. Sift the chocolate bits, reserving the chocolate powder and the bits in the sifter separately.

2. Push the ricotta through a sieve into a bowl or into a food processor bowl. Add the sugar and beat until smooth. Add the rum and blend. Fold in the chocolate bits.

3. Make the syrup: cook the sugar and water in a small heavy pot over low heat, swirling the pan occasionally until the sugar dissolves. Mix in the rum.

4. Cut the "Maddalena" into 3 even layers. Brush the top of the bottom layer with the rum syrup and put it into a 9-inch springform pan, flavored side up. Spread half the ricotta mixture over the cake. Spread half the cherries over the cheese. Brush both sides of the middle cake layer with the rum syrup and place over the first layer.

Neapolitan Cherry Ricotta Cake (continued)

Cover with the remaining cheese and cherries. Brush the bottom side of the top layer of cake with the rum syrup and place, flavored side down, on top of the second layer. Sprinkle the chocolate powder on top. Refrigerate 3 hours or overnight. *Serves 10.*

• • •

Note: Jars of steeped cherries from Bari are often available in Italian specialty markets, but the recipe works perfectly well with one 16½-ounce can pitted dark cherries, drained and steeped overnight in rum and drained, or one 12-ounce jar morello cherry jam (amarena).

Glazed Orange Cake

TORTA ALL'ARANCIA

This simple, one-layer Calabrian cake is a delicious combination of standard southern flavorings—oranges, Marsala wine, pignolis, honey, and raisins. The cake keeps well and is delightful served with a glass of good Marsala wine.

2 cups sifted cake flour
2 teaspoons baking powder
¼ teaspoon salt
1 stick unsalted butter
   (4 ounces), at room
   temperature
1 cup sugar
3 large eggs, at room
   temperature, lightly
   beaten together
4 ounces dark raisins
   (¾ cup), steeped in 4
   tablespoons Marsala wine

1 teaspoon vanilla
½ cup freshly squeezed
   orange juice
3 tablespoons pinoli nuts
   (pine nuts), lightly toasted
Grated rind of 2 oranges
   (no pith)

———

GLAZE

3 tablespoons honey
2 tablespoons orange juice

1. Preheat the oven to 350°F. Set the rack in the lower third of the oven. Butter and lightly flour the bottom and sides of an 8-inch cake pan.

2. Remove 1 generous tablespoon flour from the 2 cups and reserve. Sift the remaining flour, baking powder, and salt together twice and set aside.

3. Cream the butter until light. Gradually add the sugar and beat until the mixture is light and fluffy, scraping the sides of the bowl as necessary. Gradually and slowly add the eggs, beating continuously.

4. Drain the Marsala from the raisins and combine it and the vanilla with the orange juice. Mix the pinoli nuts with the raisins and sprinkle them with the reserved tablespoon cake flour.

5. Beginning and ending with the dry ingredients, carefully but thoroughly blend the flour mixture and orange juice mixture into the batter. Do not overbeat. Fold in the raisins, pinolis, and orange rind. Pour into the prepared pan. Bake 35 to 40 minutes, or when cake tests done (cake tester comes away clean and cake shrinks slightly from sides of pan).

6. Make the glaze by heating the honey and orange juice together until runny. As soon as the cake is removed from the oven, puncture the surface with a cake tester or other narrow skewer and drizzle on half the glaze. Cool in the pan 10 minutes. Turn out onto a rack and brush with the remaining glaze while still warm. *Serves 8.*

BUTTER CAKE CAUTIONS

So often it is a simple recipe that gives people the most trouble and I usually find that the problem is in a basic technique. The initial steps of a butter cake—creaming the butter and sugar and adding eggs—are very important to the final texture of the cake. Add the sugar gradually to the creamed butter so it is well incorporated. Really take the time to beat in the eggs one at a time so the mixture is light and fluffy. Skimping on the labor here will result in a heavy-textured, dense cake. Once the flour is added, the batter should not be overworked or the cake will be tough.

Sweet Cornmeal Cake

POLENTINA

This family favorite is usually on hand, either in the cake dish or freezer. We often top it with fresh berries, cream, or stirred custard but mostly love it plain. A rehrucken pan is a half round loaf pan with a ribbed top. It makes a pretty cake.

Cornmeal for dusting
  the pan
½ cup unsalted butter,
  at room temperature
¼ cup vegetable shortening
¾ cup sugar
3 eggs
1 tablespoon vanilla
¾ cup sifted all-purpose
  flour

¾ cup sifted corn flour
¼ cup Italian cornmeal
  (see note)
2 teaspoons baking powder
½ teaspoon salt
⅓ cup orange juice
Grated rind of 1 orange
Powdered sugar for dusting
  the cake

1. Preheat the oven to 350°F. Butter and dust with cornmeal a rehrucken pan or a 9¾ x 5½-inch loaf pan.
2. Cream the butter and shortening together well. Add the sugar gradually, beating well. Add the eggs, one at a time, and continue beating until the mixture is light and fluffy. Beat in the vanilla.
3. Sift the dry ingredients together twice. Add the dry ingredients to the batter alternately with the orange juice. Stir in the rind. Pour into the prepared pan and bake 40 to 50 minutes, or until the cake tests done. Cool in the pan 15 minutes. Turn out and when completely cool, dust with powdered sugar. *Serves 8.*

• • •

Note: Any cornmeal can be used for this cake but I prefer the finer grain Italian cornmeal. If you choose a larger grain the cake will have a coarser texture.

Neapolitan Cherry Pastries

PASTICCETTI ALL'AMARENA

You'll have to look in specialty stores to find the amarena jam (or the English version called morello jam) which gives these irresistible treats their special flavor. "Pasta frolla" is the Italian term for tender pastry made with flour, sugar, fat, eggs, and sometimes sweet wine or Marsala. "Crema," in this case, is a "crema pasticcera" or pastry cream.

PASTA FROLLA	CREMA
2½ to 2¾ cups flour	3 egg yolks
⅔ cup sugar	½ cup sugar
Grated rind of 1 lemon	6 tablespoons flour
Pinch of salt	2 cups milk
12 tablespoons cold butter	2 to 3 pieces lemon peel,
2 eggs, beaten	yellow part only
1 tablespoon white or dry	1 teaspoon vanilla
Marsala wine	

About ½ cup amarena
   (morello) cherry jam
Powdered sugar

1. Make the pastry: toss the flour, sugar, rind, and salt together on a counter. Cut in the butter with your fingertips until it is the size of small peas. Make a well in the center and add the eggs and white wine or Marsala. Toss together to incorporate the flour and liquids. Add more flour or wine as needed. Push small amounts of the mixture away from you with the heel of your hand to form sheets of butter and flour. Pull back together and repeat. Gather together and shape into a long roll. Wrap and chill about 1 hour.

2. Prepare the custard: beat the egg yolks and sugar together in a heavy 1½-quart pot until lightly ribboned. Add the flour, milk, and lemon peel. Blend well. Bring to a boil, stirring constantly. Remove from the heat, add the vanilla, and let cool, covered with wax paper or plastic wrap. Remove the lemon peel before using.

Neapolitan Cherry Pastries (continued)

3. Butter twenty 3-inch fluted tart molds well. Cut ¼-inch slices from the roll of pastry and roll each piece out until it is large enough to fill the bottom and sides of the tart molds. Line the molds. Put 1 tablespoon pastry cream into each pastry-lined mold. Put 1 teaspoon jam on top of the pastry, cover with a second piece of pastry, and pinch the edges together to seal. Bake in a 350°F oven 30 minutes, or until golden brown. Turn out of the molds when cool and dust with powdered sugar. *Makes 20.*

Raisin Nut Tartlets

NEPITELLE

These delicious Calabrian Christmas treats could quickly replace mincemeat tarts as standard holiday fare. The tarts are often baked with a lattice crust on top. I like them better with a clear view of the tasty filling, but if you wish to weave a crusty top, double the pastry recipe and freeze any extra for another time.

PASTA FROLLA

2 cups all-purpose flour
¼ cup sugar
Pinch of salt
9 tablespoons well-chilled butter, cubed
3 tablespoons dry Marsala wine
2 teaspoons grated lemon rind
1 egg, beaten

FILLING

½ cup raisins
¼ cup dry Marsala wine
⅓ cup finely chopped dried figs (about 2 ounces)
⅓ cup finely chopped walnuts (about 1½ ounces)
3 tablespoons sugar
1½ ounces bittersweet or semisweet chocolate, grated
¼ teaspoon cinnamon
Pinch of salt
Powdered sugar

1. For the pastry, sift the flour, sugar, and salt into a large bowl or onto the counter. Cut in the butter until the mixture resembles coarse meal. Make a well in the center. Add the Marsala, lemon rind, and egg. Gather the flour gradually into the well until all the flour is incorporated. Push with the heel of your hand to knead together gently but thoroughly. Gather into a ball, wrap in plastic wrap, and store in the warmest part of the refrigerator at least 30 minutes.

2. Butter twenty-four 2-inch tartlet shells. Roll the dough on a lightly floured counter to a thickness of $\frac{1}{16}$ inch. Using a floured cutter or glass, cut out 3-inch circles. Fit the circles into the prepared pans, trim the edges, and refrigerate at least 30 minutes.

3. Steep the raisins in the Marsala 30 minutes. Add the figs, walnuts, 3 tablespoons sugar, chocolate, cinnamon, and salt.

4. Preheat the oven to 400°F. Spoon 1 tablespoon filling into each shell. Bake until lightly browned, 15 to 20 minutes. Cool on a wire rack. Remove from the pans and sprinkle with powdered sugar. Serve at room temperature. These may be made 2 days ahead. *Makes 24.*

Italian boys learning to bake at the North Bennet Street School, North End, Boston.

Easter Pie

PASTIERA

Easter without "pastiera" is unheard of in a southern Italian home. The traditional pie is a symbol of man's harmony with nature's bounty. In Italy the immigrants made "pastiere" from grain because they had their own crop. In America they used rice and eventually called it "rice pie." Nonna made a delicious one with fine egg noodles, but even my Aunt Irma isn't sure how she did it. Neapolitan cooking teacher Michi Ambrosi introduced me to canned, presoaked grain which is available in Italian specialty food stores. If this had been available to the immigrants, we might never have had a southern Italian "rice pie."

PASTRY CRUST (PASTA FROLLA)

2 cups all-purpose flour
½ cup sugar
Grated rind of 1 lemon

6 ounces (12 tablespoons) butter
3 egg yolks, beaten

———

FILLING

15-ounce can of "Gran Pastiera" (see note) (or ½ cup wheat or barley grain soaked 3 days in water, then boiled in fresh water until tender, drained) or ½ cup rice boiled in 2 quarts water until tender and drained
1 cup milk
Pinch of salt

⅔ cup sugar
Grated rind of 1 orange
Grated rind of 1 lemon
1 pound fresh ricotta cheese
5 egg yolks
2 tablespoons orange-flower water
½ teaspoon cinnamon
½ pound chopped candied citron
4 egg whites

———

Powdered sugar

1. Make the pastry: sift the flour and sugar together onto a counter. Toss in the lemon rind and with the tips of your fingers,

break the butter into the flour until it is pea size. Make a well in the center and add the beaten egg yolks. Gradually incorporate the flour into the eggs until the mixture forms a pastry. Knead gently a few seconds to make it smooth. Wrap in wax paper and refrigerate 1 hour. (The dough may also be made in a food processor.)

2. Make the filling: put the prepared grain, milk, salt, 2 table-spoons sugar, and grated rinds into a 2-quart pot. Cook 20 minutes, or until all liquid is absorbed. Cool.

3. Beat the ricotta cheese with the remaining sugar until smooth. Beat in the egg yolks, cooked grain, orange-flower water, and cinnamon. Fold in the citron. In a separate bowl, beat the egg whites with a pinch of salt until stiff but not dry. Fold the egg whites gently into the grain mixture.

4. Preheat the oven to 350°F. Butter and flour a 10-inch round cake pan. Break off ¾ of the pastry and roll it out into a circle to fit the bottom and sides of the prepared pan. Trim any excess from the top. Pour the filling into the pastry. Roll out the remaining dough and cut into ¾-inch lattice strips for the top. Weave the pastry strips over the top of the filling, pinching them to the side dough. Brush with a beaten egg if desired. Bake 50 to 60 minutes, or until the filling is set and the crust is golden. Cool but do not refrigerate. Sprinkle with powdered sugar before serving. *Serves 10 to 12.*

• • •

Note: "Gran Pastiera" is an Italian product available in Italian specialty food stores. It is wheat grain that has already been soaked and cooked.

LEGEND OF THE PASTIERA

There is a particularly poetic story about the beginnings of the Neapolitan "pastiera." One ancient spring, when the air of Naples was unusually perfumed and the sky and sea exceedingly brilliant, the siren *Partenope* left her underwater throne. She entered the Bay of Naples and sang a song of praise to the wonders of nature in her city.

The people of Naples were enchanted and wanted to offer a thanksgiving. Seven of the area's most beautiful maidens presented seven gifts at the feet of Partenope. The gifts represented the products of the earth and the animal kingdom. The first was flour, symbol of wealth; the second ricotta, product of milk, the sign of abundance; the third eggs, symbol of productiveness; the fourth was grain boiled in milk to symbolize the harmonious fusion of the animal and vegetable kingdoms; the fifth, orange-flower water which perfumed the land around Naples; sixth came spices representing the homage paid to Partenope by all the people; and seventh was sugar which symbolized the sweetness of her songs that made the people dream.

Partenope was pleased with the gifts and eagerly scooped them up to bring them back to her underwater home. In her haste, she mixed them all together and they fell from her hands, forming the first "pastiera."

Peaches in White Wine

PESCHE AL VINO BIANCO

Most Italian-Americans remember, as I do, being served homemade wine as young children. First a little wine was poured from a cut glass decanter into our glasses and then water from a matching decanter was added. The proportion of wine to water increased with our ages. Sometimes, someone would cut up peaches and put them into the children's glasses of wine. This recipe takes that simple combination a bit further.

6 firm but ripe unblemished peaches
½ cup sweet white wine
¼ cup sugar
⅓ cup water

1 vanilla bean, cut in half
4 tablespoons Maraschino liqueur (or Kirsch or brandy)

1. Blanch the peaches in boiling water 3 seconds, then run them under cold water and peel. Cut the peaches in half and remove the pits.
2. Put the wine, sugar, water, and vanilla bean in a frying pan large enough to hold the peaches in one layer. Cook the liquid until the sugar melts. Add the peaches, cut side down, and bring to a simmer. Simmer, basting often, until the peaches are soft but still hold their shape (6 to 8 minutes). Remove the pan from the heat and let the peaches steep 20 minutes in the cooking liquid, basting from time to time.
3. Remove the peaches from the liquid with a slotted spoon and put them in a glass serving bowl. Return the juices to the stove and boil over high heat until the juices have reduced to less than ¼ cup. Add the Maraschino to pan, whirl together, and pour over the peaches. *Serves 6.*

• • •

Variation: Serve in individual glasses with a bit of "crema" (page 324) poured on top. Sprinkle fresh raspberries over each serving.

Stirred Custard

CREMA

"Crema" is a term Italians often apply to any smooth preparation such as a cream soup, a pastry cream, or a custard. In the case of this recipe, it refers to a stirred custard which is known in French cooking as a "creme Anglaise" (English custard). Use the "crema" over plain cake such as the "polentina" or over poached fruit or fresh berries.

3 egg yolks
¼ cup sugar
1 tablespoon flour
1 cup scalded milk

½ teaspoon vanilla extract
2 tablespoons Maraschino
   liqueur

Combine the egg yolks and sugar in a heavy saucepan, stirring just enough to blend. Sift the flour into the pan and mix well. Slowly pour in the warm milk. Put the saucepan over low heat and stir until the mixture boils and is thickened. Remove from the heat and add the vanilla and Maraschino liqueur. Strain and cool. *Makes 1½ cups.*

Glicerio Perrino's milk truck.

Maraschino-Soaked Oranges with Custard Sauce

ARANCE AL MARASCHINO CON CREMA

What a wonderful combination—oranges and Maraschino! The "crema" on top makes them just a bit more special, but don't hesitate to serve the oranges in the syrup alone. I like to serve these in a glass serving bowl because all of the color shows through.

6 large navel oranges
⅓ cup water
¾ cup sugar
Few drops of lemon juice
¼ cup Maraschino liqueur

1 recipe "crema"
    (opposite page) (optional)

1. With a sharp knife, remove the skin and all white pith neatly from the oranges. Slice the oranges into thin rounds and put them in a deep serving dish.

2. Put the water, sugar, and lemon juice into a small saucepan and cook over high heat until the sugar is melted and the liquid is unclouded. Cover the pan and allow to boil 2 minutes. Uncover the pan and cook until the liquid is syrupy (hard-ball stage). Cool slightly and add the liqueur. Pour over the oranges and chill, covered, 3 hours. Serve with "crema" if desired. *Serves 8.*

Spicy Oranges in Marsala Wine

ARANCE AL MARSALA AROMATICHE

I'm partial to fruit desserts like this one because they are usually just the right touch needed at the end of a meal when cake is too much and a plum too little. This one is particularly easy to make and wonderfully intriguing if you can find Sicilian blood oranges whose fruit is a vibrant shade of red. Serve with "biscotti" if desired.

4 large navel oranges
1 cup dry Marsala wine
¼ cup sugar
6 whole cloves

Two 3-inch cinnamon sticks
1 vanilla bean
¼ cup raisins

1. Using a sharp knife, remove the rind and all white pith from the oranges. Cut into ¼-inch-thick slices. Place in a glass bowl.

2. Cook the Marsala, sugar, cloves, cinnamon, and vanilla in a heavy saucepan, swirling occasionally, until the sugar dissolves. Increase the heat to high and boil until reduced by half, about 12 minutes. Stir in the raisins and pour over the oranges. Cover and refrigerate at least 2 hours or overnight. Discard the cloves, cinnamon, and vanilla before serving. *Serves 6.*

Maraschino-Poached Pears
with Chocolate Sauce

PERE COTTE AL MARASCHINO CON
SALSA DI CIOCCOLATA

Maraschino is Italian cherry liqueur. You could substitute Kirsch if you are unable to find Maraschino.

1 lemon
6 ripe but firm unblemished
    pears
1 cup water
½ cup dry white wine
½ cup sugar
2 tablespoons Maraschino
    liqueur

1 recipe chocolate sauce
    flavored with Maraschino
    liqueur (page 304)
6 fresh mint leaves
    (optional)

1. Remove 2 strips of peel from the lemon and set aside. Cut the lemon in half. Peel the pears, leaving the stems attached, and immediately rub with a cut lemon. Cut the pears in half, remove the core, and rub again with the lemon.

2. Put the water, wine, sugar, Maraschino, and reserved lemon peel in a skillet large enough to hold the pears in one layer. Bring to a boil and dissolve the sugar. Reduce the heat and add the pears, cut side down. Poach gently, basting often with the pan juices until the pears are tender but still slightly firm (about 10 minutes). Cool the pears in the syrup.

3. Remove the pears from the syrup and put 2 halves on each of 6 plates. Nap with the chocolate sauce and garnish with mint leaves if desired. A small dollop of unsweetened whipped cream may also be served with the pears. *Serves 6.*

• • •

Note: The pears are also delicious without the chocolate sauce. In that case, remove the pears once they are cooked and reduce the cooking syrup to a glaze. Pour the glaze over the pears and serve warm or at room temperature.

Ricotta-Filled Pears

PERE RIPIENE

These pears are a delicious and different combination of flavors. Jody Adams, my longtime friend and assistant, cut the pears in quarters before serving and was then able to pass them to a very large crowd as finger food.

1 lemon
4 large pears, 2½ pounds
   (Anjou, Comice, or
   Bartlett)
1 cup ricotta cheese, strained
3 tablespoons powdered
   sugar
2 tablespoons Maraschino
   liqueur
Pinch of salt

⅛ teaspoon freshly grated
   nutmeg
2 ounces bittersweet or
   semisweet chocolate,
   finely chopped
2 tablespoons chopped
   candied ginger
1½ cups chopped walnuts
Fresh mint leaves
   (optional)

1. Grate 1 teaspoon lemon rind and set aside. Peel the pears, cut in half, and remove the core. Rub all over with lemon juice.
2. Whip the ricotta in the bowl of an electric mixer and beat in the sugar, liqueur, salt, and nutmeg. Fold in the chocolate, lemon rind, and ginger. Fill the cavities of the pears, spreading the mixture over the entire cut surface as well. Roll the bottom and sides in the chopped nuts. Chill. Place half a pear on each dessert plate and decorate with mint leaves. *Serves 8.*

Little Fig Crosses

CROCETTE

These simple-to-make little sweets take their name from the cross shape that is made by laying the figs atop one another. I learned how to make them from Italo Scanga shortly after he learned how to make them from his sister in Calabria. This is a simple home version. Bakeries and restaurants often coat the finished figs with melted chocolate. If desired, you could serve them with chocolate sauce flavored with orange liqueur (page 304).

4 tablespoons orange marmalade	32 Calimyrna dried figs
	32 walnut halves
1 tablespoon finely chopped candied citron or 1 tablespoon grated lemon rind	4 tablespoons soft butter
	5 tablespoons powdered sugar
	¾ teaspoon cinnamon

1. Preheat the oven to 350°F.
2. Mix the marmalade and lemon rind together. Split the figs open, leaving the halves joined together at the stem end. Lay one fig down on a counter, the cut side facing up. Place a bit of marmalade mixture and a walnut half on each fig half. Lay the second fig, cut side facing up, on top of the first at a right angle. Fill like the first fig. Lay 2 more figs, unfilled, on top of the first 2 figs, cut side facing down. Enclose the filling completely. Continue to make "crosses" until all the figs are used up.
3. Use all the butter to grease a baking dish large enough to hold the figs in one layer. (The figs may be pushed very close together and overlap slightly if necessary.) Sift 3 tablespoons powdered sugar over the butter. Put the figs in the buttered dish. Mix the remaining powdered sugar with the cinnamon and sift over the figs.
4. Bake until the figs are hot, about 10 minutes. Serve warm.
Serves 8.

INDEX

PHOTOGRAPHIC ACKNOWLEDGMENTS

The photographs reproduced in this book were provided with the permission and courtesy of the following:

Library of Congress: v, xii, 83, 111
Providence Journal Bulletin: vii, 18, 40, 43, 55, 106, 118, 125, 130, 153, 158, 247, 269, 285
Mr. Gary D. Smith: 2, 4, 11, 15, 187, 198, 262, 270, 306, 326
Mr. Salvatore Mancini: 13, 175, 288
The Metropolitan Museum of Art, The Jefferson R. Burdick Collection, Gift of Jefferson R. Burdick, 1963: 20, 61, 148, 192, 202, 208, 227
Ms. Kathryn Parise: 27, 245 (both)
Collection of Stephen and Julie Brigidi. Photo by Nanette McAuliffe: 38
Mr. Lombard Gasbarro: 43, 165, 206
FPG International: 44, 46, 66, 97, 200, 243, 260
Ms. Donna Scarpetti Rizzo: 51, 53
The Echo: 76, 212
Collection of Business Americana, Archives Center, National Museum of American History, Smithsonian Institution: 84, 116, 129, 215, 321
The Rossi family: 86, 88
Slater Mill Historic Site: 94
Museum of the City of New York: 104
Mr. Gary A. Mantoosh: 142 (both)
Eureka Bank North Beach Museum: 167
Mrs. Irma Verde: 177, 178, 290
Mrs. Rozann DiGiglio Buckner: 195
Lewis W. Hine Collection, United States History, Local History & Genealogy Division, The New York Public Library, Astor, Lenox and Tilden Foundations: 204
Ms. Mary Codola: 237
Italian American Collection, Special Collections, The University Library, The University of Illinois at Chicago: 239, 253
Mr. Joseph R. Muratore: 251, 283, 324
Mr. Anthony Fama: 274, 276
The Rossi Family: 308, 309
The Schlesinger Library, Radcliffe College: 319

A NOTE ABOUT THE AUTHOR

Nancy Verde Barr was born and grew up in Providence, Rhode Island. She graduated from the University of Rhode Island and studied cooking with Marcella Hazan and Madeleine Kamman, among others, and has worked as Executive Chef to Julia Child and as a food consultant for various television programs. Nancy Barr has taught cooking in Rhode Island, Boston, and New York, and has had articles published in *Gourmet, Cook's Magazine, Food & Wine, Bon Appetit*, and *Yankee* magazine, as well as contributing recipes to Time-Life cookbooks. This is her first cookbook.

A NOTE ON THE TYPE

The text of this book was set in Sabon, a typeface designed by Jan Tschichold (1902–1974), the well-known German typographer. Because it was designed in Frankfurt, Sabon was named for the famous Frankfurt type founder Jacques Sabon, who died in 1580 while manager of the Egenolff foundry. Based loosely on the original designs of Claude Garamond (c. 1480–1561), Sabon is unique in that it was explicitly designed for hot-metal composition on both the Monotype and Linotype machines as well as for film composition.

Composed by Dix Type, Syracuse, New York

Printed and bound by The Courier Companies, Inc.
Westford, Massachusetts

Design by Dorothy Schmiderer Baker

KNOPF COOKS AMERICAN

The series of cookbooks that celebrates the culinary heritage of America, telling different aspects of our story through recipes interspersed with historical lore, personal reflections, and the recollections of old-timers.

"Our food tells us where we came from and who we are . . ."